Student Companion to

Charles
DICKENS

Student Companion to
Charles
DICKENS

Ruth Glancy

Student Companions to Classic Writers

Greenwood Press
Westport, Connecticut • London

Library of Congress Cataloging-in-Publication Data

Glancy, Ruth F., 1948–
      Student companion to Charles Dickens / Ruth Glancy.
          p.   cm.—(Student companions to classic writers, ISSN
      1522–7979)
      Includes bibliographical references (p.   ) and index.
      ISBN 0–313–30611–7 (alk. paper)
      1. Dickens, Charles, 1812–1870—Examinations—Study guides.
      I. Title.   II. Series.
      PR4581.G57   1999
      823′.8—dc21   99–27188

British Library Cataloguing in Publication Data is available.

Library of Congress Catalog Card Number: 99–27188
ISBN: 0–313–30611–7
ISSN: 1522–7979

First published in 1999

Greenwood Press, 88 Post Road West, Westport, CT 06881
An imprint of Greenwood Publishing Group, Inc.
www.greenwood.com

Printed in the United States of America

∞™

The paper used in this book complies with the
Permanent Paper Standard issued by the National
Information Standards Organization (Z39.48–1984).

10 9 8 7 6 5 4 3 2 1

Cover portrait of Charles Dickens by W. P. Frith, 1859.

Contents

Series Foreword

This series has been designed to meet the needs of students and general readers for accessible literary criticism on the American and world writers most frequently studied and read in the secondary school, community college, and four-year college classrooms. Unlike other works of literary criticism that are written for the specialist and graduate student, or that feature a variety of reprinted scholarly essays on sometimes obscure aspects of the writer's work, the Student Companions to Classic Writers series is carefully crafted to examine each writer's major works fully and in a systematic way, at the level of the nonspecialist and general reader. The objective is to enable the reader to gain a deeper understanding of the work and to apply critical thinking skills to the act of reading. The proven format for the volumes in this series was developed by an advisory board of teachers and librarians for a successful series published by Greenwood Press, Critical Companions to Popular Contemporary Writers. Responding to their request for easy-to-use and yet challenging literary criticism for students and adult library patrons, Greenwood Press developed a systematic format that is not intimidating but helps the reader to develop the ability to analyze literature.

How does this work? Each volume in the Student Companions to Classic Writers series is written by a subject specialist, an academic who understands students' needs for basic and yet challenging examination of the writer's canon. Each volume begins with a biographical chapter, drawn from published sources, biographies, and autobiographies, that relates the writer's life to his or her work. The next chapter examines the writer's literary heritage, tracing the literary influences of other writers on that writer and explaining and discussing the literary genres into which the writer's work falls. Each of the following chapters examines a major work by the writer, those works most frequently read and studied by high school and college students. Depending on the writer's canon, generally between four and eight major works are examined, each in an individual chapter. The discussion of each work is organized into separate sections on plot development, character development, and major themes. Literary devices and style, narrative point of view, and historical setting are also discussed in turn if pertinent to the work. Each chapter concludes with an alternate critical perspective from which to read the work, such as a psychological or feminist criticism. The critical theory is defined briefly in easy, comprehensible language for the student. Looking at the literature from the point of view of a particular critical approach will help the reader to understand and apply critical theory to the act of reading and analyzing literature.

Of particular value in each volume is the bibliography, which includes a complete bibliography of the writer's works, a selected bibliography of biographical and critical works suitable for students, and lists of reviews of each work examined in the companion, both from the time the literature was originally published and from contemporary sources, all of which will be helpful to readers, teachers, and librarians who would like to consult additional sources.

As a source of literary criticism for the student or for the general reader, this series will help the reader to gain understanding of the writer's work and skill in critical reading.

1

The Life of
Charles Dickens

When Charles Dickens began the story of the orphan Oliver Twist in 1837, he was the first writer to consider a child a suitable hero for a novel. Children had always been featured in fairy tales, but Dickens was the first novelist to spend more than a page or two on his hero's childhood. Since then, stories about childhood have become commonplace, but few writers have achieved Dickens's power in re-creating the point of view and emotional turmoil of the child, especially the frightened, abandoned, or mistreated child. He was equally good, though, at entering the imaginatively rich and lively world of the happy child. In his own life he had been both abandoned and nurtured, and the vividness with which he constantly relived his childhood experiences, both bad and good, made possible so many of his most memorable child characters. His strong imaginative links to his childhood continued throughout his life and colored his adult perception of the world and his moral outlook.

Dickens's family on his father's side had been servants, but powerful ones, in the wealthy Crewe family in Cheshire. His grandfather William Dickens, butler to the Crewes, married Elizabeth Ball in 1781, and she became their housekeeper. Dickens knew his grandmother as an old lady when she lived in London, and her talent as a storyteller influenced the growth of his imagination. From her he heard the ghost stories, fairy tales, and old legends that added a surreal dimension to his novels.

When he was nineteen, Dickens's father left his mother's home with the Crewe family to become a clerk in the London office of the Treasurer of His

Majesty's Navy. Here he met Thomas Barrow, whose sister Elizabeth he married in 1809 after he had moved to the Portsmouth office, on the south coast. England was at war with Napoleon, and John Dickens's job was to pay the British sailors when they returned home.

The Dickens family lived at Mile End Terrace, which is now the Dickens Birthplace Museum because first Frances (Fanny) was born there, followed by Charles on 7 February 1812. Another baby, Alfred, was born in 1814 but lived only a few months. In 1815, with the defeat of Napoleon and the end of the war with America, John Dickens was moved back to the London office. Two years later, after the birth of another daughter, the family moved to Kent, where Dickens's most powerful childhood memories were formed. They settled in Chatham, a rather rowdy but colorful seaside town that was home to several regiments of soldiers as well as the navy. From 1817 to 1821 they lived in Ordnance Terrace, where another son and daughter were born.

Chatham, its surrounding countryside, and neighboring county town of Rochester appear over and over again in Dickens's fiction and in his essays, where Chatham is "Dullborough Town." It was never dull to the young boy, though, who delighted in the eccentric characters he saw around the dockyard and in the inns, houses, cathedral, and castle ruins that he explored. His imagination was also formed by his young nursemaid Mary Weller, whose gruesome tales—simultaneously terrifying and irresistible—find their way into many of his novels and are recounted in his essay "Nurses' Stories." His next-door neighbor in Ordnance Terrace was Lucy Stroughill, a beautiful little blonde girl who influenced many of his heroines, most notably Lucie Manette in *A Tale of Two Cities*.

Because he was soon to enter a very different life, Dickens always remembered the Chatham days as the most carefree and enjoyable of his life. He read the novels of the eighteenth century as well as old tales like *The Arabian Nights*, wrote and acted in small plays, and enjoyed magic lantern shows and pantomimes. He and Fanny were well known in the neighborhood for their singing, and they would entertain at home and at the local inn. Best of all, he had a young and sympathetic school master, William Giles, under whom he flourished. With John Dickens's promotions in the Navy Pay Office, the family, which now included a new baby, Alfred Lamert, seemed to be going up in the world.

Dickens's father was immortalized in the character of Mr. Micawber in Dickens's most autobiographical novel, *David Copperfield*. Sociable, generous, and friendly, John was ambitious to rise in society and be a "gentleman," and in Chatham he had acquired such a status. Unfortunately, though, he was also like Mr. Micawber in wanting to live beyond his means and keep up appearances, the cause of most financial disasters. At Chatham he borrowed a large sum of money, which he did not repay, relying on his brother-in-law Thomas Barrow to pay it for him. The family moved back to London in 1822, selling off some of their furniture and shipping the rest by boat.

Even more dismal times lay ahead for the Dickenses, who settled into the poor neighborhood of Bayham Street, Camden Town, three miles north of central London. Dickens recognized that his father, while kind to his children and fond of them, was a feckless and irresponsible man, as he was later to explain to his friend John Forster:

I know my father to be as kindhearted and generous a man as ever lived in the world. Everything that I can remember of his conduct to his wife, or children, or friends, in sickness or affliction, is beyond all praise. . . . But, in the ease of his temper, and the straitness of his means, he appeared to have utterly lost at this time the idea of educating me at all, and to have utterly put from him the notion that I had any claim upon him, in that regard, whatever. So I degenerated into cleaning his boots of a morning, and my own; and making myself useful in the work of the little house; and looking after my younger brothers and sisters (we were now six in all); and going on such poor errands as arose out of our poor way of living. (Forster 1.13)

Many children in Dickens's works are similarly expected to be parents to their younger siblings and stagger about under the weight of large and demanding babies. Dickens's older sister was more fortunate: Because of her musical talent, Fanny was sent as a boarder to the Royal Academy of Music in 1823, an opportunity that Dickens regarded with envy.

In an effort to pay the many creditors, the family moved to Gower Street so that Mrs. Dickens could open a school, but although Charles was sent out to deliver advertisements for it, "nobody ever came to school, nor do I recollect that anybody ever proposed to come, or that the least preparation was made to receive anybody" (Forster 1.16). Dickens's hopes that he would return to school were completely dashed soon after when he was sent to work at Warren's, a shoe-blacking factory managed by James Lamert, a relative by marriage of Dickens's aunt and a close friend of the family. Michael Allen suggests that Charles started work on 9 February 1824, a few days before his father was arrested for debt and confined in the Marshalsea Prison. Mrs. Dickens and the three younger children (the baby had died) moved into the prison also, but Dickens went to live with Mrs. Roylance, an eccentric and rather formidable lady (who became Mrs. Pipchin in *Dombey and Son*), near Bayham Street. At first, he walked five miles to work and back each day as well as the much longer walk to the prison and to visit Fanny at the music academy on Sundays. Later, he moved to lodgings near the prison. Thus at the age of twelve, Dickens was suddenly dropped into an adult world of poverty, crime, and disillusionment that was to have a profound effect on his fiction.

The blacking factory was a dark, rat-infested building near the river at Hungerford Stairs. Dickens's companions there were rough street boys (one was called Fagin), and his job was repetitive: pasting labels on the bottles of shoe-blacking. Although the factory moved to better premises in Covent Garden, it was a soul-destroying job for a well-read and educated boy; even after his father was released from prison, he was kept on there, suggesting to his young mind that he would never be educated again. John Dickens was released from the Marshalsea in May 1824, but Dickens seems to have stayed at Warren's until the following spring, a thirteen-month period.

That this episode in his life was unbearably painful for him to recall is evident from his inability to talk about it to anyone, even to his wife and family, although he refers to Warren's often in his novels and re-created the experience in *David Copperfield*. In 1847, he wrote an autobiographical fragment for John Forster that expressed the pain he felt at what he saw as his parents' neglect:

It is wonderful to me how I could have been so easily cast away at such an age. . . . No words can express the secret agony of my soul as I sunk into this companionship; compared these everyday associates with those of my happier childhood; and felt my early hopes of growing up to be a learned and distinguished man crushed in my breast. The deep remembrance of the sense I had of being utterly neglected and hopeless; of the shame I felt in my position; of the misery it was to my young heart to believe that, day by day, what I had learned, and thought, and delighted in, and raised my fancy and my emulation up by, was passing away from me, never to be brought back any more; cannot be written. My whole nature was so penetrated with the grief and humiliation of such considerations, that even now, famous and caressed and happy, I often forget in my dreams that I have a dear wife and children; even that I am a man; and wander desolately back to that time of my life. (Forster 1.21–23)

Another lasting scar from the blacking-warehouse episode was formed when John Dickens finally took his son out of the warehouse with the intention of sending him to school, but Mrs. Dickens wanted to send him back to Warren's. Although Dickens was fond of his mother and she was generally regarded as a kind woman with a talent for mimicry and storytelling, he never forgot this betrayal.

Life resumed a more normal course when Dickens's father, with the help of a legacy and a pension from the Admiralty, was able to provide for his family again. Dickens attended Wellington House Academy and enjoyed the life of an ordinary schoolboy for a little over a year; then, in 1826, his father lost his position as a journalist with a daily paper and another income was required. At just fifteen, Dickens became an office boy for a law firm, but with a view to a career in journalism, he learned shorthand and became a reporter in Doctor's Commons, where non-criminal law cases were heard. Dickens satirized the incompetence and corruption of Doctor's Commons in many of his works, and at the time he found the work tedious and dispiriting. As soon as he turned eighteen in February 1830, he obtained a reader's ticket for the British Museum. For the next four years, he spent much of his spare time there, making up for his lack of formal education by reading voraciously. He was able to indulge his passion for acting by visiting the many theaters in London and by acting himself in amateur performances and singing with his sister Fanny, who had by then graduated as a singer from the Royal Academy of Music. Dickens loved to relate how he nearly became an actor instead of a writer: He had an audition with the famous actor Charles Mathews at the Lyceum Theatre, but a bad cold prevented Dickens from attending.

A more lucrative career than acting opened up shortly after, when Dickens was hired as a parliamentary reporter, first for his uncle's newspaper, the *Mirror of Parliament,* where his father was working as a reporter, and then for a new publication as well, the *True Sun,* which he joined in March 1832. He was an excellent shorthand reporter and made a name for himself very quickly. Ambitious to rise in the world, he was spurred on by having fallen hopelessly in love with Maria Beadnell, a pretty but flighty daughter of a banker. He had met her when he was only seventeen, and his youthful infatuation is movingly portrayed in David Copperfield's love for Dora Spenlow. Maria's parents did not consider the young reporter a suitable connection, so they sent her to Paris to finish her education. The romance struggled on, Dickens devoted and Maria tormenting and capricious, until in 1833 he reluctantly accepted that his love would never be returned. Dickens was later to credit this bitter hurt with his difficulty in being openly affectionate, even with his children.

Dickens's career as a parliamentary reporter gave him an intimate view of the workings of government as well as extending his already vast knowledge of London, its places and people. He began to write short sketches about London life, and in 1833, he submitted one for publication, dropping it, as he was later to recall in the Preface to *The Pickwick Papers*, "stealthily one evening at twilight, with fear and trembling, into a dark letterbox, in a dark office, up a dark court in Fleet Street." In the same Preface he describes how when "A Dinner at Poplar Walk" was printed in the December issue of the *Monthly Magazine,* he walked in Westminster Hall for half an hour because his eyes were "so dimmed with joy and pride, that they could not bear the street, and were not fit to be seen there." Although he received no payment for the story, he was delighted to be invited to write six more. In 1834, he became a reporter for the well-established newspaper the *Morning Chronicle* and published a series of sketches there and in the new *Evening Chronicle*, for which he was paid. The stories appeared anonymously at first, until he decided on the pseudonym "Boz," the nickname of his youngest and favorite brother, Augustus. Dickens had called him "Moses" after a character in Oliver Goldsmith's *The Vicar of Wakefield*, which, in the small child's pronunciation, had become "Boses" and then "Boz." Between 1833 and 1836, he wrote fifty-six amusing and vivid pieces about London people and places for several newspapers and magazines; they were so well received that, in 1836, they appeared in book form in two series entitled *Sketches by Boz*.

The *Evening Chronicle* was established by George Hogarth, a Scottish lawyer, writer, and friend of Sir Walter Scott, who had recently moved to London as a critic for the *Morning Chronicle*. Dickens became friendly with the family, which included three daughters: Mary, Georgina, and Catherine, the oldest, with whom he began a courtship. They were very different in ways that would eventually destroy the relationship, but in the early days, they seemed happily compatible.

Dickens now had a good income for his age and was called upon to help his improvident parents and younger siblings, who were once again in financial difficulties because of John Dickens's failure to provide for them. (Dickens continued to shore up his father financially until John Dickens's death in 1851.) His next commission came from Chapman and Hall, a London firm that would remain his publisher for most of his life. He was invited to write a series of humorous pieces to accompany illustrations of sporting scenes by a well-known artist, Robert Seymour. He immediately took control of the project, insisting that the topic be expanded and that the illustrations accompany the text rather than the other way round. Chapman agreed, and *The Posthumous Papers of the Pickwick Club* began publication in twenty monthly installments, in March 1836. On the strength of this more assured income, Dickens and Catherine Hogarth were married on 2 April 1836, at St. Luke's Church, Chelsea, and began married life in Dickens's rooms in Furnival's Inn.

Tragedy struck before publication of the second number (installment) with the suicide of the artist Robert Seymour, triggered by being asked to redo one of the illustrations. R. W. Buss illustrated number three, but he was replaced by Hablot Knight Browne, who became Dickens's main illustrator and "Phiz" to Dickens's "Boz." Although sales of *The Pickwick Papers* were slow at the beginning, Dickens had other literary work. He was still a very busy parliamentary reporter for the *Morning Chronicle*; he had written a farce and an operetta; and his first entry on the stage of social comment was a pamphlet opposing a bill that would prohibit all recreation on Sunday. *Sunday Under Three Heads* was the beginning of Dickens's championing of the poorer classes, who would have been deprived of their only opportunity to enjoy any amusement on their one day of rest from work. Dickens's pamphlet attacked both the wealthy promoters of the bill and a hypocritical clergy, who would both have been unaffected by it.

In the summer of 1836, Dickens introduced Sam Weller into *The Pickwick Papers*, and within weeks the book became a best-seller, its circulation shooting from a few hundred copies per number to forty thousand. The early numbers were snapped up, and Dickens was famous throughout the country. In a craze that resembled the late twentieth century more than the nineteenth, Mr. Pickwick and his friends became the source of souvenirs, parodies, and songs. Dickens did not exaggerate when he wrote to John Macrone, the publisher of *Sketches by Boz*, "PICKWICK, TRIUMPHANT" (*Letters* 1.147). He started to move in London literary circles as a result of his sudden fame and gained many valuable friends, the most important of whom was John Forster, a literary critic on *The Examiner* who had reviewed *Sketches by Boz* very favorably. He would become Dickens's closest friend, adviser, and first biographer.

The year 1837 was one of sunshine and shadow. On 1 January, Dickens became the editor of the monthly magazine *Bentley's Miscellany*, for which he began *Oliver Twist* that month while still working on *Pickwick*, which did not conclude until October. On 6 January, his first son, Charles, was born, and in March, his one-act burletta (comic opera) *Is She His Wife?* opened at the St. James Theatre. In April, the family moved to 48 Doughty Street, which is now the Dickens House Museum. After attending a performance of the burletta on 6 May, Mary Hogarth, who was living with Dickens and Catherine, took suddenly ill and died the next day. The loss of the sister whom Dickens called "the grace and life of our home" (*Letters* 1.257) was devastating for the whole family; for Dickens, it was the loss of the person he felt most understood and inspired him. He wrote to a close friend, "Thank God she died in my arms, and the very last words she whispered were of me. . . . I solemnly believe that so perfect a creature never breathed. I knew her inmost heart, and her real worth and value. She had not a fault" (*Letters* 1.259). Dickens never fully recovered from her death, and her sweet nature and youthful promise became attributes of many of his heroines who often shared her age, seventeen, and sometimes her name. Dickens suspended the writing of his two novels for a month after her death, and the family found some solace in escaping to France and the seaside town of Broadstairs, Kent ("Our English Watering-Place"); both became favourite haunts. That memorable year, 1837, finished on a high note, however, with the conclusion of *The Pickwick Papers* in November, which was celebrated at a grand dinner attended by many of London's leading writers. At the age of only twenty-five, Dickens was the toast of the literary world.

Always full of ideas for his writing, while still at work on *Oliver Twist* Dickens travelled to Yorkshire to visit the notoriously abusive boarding schools that he would attack in his next twenty-part serial for Chapman and Hall, *The Life and Adventures of Nicholas Nickleby*. The first number appeared at the end of March 1838 and sold nearly fifty thousand copies on its first day. It was a stressful time for Dickens, the father of two young children (his first daughter, Mary, or "Mamie" as she came to be called, was born in March 1838), who was simultaneously editing *Bentley's Miscellany*, fulfilling small writing commissions, and producing monthly numbers of two novels. He was also working on a third, *Barnaby Rudge*, which he had originally promised to John Macrone in 1836 but had transferred to Bentley, promising to publish it in the *Miscellany* when *Oliver Twist* was finished, in November 1838. But, as Dickens said, not even Sir Walter Scott could have kept up such a pace for long. After many battles with Richard Bentley, he resigned as editor of the *Miscellany* early in 1839; later that year his second daughter, Kate, was born, and the family moved to Devonshire Terrace, Dickens's home for the next fifteen years. His fourth child, Walter, was born there in 1841.

Having broken with Richard Bentley, Dickens suggested to Chapman and Hall that he edit a new periodical in the tradition of the eighteenth-century magazines that he had always enjoyed, such as *The Spectator*. *Master Humphrey's Clock*, which began in April 1840, revolved around a group of eccentric but kindly old storytellers who meet at Master Humphrey's house to talk about contemporary events and read stories from manuscripts hidden away in the old clock. When Master Humphrey's short autobiography, *The Old Curiosity Shop*, proved very popular, immediately increasing the flagging sales of the magazine, Dickens abandoned the original plan and turned the short tale into a novel instead, quietly removing Master Humphrey as the storyteller. It became Dickens's most popular novel to date and achieved record sales of 100,000 each week. It was followed by *Barnaby Rudge* in 1841, partly written while Dickens and Catherine were touring Scotland and being feted in Edinburgh. When the novel concluded at the end of the year, *Master Humphrey's Clock* wound down also with the death of Master Humphrey.

Barnaby Rudge had been simmering in Dickens's brain since 1836. Now, just five years later, he had not only completed that work but had written four other long novels as well. The last two novels were in weekly installments for the periodical, always a more stressful format than the more leisurely monthly issue. He was ready for a rest. In January 1842, he and his wife sailed on the S.S. *Britannia* to Boston to begin a six-month tour of eastern North America that would let him meet his rapturous American readers and write a book about his impressions for Chapman and Hall. They travelled by steamboat and train mainly through the eastern states, visiting New York; Philadelphia; Washington; Richmond, Virginia; Baltimore; Pittsburgh; Cincinnati; St. Louis; and Columbus. After a month of exhausting travel, they arrived at the Canadian side of Niagara Falls at the end of April, crossed Lake Ontario by steamboat, and visited Toronto and Kingston, at that time the capital of the Province of Canada. They took the steamboat down the St. Lawrence River to Montreal, where Dickens stage-managed and acted in two evenings of plays with his friend the Earl of Mulgrave and an amateur acting company of officers from the local garrison. The Dickenses sailed home from New York at the beginning of June.

Dickens spent the summer at Broadstairs with his children, writing his impressions of his tour in *American Notes for General Circulation*. He had been royally treated wherever he went and made many lasting friendships, including Longfellow, the publisher James Fields, and Harvard professor C. C. Felton. The American press was critical of Dickens, however, because he campaigned for international copyright to try to stop the endless pirating of his books. Their antipathy did much to alter the wholly favorable opinion that Dickens had held of America before he visited it. He was also appalled by the American prison system, especially the solitary system practiced in Philadelphia. His "notes" were often critical of American society and customs; it turned out not to be the golden land that he had envisioned, free from the evils that he attacked in his own country. His disappointment is evident in *American Notes*, which was not well received by his American readers and which lost him some American friends, notably Washington Irving.

After an enjoyable autumn holiday, Dickens began monthly installments of *Martin Chuzzlewit*, the first number appearing in January 1843. When the early numbers did not sell as well as he had hoped, he revived interest in the story by sending his hero to America, where he renewed his attack on American culture and institutions, just as he was also beginning to attack those at home.

Dickens's concern with the conditions of the working poor increased at this time, inspired by government reports on child labor and the sanitary conditions in the slums. His friend Dr. Southwood Smith had sent him a copy of the Second Report of the Children's Employment Commission, which had left Dickens "so perfectly stricken down" that he thought of publishing a pamphlet entitled "An appeal to the People of England, on behalf of the Poor Man's Child" (*Letters* 3.459). After he visited a Ragged School for poor London children in September, Dickens was ready to draw attention to their plight and also to make up for his loss of income from the novel by writing a long story for the Christmas market. *A Christmas Carol* took just two months to write and appeared just before Christmas 1843. It was an immediate success, selling out its first edition of six thousand copies before the new year. It was not the financial success that Dickens had been hoping for, however, because it was an expensive publication, beautifully illustrated and decorated for the Christmas book market. The ten thousand copies that were published in three editions in December 1843 and January 1844 brought in only half the thousand pounds that Dickens had been hoping for. But the immense popularity of the Christmas book more than compensated Dickens for its failure to pay the bills of his family, which had increased to five children with the birth of Francis Jeffrey Dickens in January 1844. Because of his own father's improvidence Dickens worried about being able to provide for his family all his life, long after his fame brought him a comfortable income.

With the conclusion of *Martin Chuzzlewit* in June 1844, Dickens took a two-year break from the rigors of novel-writing. He moved to Genoa, Italy, where the good climate and the change of scene brought him much-needed rest and allowed him to live more economically than in England (as well as escaping the financial demands of his father). At first the family lived beside the sea at Albaro, in an imposing old villa that Dickens likened to a pink jail, but in the autumn they moved to the Palazzo Peschiere, a beautiful house overlooking Genoa. Here he wrote the Christmas book for 1844, *The Chimes*, returning alone to London for a few weeks in December to see to its publication and to read it aloud to a select group of his friends. The readings were very well received: he wrote to his wife, "If you had seen Macready last night—undisguisedly sobbing, and crying on the sofa, as I read—you would have felt (as I did) what a thing it is to have Power" (*Letters* 4.235). This success led to Dickens's decision to read aloud for profit later in his career.

After further extensive touring in Europe, his impressions of which he recorded in *Pictures from Italy* in 1846, the family returned to London in May 1845. As well as enthusiastically appearing in several amateur theatricals and writing *The Cricket on the Hearth* for Christmas 1845, Dickens briefly edited a new liberal newspaper, the *Daily News*, published by his own publisher, Bradbury and Evans. But he was becoming anxious to work on a long novel again and resigned in February 1846, after just one month. He continued to write for the paper, contributing articles promoting the Ragged School movement and the abolition of capital punishment.

The new novel brewing in Dickens's mind was *Dombey and Son*, and once again he went abroad to save money (his sixth child, Alfred, had been born in October 1845) and find some peace and quiet in which to write. This time he chose Lausanne, settling in a pleasant house, the Villa Rosemont, on a hill outside the town. Although Dickens told his correspondents that he could write "a long book . . . better in retirement" (*Letters* 4.539) and was going in search of mountain knowledge in all four seasons, the escapes abroad were not wholly conducive to work. When he was writing *The Chimes* in Genoa, he acknowledged wanting "a crowded street to plunge into at night" (*Letters* 4.200), and even among the mountain grandeur of Switzerland he complained of "the absence of streets and numbers of figures. I can't express how much I want these"

(*Letters* 4.612). He had good friends in Switzerland, however, and with them, he and his wife explored the Swiss and French Alps. Their visit to the Saint Bernard Convent and Martigny is recalled in *Little Dorrit* and his last Christmas story, *No Thoroughfare*. In the last months of 1846, he wrote another Christmas book, *The Battle of Life*.

The Dickens family moved to Paris in November, where they rented a house while Dickens returned to London to see to the publication of the Christmas book and to oversee Albert Smith's authorized dramatization of it, which was a great success. He rejoined his family in Paris for the rest of the winter and wrote about the death of the character Paul Dombey there, with the byways of Paris taking the place of his more familiar London streets, as he told his readers in his 1858 Preface: "when I am reminded of what it was that the waves were always saying, I wander in my fancy for a whole winter night about the streets of Paris—as I really did, with a heavy heart, on the night when my little friend and I parted company for ever." John Forster visited Dickens in Paris, and together they explored not just the tourist spots, but also the morgue and the prisons, appropriate settings for his portrait of revolutionary Paris in *A Tale of Two Cities*.

Back in England, the writing of *Dombey and Son* occupied Dickens until April 1848. His seventh child, Sydney, was born in April 1847, and his eighth child, Henry, in January 1848. Over the next two years, he was also kept busy acting in and managing amateur stage productions in London, Manchester, Liverpool, and Scotland; the profits usually went to various charities or personal benefits such as the endowment of a curatorship for Shakespeare's house in Stratford. His main charity work, though, was to help Angela Burdett-Coutts, a wealthy friend and philanthropist, establish a home for homeless women in London. The intention of Urania Cottage was to help the women regain a normal life (some were prostitutes; others were petty criminals or just destitute girls). When Dickens reported on the fate of the fifty-six residents of the house in its first six years, thirty had successfully married or emigrated, the original goal of the plan. He was actively involved in running the home, which was far from trouble-free but which he approached with good sense as well as compassion. His experiences with Urania Cottage led to his sympathetic treatment of Little Em'ly and Martha in *David Copperfield*.

Another of Dickens's interests in these years was the publication in a "Cheap Edition" of all his works so far; Dickens's intention was to bring his novels to the audience for whom they were primarily written. He dedicated them to "the English people," with the hope that they would be accessible to all homes. He wrote new prefaces for them, which stressed the social issues of the day.

Because of the pressures of writing *Dombey and Son*, Dickens reluctantly decided against writing a Christmas book in 1847, although he had the idea for

The Haunted Man in 1846; it appeared in December 1848. Dickens's sister Fanny contracted consumption in the summer of 1848 and died in September. Her loss was one reason for Dickens's increasing interest at this time in the action of memory and the complex emotions of regret and consolation. This interest was central to the Christmas book and also to *David Copperfield*, which he began early in 1849 and continued in monthly instalments until the end of October 1850. In 1849, he also wrote *The Life of Our Lord* for his children, but it was not published until 1934.

Ever since his early days as editor of *Bentley's Miscellany*, Dickens had wanted to edit his own periodical. *Master Humphrey's Clock* ran briefly as a magazine, and in 1845, he had considered starting a weekly journal to be entitled *The Cricket*, but John Forster was against it, and the idea became the 1845 Christmas book instead. Between *Dombey and Son* and *David Copperfield*, he contributed several articles to the *Examiner* (for which John Forster was now editor) on the subjects dear to his heart: the relationship between ignorance and crime, the iniquities of the "baby farm" system (which he had attacked in *Oliver Twist*), and other injustices of the time. But he wanted a journal over which he would have full editorial control, a journal that would embody his strongly felt belief that he could improve the lives of the hundreds of thousands of people who loved his work. He wanted not just to attack social evils, but also to cheer, encourage, and especially to nurture the imagination. His dream was realized in *Household Words*, a "weekly miscellany of general literature," which first appeared in March 1850. In the first two years, Dickens contributed *A Child's History of England*, written for his children, as well as about one hundred stories and essays.

In the spring of 1851, Dickens lost first his father and then his eight-month-old baby daughter Dora, who had been sickly since birth. The news of Dora's unexpected death was brought to him as he presided at a dinner for the General Theatrical Fund, one of the many speaking engagements that Dickens undertook for charity. He was caught up also in amateur theatricals to raise money for a new project, The Guild of Literature and Art, which was intended to provide financial aid to artists and writers. He and a group of friends performed Edward Bulwer-Lytton's *Not so Bad as We Seem* and a farce by Dickens and Mark Lemon entitled *Mr. Nightingale's Diary*, which the audiences loved; even Queen Victoria attended. Dickens stage-managed both plays and also acted in them; he played six parts in the farce.

Always anxious to be working on a new novel, Dickens found himself seized by "violent restlessness, and vague ideas of going I don't know where" (*Letters* 6.463), which he recognized as symptoms of ideas brewing. His interest in the living conditions of the urban poor and the red tape of government and the courts that prevented their improvement was central to *Bleak House*, which ran in monthly numbers from March 1852 until September 1853. While the novel was in progress, a serious outbreak of cholera made Dickens's attack particularly timely. *Bleak House* was followed by *Hard Times*, published weekly in *Household Words* from April to August 1854; at the end of the following year, *Little Dorrit* began in monthly installments. Boulogne, on the French coast, was now his retreat when he needed a break, and he also returned to Switzerland and Italy with his friends Wilkie Collins and Augustus Egg. In between writing these dense and complex novels, he was still busy with the home for homeless women, meticulously editing *Household Words*, appearing in amateur theatricals (including Wilkie Collins's play *The Lighthouse*, in which Dickens had the leading role), and giving numerous invited speeches. He again tested the idea of reading aloud from his works (already tried with *The Chimes*) with *A Christmas Carol* in 1853, which he shortened into a special reading version and presented in Birmingham for charity. The tremendous success of his charity readings led to his later reading tours for profit on both sides of the Atlantic.

In 1855, Dickens received a letter from Maria Beadnell, the passion of his youth. She was now a married matron, but before they met again, their correspondence rekindled Dickens's old feelings for her; he was swept back to 1830 and pictured her as the beautiful young girl he had loved so devotedly. When they did meet, he was shocked to find that his old charmer was now plump and unattractive; worst of all, though, she was also talkative and silly. His recognition of the humor of his "great expectations" found a comic outlet in Arthur Clennam's rediscovery of Flora Finching in *Little Dorrit*.

Dickens's friendship with Wilkie Collins deepened in the 1850s, partly due to Dickens's then very troubled marriage. Collins was unorthodox in his own domestic arrangements (he had mistresses, never wives), so Dickens found him more understanding than his more conservative friends. They were both interested in heroism, and in the last half of the 1850s they collaborated on many stories and sketches on that subject for *Household Words*, often using their friendship to write adventure tales based on male relationships. The 1857 Christmas number, *The Perils of Certain English Prisoners*, was a collaboration to commemorate the heroism of the British in the Indian Mutiny of that year, and earlier that year, they wrote and acted in a play, *The Frozen Deep*. Dickens's role was particularly emotional as he was the unlikable Richard Wardour who sacrifices his own life to save his rival in love, Frank Aldersley, played by Wilkie Collins. As Dickens lay dying on the stage night after night, wept over by his lost love, he conceived the idea of Sydney Carton for *A Tale of Two Cities*. *The Frozen Deep* was so successful (even Queen Victoria asked to see it) that they took it to Manchester for public performances, employing a professional acting family, Mrs. Ternan and her two daughters, to play the female roles in place of Dickens's daughters and sister-in-law, for whom public performance would not have been considered proper.

Already restless and unhappy in his marriage, Dickens was smitten by the younger Ternan sister, eighteen-year-old Ellen. When the emotional intensity of playing Richard Wardour ended in August, he escaped with Wilkie Collins to the north for a short holiday, explaining to his friend, "when I *do* start up and stare myself seedily in the face, as happens to be my case at present, my blankness is inconceivable—indescribable—my misery, amazing" (*Letters* 8.423). They stayed in Doncaster, where Ellen Ternan was performing in a play, and together they wrote "The Lazy Tour of Two Idle Apprentices" for *Household Words*. One of Dickens's stories for that publication told of a man who wills his wife to die. His marriage to Catherine struggled on for a few months (he renovated their house in London to give them separate bedrooms). But by March, he admitted to Wilkie Collins that he could neither write nor sleep and had "never known a moment's peace or content, since the last night of The Frozen Deep" (*Letters* 8.536). The break with Catherine came in May, when she moved out with their oldest son, while the other children remained with Dickens and their aunt Georgina.

Dickens attempted to stop speculation about his relationship with Ellen Ternan (and even his sister-in-law Georgina was implicated in some rumors) by publishing a statement regarding his personal affairs in many of the London newspapers. When his publishers Bradbury and Evans refused to publish the statement in their comic paper, *Punch*, he broke off his relationship with them, closed *Household Words*, and returned to his former publisher, Chapman and Hall, with whom he began a new journal, *All the Year Round*. To get this venture off to a good start, he opened it with a new novel in weekly parts: *A Tale of Two Cities* ran in *All the Year Round* from 30 April to 26 November 1859, with a circulation of 100,000 copies a week. The novel incorporates Dickens's marital problems in many significant ways, and the three male protagonists can all be seen as aspects of Dickens himself as he struggled with the conflict of leaving his wife for Ellen Ternan, with whom he was now deeply committed.

Dickens had always possessed exceptional energy and drive. He would regularly walk twenty miles, often at night (even when he had a frost-bitten foot in 1865, he still walked ten miles every morning), and, of course, his literary production and editing work was considerable as well. He found activity the only answer to his emotional turmoil, and so in 1858, he decided to extend his sporadic but very popular readings for charity into a professional career. His friend John Forster disapproved of them, but Dickens found the readings a welcome outlet for his unhappiness. As in acting, he could lose himself in the roles of his characters, whose different voices and facial expressions he could produce to great effect. The laughter and tears of the audience also gave him a sense of connection with them that he had always sought in his writings. The readings were lucrative, a welcome bonus to the father of a large family and the new owner of Gad's Hill Place in Kent, the house he had dreamed of owning when he was a small boy. They were also exhausting: The 1858 tour took him through England, Wales, and Scotland for more than one hundred performances.

Dickens did not attempt a serial novel while on a reading tour, but he was always busy with *All the Year Round*, and in 1860, he wrote a delightful series of seventeen personal essays for it under the title *The Uncommercial Traveller*. These essays contained recollections of his childhood, of places he had visited and people he had met that he was happy to retain. In the same year, he disposed of the letters and papers that he did not want to immortalize, burning them in a huge bonfire at Gad's Hill. At the end of the year, *Great Expectations* followed Wilkie Collins's very successful *The Woman in White* in the journal, running from 1 December 1860 to 3 August 1861.

Dickens's family were by now leaving the nest. Charley, the oldest, had attended Eton and was now employed by Barings, a London importing firm that sent him to the Far East for a few months. Sydney joined a training ship as a cadet that year and remained in the navy; he died at sea in 1872. Walter was in the army in India, where he died on New Year's Eve 1863. Not knowing of his death, his brother Frank went to join Walter in India in 1863 and later became a policeman with the North West Mounted Police in western Canada. Alfred, at school in France in 1860, emigrated to Australia in 1865. Henry, also at school, went on to Cambridge University and a very successful legal career; he became a Queen's Counsel and was knighted. Edward (Plorn), the youngest child and a disappointment as a scholar, was dispatched to Australia, regretfully, by his father in 1868. Mary (Mamie) was at home; she never married and remained her father's companion until his death (after the breakup of the marriage, she did not visit her mother until Dickens had died). In 1860, her sister Kate married Wilkie Collins's younger brother Charles, a painter and writer; a few days later, Dickens's brother Alfred died, leaving a widow and five children, for whom Dickens felt financially responsible.

Dickens's relationship with Ellen Ternan continued in secret until his death. He probably bought a house for her, her mother, and sisters in London in 1859, and he was closely attached to the family throughout the 1860s. It is likely that she lived in France from 1862 to 1865 and that he visited her there frequently, although no proof has yet come to light that she was there and Ellen herself never referred to these years later. Dickens travelled alone on many of his trips across the Channel and referred to them mysteriously in letters; sometimes his sister-in-law Georgina and his daughter Mary went with him. His letters also indicate some sort of emotional crisis in the autumn and winter of 1862, and Dickens's son Henry and his daughter Kate (his two most reliable and affectionate children) both said later that Ellen gave birth to a baby boy, who died. If this occurred—and when—have never been proven.

Reading tours occupied much of 1862 and 1863, until he began work on a long novel, *Our Mutual Friend*, the first twenty-number work since *Little Dorrit*. *Our Mutual Friend* began publication in monthly numbers at the end of April 1864 and continued until November 1865. He nearly lost the manuscript of one part of it when, on 9 June 1865, the train in which he, Ellen Ternan, and her mother were returning from France was derailed at Staplehurst, Kent. In a postscript to the novel, Dickens described having to rescue the manuscript from their carriage, which hung suspended over a gap into which the other carriages had plunged. He spent the afternoon tending to the dead and dying; ten were killed and about fifty were injured, including Ellen, whose identity Dickens worked hard to keep secret. The accident damaged Dickens's nerves so badly that the anniversary of it continued to distress him, and he died on the fifth anniversary, 9 June 1870. It also inspired the 1866 Christmas number, *Mugby Junction*, which contained his chilling ghost story about a train accident, "The Signal-Man."

Dickens resumed his public reading tours in 1866 and 1867. In between, he was secretly visiting Ellen, now living near London. For some time, he had been contemplating (but rather fearing) a reading tour of America. Finally, in September 1867, he left for Boston, lured by the considerable financial rewards the tour would offer. It was a gruelling schedule of readings, involving considerable travelling through Massachusetts, Connecticut, Maine, and New York, with a side trip to Niagara Falls for sightseeing. Ill health, including a very swollen foot and a persistent cold, dogged him for much of the tour, but it was enormously successful. He returned to England at the beginning of May to find his latest Christmas story collaboration with Wilkie Collins, *No Thoroughfare*, a hit in its dramatic versions at home and in Paris.

Dickens's last series of provincial readings—seventy-two in all—took him all around England and up to Scotland between October 1868 and April 1869, when his doctor warned him that the readings must be stopped at once. Dickens was suffering from giddiness and deadness in the left side of his body, but he was reluctant to give up the readings, which he found profoundly satisfying if also exhausting both physically and emotionally. Despite these warnings, he performed twelve readings in London between January and March 1870, but his pulse rate would rise from seventy-two to 124 during the reading of the murder of Nancy from *Oliver Twist*, and he would have to lie down afterward.

Since 1865, Dickens had written his Christmas stories and other short pieces in a Swiss chalet in his garden at Gad's Hill Place, a present from his Swiss friend Charles Fechter. It was here that he began his last novel, *The Mystery of Edwin Drood*, for which he had "a very curious and new idea," in the autumn of 1869. The first monthly installment appeared on 1 April 1870, to great acclaim; his reading public had been without a Dickens novel for nearly five years. On 3 June he told his daughter that he hoped it would be a success if he lived to finish it. It was not to be; he collapsed on 8 June at Gad's Hill and died the next day without regaining consciousness, the manuscript of *The Mystery of Edwin Drood* open on his desk. His last two pages speak movingly of sunlight and shadow. They recall the ending of his first novel, *The Pickwick Papers*, in which Dickens had said farewell to his good friend Mr. Pickwick with the words "there are dark shadows on the earth, but its lights are stronger in the contrast. Some men, like bats or owls, have better eyes for the darkness than for the light; we . . . are better pleased to take our last parting look at the visionary companions of many solitary hours, when the brief sunshine of the world is blazing full upon them." Unexpectedly taking his parting look at Dick Datchery, Dickens suitably invokes the dying words of Sydney Carton for his own goodbye: "A brilliant morning shines on the old city. . . . Changes of glorious light from moving boughs, songs of birds, scents from gardens, woods, and fields . . . penetrate into the cathedral, subdue its earthy odour, and preach the Resurrection and the Light." A week later, he was laid to rest among the sunlight and shadows of Westminster Abbey, just fifty-eight years old.

2

Literary Heritage

Dickens's career as a novelist, public speaker, editor, and journalist spanned thirty-seven years, from a few years before Queen Victoria's succession to the throne in 1837 to his death in 1870. When he died, he was the most popular writer that the English-speaking world had ever known other than Shakespeare, with whom he is often compared for the tremendous range of their characterization, their understanding of human nature, the broadness of their comedy, and the intensity of their tragedy. Both writers also have unique, unmistakable voices whose expressions have become "household words" (Shakespeare's phrase, borrowed by Dickens for the title of his magazine) for generations of people who may no longer even read the works from which the words come. As the poet T. S. Eliot noted, one phrase either by the characters or about them can bring them vividly to our minds: no reader of *David Copperfield* ever forgets that Uriah Heep is "ever so 'umble" and "Barkis is willin'."

When Dickens leapt into almost overnight fame with *The Pickwick Papers*, one curmudgeonly critic said that he had gone up like a rocket but he would come down like the stick. He never did. Over the years, of course, his readers would prefer some of his novels to others, but the audience he cared about, the poorer and often illiterate people who would hear his novels read aloud in the local pub or neighbor's living room, never wavered in their love of his rich and original work. Most of all, they appreciated his humor, a quality that has sometimes been overlooked in the more serious literary analyses of Dickens in the twentieth century. Many of his contemporary readers disliked the darker vein of Dickens's later novels and urged him to return to the lighter, comic style of *Pickwick*, but Dickens himself recognized that the world had changed dramatically in his own lifetime and that the England of the 1850s was no longer the rural, slow-moving world of the stagecoach and country inn. The big industrial city and northern mill towns were home to most of his readers now, and he had to try to make life a little more interesting for them as well as drawing public attention to their problems and injustices. In every word he wrote, his aim was to combat Utilitarian practicality (to Dickens the most harmful attitude of his age) by encouraging the imagination and bringing the everyday to vivid life.

Dickens was one of many writers who were growing up in the 1820s and 1830s to become exemplary novelists in the 1840s to 1860s, the high tide of the Victorian novel in the works of Dickens, Thackeray, the Brontës, Elizabeth Gaskell, Charles Kingsley, Anthony Trollope, George Eliot, and Wilkie Collins. There had been a lull in novel-writing since the deaths of Jane Austen in 1817 and Sir Walter Scott in 1832. Novels were still being written, of course, but they have not stood the test of time. The so-called silver-fork school, or fashionable novel, dealt exclusively with high society, at first to admire it but later to expose its follies and evils. Another school was the Newgate novel, which explored the other extreme of pre-Victorian society: the criminal classes. Dickens made fun of the fashionable novel in his portrait of the upper-class fops Sir Mulberry Hawk and Lord Frederick Verisopht in *Nicholas Nickleby*, while in *Oliver Twist* he wanted to give his readers a more realistic portrait of criminal life than was offered in the Newgate novel.

As a novelist, Dickens was influenced by the eighteenth-century writers that he (as well as David Copperfield) read as a child. Smollett, Fielding, Sterne, and Defoe in Britain and LeSage and Cervantes on the Continent gave him his latent sense of the novel as providing a social panorama; a critique of society and human failings such as hypocrisy, vanity, and greed; and a vivid re-creation of place and character. While Smollett's and Cervantes's love of the grotesque and eccentric can be seen in all of Dickens's work—and other early influences continued to be important—a shift from his early masters to a reliance on his own methods and interests occurred before the end of his first novel, *The Pickwick Papers*, with its deepening interest in family relations and the introduction of darker themes, symbolized in the prison.

In 1836, Dickens revolutionized the world of novel-publishing when *The Pickwick Papers* gradually transformed during the course of twenty monthly installments from a series of unrelated episodes to a novel in the loosely structured picaresque tradition of *Don Quixote*, where a hero travels the world getting into various scrapes and adventures. Novels had been published in serial format before, but they were always reprints of novels such as Sir Walter Scott's popular Waverley series. Publishers were understandably loathe to risk publishing a novel in monthly parts when there was no guarantee of quality or even completion. With the success of *The Pickwick Papers*, publishers were quick to commission Dickens to write more "novels" (by the time it was completed, *Pickwick* did have a coherent story line), and from then on, he wrote all his novels for either monthly publication or weekly serialization in magazines. Despite the pressure of writing in serial form (the constant deadlines, the need to sustain interest, the difficulty of plotting when the writer could not go back and alter what he had written), monthly numbers (installments) became the most popular form of novel-publication for many years. Dickens liked it because poorer people could afford to buy the monthly numbers when a complete volume would have been too expensive; publishers liked it because they had the sales of both the numbers and the complete novel. Some people criticized it at the time as a denigration of the noble art of literature; monthly installments seemed to them like journalism or newspaper writing, ephemeral rather than written to last. But the success of Dickens's novels in serial form fundamentally altered publishing at a time when other changes were also being made (the shift from booksellers as publishers to proper publishing firms, for example), and in the 1840s and later, many other writers issued at least some of their novels in parts. The part issues of novels sometimes appeared alone, as was the case with *The Pickwick Papers*, but they were often just one section of a weekly or monthly magazine. *Oliver Twist* appeared monthly in *Bentley's Miscellany*, and *The Old Curiosity Shop* and *Barnaby Rudge* both appeared in weekly installments in *Master Humphrey's Clock*. Other magazines such as the *Cornhill* and *Blackwood's* followed suit and often competed for a chance to publish the next novel of the popular writers of the day. Dickens published *Hard Times, A Tale of Two Cities*, and *Great Expectations* in weekly installments in his journals *Household Words* (1850–1859) and *All the Year Round* (1859–1870), and he encouraged and promoted other Victorian novelists such as Elizabeth Gaskell, Edward Bulwer-Lytton, Charles Reade, Charles Lever, and Wilkie Collins, most of whose novels appeared there, including the classics *The Woman in White* and *The Moonstone*. Like television in the twentieth century, the serial novel of the nineteenth century was both praised for being more democratic and reaching a much wider audience than had been possible before, and condemned for exactly that feature: How could wildly popular novels like Dickens's be considered "good literature"? Although such criticism from snobbish critics rankled Dickens, his huge following of fans from bishops to barmaids more than made up for it. Despite the difficulties of writing in installments, especially weekly ones, Dickens never abandoned serial publication, begun really by accident in *The Pickwick Papers*.

As well as novels and poems, *Household Words* and *All the Year Round* contained articles on a wide range of contemporary topics. Dickens held very strict editorial control and influenced many young journalists who either worked on his staff, such as G. A. Sala and Henry Morley, or who contributed pieces, such as Mark Lemon, Harriet Martineau, and a host of other well-known Victorian writers. He corrected and revised every article that was published, often so carefully that the result looked like "an inky fishing-net" (Forster 2.384). In the pages of these journals a reader will find essays on every facet of Victorian life, including science, travel, politics, entertainment, religion, art, the law, and education, all inspired by Dickens's constant injunction to his sub-editor W. H. Wills to "KEEP 'HOUSEHOLD WORDS' IMAGINATIVE!" (*Letters* 7.200) and "Brighten it, brighten it, brighten it!" (*Letters* 7.126). At the same time, Dickens insisted on accuracy; he told Wills that "nothing can be so damaging to Household Words as carelessness about facts. It is as hideous as dulness" (*Letters* 7.51). Lord Northcliffe, founder of two of Britain's most popular newspapers, considered Dickens the greatest magazine editor of all time.

One of Dickens's most important influences on literature and society has been his love of Christmas. Before *A Christmas Carol*, his perennially popular 1843 story written specifically for the season, Christmas books had been elaborate affairs, richly bound and illustrated annuals that published poems and short pieces. Like the silver-fork school of novels, they were aimed at the upper classes and were scoffed at by serious writers such as Wordsworth and Sir Walter Scott, who contributed to them anyway. They were often Gothic in content and unrelated to the season, their appeal being their coffee-table format. After *A Christmas Carol*, Victorian publishers recognized a new genre: Dickens's attractive small book that openly preached Christian charity and kindness became the new model, and many writers produced similar books over the next few years. William Makepeace Thackeray's Christmas books were satirical sketches very different from Dickens's books, but Elizabeth Gaskell, Anthony Trollope, Wilkie Collins, and many other writers were commissioned to write in imitation of *A Christmas Carol*. In his autobiography, Trollope described the order as humbug, but it was the publishers rather than Dickens who tried to find a formula for the Christmas book. Dickens departed from descriptions of Christmas festivities in his very next book, *The Chimes*, which was set at New Year and depicted a harsh Utilitarian world rather than a cozy Yuletide scene.

Dickens was particularly influential also in the rise of the short story in the nineteenth century. It was a form that was only then becoming popular, and as late as 1862, a critic in *The Times* still did not see the story as a separate genre with particular techniques and effects. Reviewing the stories in Dickens's Christmas number for that year, he excused what he considered their poor quality on the grounds that "they occupy each but four or five pages. What is a tale-writer to do in four or five pages? Think what the first chapter of a novel is—how dull it is generally." Dickens had always particularly valued the short-story genre in the fairy tales of his childhood, ghost stories, and *The Arabian Nights*, and from his first publication (one of the *Sketches by Boz*) to his 1868 story "George Silverman's Explanation," he explored the possibilities of the form as confessional fiction, supernatural hair-raiser, fairy tale, comic sketch, and many other variations. In his journals *Household Words* and *All the Year Round*, he provided and encouraged the writing of stories, especially in the annual Christmas numbers, which commissioned stories from a wide variety of writers. Elizabeth Gaskell, Wilkie Collins, and many other Victorians discovered their talent as short-story writers through contributing to Dickens's journals, and again other publishers took up the idea of using a framework to unify short stories into a book or a special number. Reviewing Dickens's Christmas number *Mugby Junction* in *The Times* on 5 December 1866, E. S. Dallas compared it favorably to the proliferation of other Christmas numbers because it relied on the quality of the writing for its appeal:

Regularly as the year draws to a close we are inundated with a peculiar class of books which are supposed to be appropriate to the goodwill and joviality of the season. Most of these publications are quickly forgotten; and, indeed, are so full of display that they deserve no better fate. But amid the crowd of ostentatious and ephemeral works there appears an unpretending little brochure. The plainest, the homeliest, the cheapest, the least promising of the Christmas books—it is the best of all, the liveliest, the longest-lived, and the most successful. It is so because it is instinct with the fine spirit and the rare genius of the most popular of English authors. (*The Times*, 5 December 1866)

Several of Dickens's stories were written for American publishers, the short-story form having struck a firm root there in the work of Edgar Allan Poe (whose stories some of Dickens's early attempts closely resemble), Nathaniel Hawthorne, and Herman Melville. An earlier American writer, Washington Irving, had a strong influence on Dickens's early sketches in *Sketches by Boz* and *The Pickwick Papers*, which often recall Irving's portrait of English life in *The Sketch Book of Geoffrey Crayon* and *Bracebridge Hall*.

The adjective "Dickensian" has come to mean many things. Often it refers to atrocious living conditions, which Dickens described in more vivid detail than any other writer of his age. Despite the objections of some of his early readers who considered social realism out of place in literature, Dickens was not afraid to enter the prison or the slum in his novels and depict them as he had actually found them. From Mr. Pickwick's eye-opening but brief sojourn in the Fleet Prison, to Oliver Twist's terrified imprisonment in Fagin's dark den, and Jo's "home," the miserable, disease-ridden corner of London called Tom-

All-Alone's in *Bleak House*, Dickens painted unforgettable and valid pictures of life for the outcast and forgotten of Victorian society. *Oliver Twist* was his first novel to deal directly with a contemporary social evil, in this case, the New Poor Law and its effect on the people it was intended to help. Increasingly, Dickens's novels took up the issues of the day until, in *A Christmas Carol* and the novels that followed it, he learned to weave together theme, character, and plot into coherent visions of Victorian life, especially the lives of those on the margins of society: criminals, children, and the working poor. Many other novelists shared his belief that, through fiction, they could draw attention to social evils and also support and entertain a class of people whose day-to-day lives were tedious and wretched. Benjamin Disraeli, Elizabeth Gaskell, and Charles Kingsley were a few of the novelists who, in the 1840s, joined Dickens in describing the division in English society as "The Two Nations" (Disraeli's term) or "North and South" (Mrs. Gaskell's term). The "condition of England" novels all depicted "hard times" for the working people of mid-century; they were new in fiction and helped to bring about social reform.

"Dickensian" has also come to mean abundance and variety in style and character, a lively and animated vision of the eccentricities and potential of human nature told in highly metaphorical language where inanimate objects regularly come to life. Dickens's metonymic method of writing (where external signs denote internal character, just as Pip imagines his dead parents as resembling the script on their tombstones) has led some readers to accuse him of failing to understand or communicate the inner life of his characters. But, increasingly, Dickens's shrewd and complex insight into human psychology (found often in his exploration of dreams and symbols) has been recognized and valued, just as it was recognized in the nineteenth century by the great Russian novelists Leo Tolstoy and Fyodor Dostoevsky, both ardent admirers of Dickens. The famous Russian filmmaker Sergei Eisenstein praised Dickens's use of cinematic devices such as close-up, the effect of which is the creation of atmosphere: "and 'atmosphere'—always and everywhere—is one of the most expressive means of revealing the inner world and ethical countenance of the characters themselves."[1] Many advances in literary technique commonly thought to belong to the twentieth century can be found in Dickens's work, such as stream of consciousness, multiple narrators, and linguistic experiment. His influence on such innovative writers as James Joyce and John Irving, in the novel, and T. S. Eliot, in poetry, has been profound.

Dickens has also been credited with helping to establish the genre of detective fiction. He and his friend Wilkie Collins (who wrote one of the earliest detective novels, *The Moonstone*) both enjoyed the complex plotting required in the mystery story, and Dickens's later novels all involved the uncovering of hidden secrets. Inspector Bucket in *Bleak House* is usually regarded as the prototype of the modern detective, and the unfinished *The Mystery of Edwin Drood* seems to be a crime novel. But, for Dickens, the intricate plots were not the main interest; rather, they were vehicles for exploring questions of identity and illustrating a complex vision of a society that seems fragmented but that the secrets reveal is actually connected in profound ways.

In his own time, Dickens demonstrated the nineteenth-century shift from the Romanticism of the early part of the century to a sometimes grudging acceptance of the Industrial Age and belief in progress that marked the Victorian period. One of his most beneficial contributions was to keep alive the Romantic belief in the importance of the imagination and the value of the child in an era that was often critical of both. But as well as criticizing the follies of his own age, Dickens departed from Romanticism by becoming the novelist of the city and a champion of modern life, recognizing that the human heart will continue to beat alongside the whirr of the factory loom or the hum of the computer. Rather than escaping to the countryside, Dickens increasingly saw the need for finding and nurturing the imaginative core of life that can prevail even in the center of the modern industrial city. People will always resist the modern tendency to reduce them to statistics or replace them with machines, but they need support and encouragement. In 1859, he wrote to a friend, "I hope I have done my part to make the rising generation 'more childish,' in rendering them a little more imaginative, a little more gentle, and a little less conceited and hard, than they would have been without me. I desire to do nothing better" (*Letters* 9.1).

NOTE

1 "Dickens, Griffith, and the Film Today," *Film Form* (London, 1951), 199.

3

The Early Novels from *The Pickwick Papers* (1837) to *Martin Chuzzlewit* (1844)

THE PICKWICK PAPERS (1837)

The Pickwick Papers is a remarkable first novel: original, bursting with energy and humor, swept along by characters who have become as immortal as the "inimitable Boz" who invented them at the age of only twenty-four. The book is colored by its opening image, the "first ray of light which illumines the gloom, and converts into a dazzling brilliancy that obscurity in which the earlier history of the public career of the immortal Pickwick would appear to be involved." It was as though the young novelist, while no longer obscure in London thanks to *Sketches by Boz*, yet had some notion that in *Pickwick* he would achieve the extraordinary fame that was accorded to him even before the book was completed.

Dickens grew into novel-writing from his beginnings as a journalist and only gradually developed a novelist's sense of structure, plot, and deliberate form. When, in 1836, he was commissioned to write *The Pickwick Papers* as a monthly series, he was not writing a novel with a preconceived central idea that would be worked out through careful plotting, foreshadowing, and character development; he was writing a series of episodes held together by the most tenuous of threads. The episodes would concern the members of the "Pickwick Club," and they would involve comic misunderstandings and slapstick humor in the manner of the popular stories of the day. He decided on the idea of a club because he was taking over an idea for a serial that had already been devised by the publisher Chapman and Hall and an illustrator, Robert Seymour. In his Preface to the 1847 edition of the novel, Dickens describes how he was invited by Mr. Chapman and Mr. Hall to write the commentary for a series of prints about a Nimrod Club, whose members were incompetent sportsmen who would get into all sorts of difficulties with hunting and fishing. Pointing out that this idea was not very original and that he was no sportsman, the new young author told the publishers, "I would like to take my own way, with a freer range of English scenes and people, and was afraid I should ultimately do so in any case, whatever course I might prescribe to myself at starting." The argument was quickly resolved: "My views being deferred to, I thought of Mr. Pickwick."

That Dickens "thought of Mr. Pickwick" is one of literature's most famous understatements. But Pickwick and his sidekick Sam Weller were also a part of a tradition in the early novel of an innocently bumbling but wholly good master and his worldly-wise and canny servant or companion, like Cervantes's Don Quixote and Sancho Panza or Fielding's Parson Adams and Joseph Andrews. These earlier works were usually episodic stories, centering on the hero's journey, not necessarily a quest but often just a rambling adventure in which the hero's innocence would lead him into embarrassing scrapes, often with con men who recognized an easy victim. For the first few numbers, *The Pickwick Papers* relied on the stock devices of these early stories, and although the familiar episodes of the eighteenth-century novel continued to dominate the book, it very quickly took on a very different aspect as well, one that looked ahead to the nineteenth-century novel and to Dickens's own development as a serious novelist.

Mr. Pickwick begins as a good-natured bumbler, constantly getting into trouble from which Sam Weller or his friends have to extricate him, such as finding himself in a spinster's bedroom in the middle of the night or enjoying a little too much punch and waking up in a wheelbarrow at the pound. But as the novel proceeds, Pickwick ceases to be the butt of the jokes and becomes a more active moral center of the novel when his landlady, Mrs. Bardell, sues him for breach of promise of marriage (she misunderstood his faltering request to be allowed to bring a manservant, Sam Weller, into his lodgings). The trial between Bardell and Pickwick is one of the most famous comic scenes in English literature and one that Dickens took great delight in performing during his public reading tours. When the court decides in favor of Mrs. Bardell and awards costs against Pickwick, he refuses to pay her rascally lawyers, Dodson and Fogg, choosing an indefinite sentence at Fleet Prison. He is released when a greater challenge to his honor is offered: Mrs. Bardell is about to be imprisoned for not paying the legal fees, and she can only be kept out of jail if Mr. Pickwick pays them. As a gentleman, of course, he has no option but to pay Dodson and Fogg's bill.

At first, Mr. Pickwick had been merely a friend to the three comical, bumbling members of the Pickwick Club, Mr. Winkle, Mr. Snodgrass, and Mr. Tupman; as the novel proceeds, he becomes a father figure to them, in sharp contrast to the destructive fathers of some of the interpolated stories. The themes of marriage, parents, and children, so dominant in all his works, emerge here as Mr. Pickwick becomes the surrogate father who brings about the happy marriages of his young men. His relationship with Sam Weller develops into a bond of affection and loyalty, crowned by Sam's deliberate imprisonment for debt so that he can remain with his master. Sam's own father, Tony Weller, who, with Sam himself, is one of Dickens's happiest creations, gains in understanding and dignity through his association with Mr. Pickwick.

Dickens's lifelong interest in the darker side of our natures—in madmen, murderers, the guilty mind, and the troubled psyche—is evident early in the novel, in the interpolated stories, a stock device of the novels Dickens loved, such as *Don Quixote* and *Gil Blas*. Evil in the novel is at first either set apart in stories (to which the characters are often not really listening) or largely comical and easily dealt with, from the enterprising con man Mr. Jingle (whose disjointed language is an early example of Dickens's skill with dialogue to embody character) to the vagaries of the law in Mr. Pickwick's trial and the injustices of the parliamentary system in the hilarious Eatanswill election. But in the Fleet prison, Mr. Pickwick encounters a darker side of society that he had not known before. Prisons, and prisons of the mind, would continue to dominate Dickens's fiction for the rest of his career.

In his Preface to the 1867 edition of the novel, Dickens drew attention to the Reverend Stiggins, the first of his many satirical portraits of hypocritical preachers and their loyal followers. While the Reverend preaches temperance, he is also very fond of rum; Dickens's main complaint here and in his later works, however, is with the dangerous hypocrisy of the Reverend's religion, which does such a disservice to genuine Christianity. Quoting Jonathan Swift, Dickens refers to Stiggins as one of the many who "have just enough religion to make them hate, and not enough to make them love, one another."

The Pickwick Papers will always be read and appreciated for its affectionate portrait of pre-Victorian England: a time when the Industrial Revolution had not yet made its mark on the landscape and the people; when the stagecoach plied the rough roads of the country (ably driven by Tony Weller, whose language is peppered with metaphors from his calling); when Christmas at Dingley Dell kept alive the rural traditions of a well-ordered and peaceful way of life, so different from the urban meal enjoyed by the Cratchits sixteen years later. It is the novel of a young man newly married, with the world before him, in which the romances end happily, absent or failing fathers are replaced by kind and loving ones, and at the end of the story, the "dark shadows" of the earth merely make the lights "stronger in the contrast." The shadows may grow longer in the later novels, but Dickens never lost his faith in man's capacity for virtue and kindness, as immortalized in Mr. Pickwick.

THE LIFE AND ADVENTURES OF NICHOLAS NICKLEBY (1839)

While still working on *Oliver Twist*, Dickens began *Nicholas Nickleby*, like *Pickwick*, a twenty-part novel that ran in monthly installments from April 1838 to October 1839. Like *Pickwick*, the new novel was heavily influenced by the loosely structured and satirical eighteenth-century novels of Fielding and Smollett, but it was also imbued with Dickens's love of the theater in its memorable descriptions of stage life and people, and in its highly melodramatic plot.

Dickens's first notion for *Nicholas Nickleby* derived from a contemporary evil. While *Oliver Twist* had exposed the horrors of the workhouse and the baby farm, the new novel began by uncovering another source of child suffering, the notorious "cheap schools" of Yorkshire where for nearly a hundred years orphaned or unwanted (often illegitimate) children had been farmed out and forgotten. Dickens visited the schools with his illustrator, Hablot Knight Browne, early in 1838. In his Preface to the 1848 edition of the novel, he explains how, at that time, anyone could set up as a schoolmaster; no qualifications were required. Therefore, in a race of "blockheads and imposters" the Yorkshire variety "were the lowest and most rotten round in the whole ladder. Traders in the avarice, indifference, or imbecility of parents, and the helplessness of children; ignorant, sordid, brutal men . . . they formed the worthy corner-stone of a structure, which, for absurdity and a magnificent high-handed *laissez-aller* neglect, has rarely been exceeded in the world."

Dickens brought the schools vividly to life in the brutal Wackford Squeers, headmaster of Dotheboys Hall, when Nicholas (another fatherless boy, with a foolish and ineffectual mother) is sent there by his evil Uncle Ralph to earn his living as schoolmaster's assistant. Squeers is assisted in his unrelenting cruelty to the boys by his wife, but both get their comeuppance from Nicholas, who beats Squeers within an inch of his life. The boys force brimstone and treacle—their vile medicine—down the throat of Squeers's wife. The sufferings of the children of the Yorkshire school system are graphically realized in Smike, a painfully thin, half-witted boy whom Squeers enslaves in exchange for his fees, which have not been paid for many years. When Smike tries to run away, Squeers thrashes him, leading to Nicholas's retaliation. It is later revealed that

Smike is the illegitimate son of Nicholas's Uncle Ralph, a moneylender and source of all the evil doings in the novel, who hangs himself at the end.

The plot of *Nicholas Nickleby* is complicated and theatrical, with a cast of predictable characters from the evil Uncle Ralph, who orchestrates most of the action, to the scheming aristocrat Sir Mulberry Hawk and his sycophant Lord Frederick Verisopht, whose names indicate their source in the eighteenth-century novel. While Nicholas is pursued by the amorous daughter of Wackford Squeers in Yorkshire, his sister Kate, a milliner's assistant at the Mantalinis in London, attracts the amorous notice of Mr. Mantalini, but she is more dangerously threatened by the predatory Sir Mulberry Hawk. Kate is rescued from his evil plot by her brother, who has returned to London with Smike. Hawk arranges for Squeers to capture Smike in retaliation, but the plot is foiled.

An early working out of the theme of the January/May marriage, which Dickens would return to in *The Cricket on the Hearth* and *David Copperfield*, thickens the plot when Nicholas falls in love with the beautiful Madeline Bray, based on Dickens's beloved sister-in-law Mary Hogarth, who had died the previous year and whom Dickens dreamed about when he was visiting Yorkshire. Madeline's father is typical of Dickens's dangerously selfish fathers, a weak-willed and sickly man who is prepared to sacrifice his daughter in marriage to an old, lecherous, and avaricious moneylender, Arthur Gride, who has secret knowledge that Madeline is an heiress. The plot, masterminded by Uncle Ralph, is foiled by Nicholas, who marries her.

There is much humor and pathos in this melodrama, but the finest comedy occurs in Dickens's rendering of his favorite pursuit, the contemporary theater. Nicholas and Smike join Vincent Crummles's touring company, which includes the versatile Miss Snevellici and Ninetta, the infant phenomenon, who is not as much an infant as Vincent would like the audience to believe. She and Mr. Crummles were probably based on the actor-manager T. D. Davenport and his daughter. Mr. Crummles's troupe regularly draws crowds to see "positively the last appearance" of an actor or play. Dickens's affection for the theater and its people is evident in the highly comic descriptions, of their extravagances, theatrical conventions, deceptions and attachments, a lively portrait that will be repeated with less exuberance in Mr. Sleary's circus in *Hard Times*. Just as the circus provides the imaginative entertainment vital to a healthy society, the theater also serves as an antidote to the cruelties and rapaciousness of Squeers, Ralph Nickleby, and their accomplices, who threaten to destroy Nicholas, Kate, and Madeline, and whose cruelty and neglect destroy poor Smike.

As always in Dickens, the novel teems with memorable minor characters. In addition to the many theatrical portraits, there is Mrs. Nickleby, based on Dickens's own mother, a foolish, garrulous woman given to conversational flights that go nowhere (a precursor to Flora Finching in *Little Dorrit*), well-meaning but vain and essentially useless as a mother. It is her fault that her children are put at the mercy of the villainous Uncle Ralph at the beginning of the novel. She is pursued romantically by a lunatic neighbor whose courting involves flinging vegetables over the wall for her. Newman Noggs, Ralph's clerk, has, through drink and carelessness with money, lost his gentlemanly status, but he is now stirred to right action by the plight of Nicholas and Kate. Less convincing are the representatives of goodness, the benevolent Cheeryble brothers who employ Nicholas and act as fairy godfathers to help bring about the happy resolution of the story. Kate marries their equally honorable and benevolent nephew, Frank. Recognizing that the Cheeryble brothers seem too good to be true, Dickens noted in his Preface that they were based on real people, brothers he knew in Manchester.

The strength of *Nicholas Nickleby* lies in the language, particularly the dialogue of the huge cast of characters. Few readers forget Squeers's rapture over the watered-down milk on which he starves the boys—"Here's richness!"—or his daughter's long letter to Ralph Nickleby after Squeers's thrashing by Nicholas, informing him that "it is doubtful whether he will ever recuvver the use of his legs which prevents him holding a pen." Mrs. Squeers, she writes, was also assaulted by Nicholas, who "drove her back comb several inches into her head. A very little more and it must have entered her skull."

Although the abuses of the schools were well known, Dickens was correct to take some credit for their improvement when he wrote his 1848 Preface. The tremendous popularity of the novel drew attention to them; the description was recognized as being accurate if exaggerated; and many children were withdrawn and the schools were closed. Thackeray credited Dickens with the reforms in his 1852 lecture "Charity and Humour," where he also notes that his ten-year-old daughter Minnie read *Nicholas Nickleby* over and over again.

THE OLD CURIOSITY SHOP (1841)

Nicholas Nickleby closes with children visiting the grassy grave of poor Smike, the child victim of adult cruelty and neglect. In Dickens's next novel, the death of the child heroine, Little Nell, while not planned from the start, has become one of the most famous and controversial scenes in literature.

The Old Curiosity Shop began as a short story for Dickens's weekly periodical *Master Humphrey's Clock*. The title character was a kindly, secretive, infirm old man who invited a few lonely old friends to form a storytelling club in his old house. The idea was that they would take manuscripts from the depths of the old clock and weave bright stories from the darkness of their past sufferings, just as the butterflies "have sprung for the first time into light and sunshine from some dark corner of these old walls." It was crucial to Dickens's conception of storytelling that the stories had to be autobiographical, the stirrings of memory that would result in greater compassion and understanding. Dickens's own grief at the loss of Mary Hogarth in 1837 no doubt partially accounts for his obsessive need to find, in sad memories, a source of strength and consolation and for his decision to center the story around a young, innocent girl. The story of Little Nell and her grandfather was at first only one of the manuscripts taken from the clock case, narrated by Master Humphrey as a story in which he had a personal interest. Sales of the periodical had been dropping, but when they revived dramatically with the introduction of Little Nell, Dickens decided to drop all the other material and turn the new story into a novel, quietly removing Humphrey as the narrator. In no time, *The Old Curiosity Shop* was a triumph, with weekly sales reaching 100,000 copies.

The novel has similarities with *Nicholas Nickleby*. Again, a child (Nell is thirteen) is forced prematurely to deal with a hostile and difficult world because of a well-meaning but incompetent adult, Nell's grandfather, a compulsive gambler. The villainous schoolmaster Squeers, a grotesque compound of vicious cruelty and comic vitality, is deepened into a broader and more far-reaching evil in Daniel Quilp, the dwarfish and hideous creditor of Nell's grandfather. He is the devil himself who devours eggs, shells and all, gigantic whole prawns, and boiling tea. As Smike tries to evade Squeers in *Nicholas Nickleby*, Nell and her grandfather spend most of the time in this novel fleeing from Quilp, who, like so many Dickensian villains, tracks them relentlessly after foreclosing on their home, the old curiosity shop. The imaginative world of the theater to which Smike and Nicholas escape becomes, for Nell and her grandfather, a variety of entertainments that are not always a refuge: One of the owners of a Punch and Judy show threatens to tell Quilp of their whereabouts; but Mrs. Jarley, the kindly proprietor of a travelling wax-works, employs and aids Nell.

Little Nell, like Oliver Twist, is the personification of goodness, the innocent child in a world fraught with predatory adults and other dangers. This central theme is embodied in the opening description (emphasized by the first illustration) of Nell in the old curiosity shop, "the child in the midst of a crowd of uncongenial and ancient things" (*Letters* 2.49), as Dickens wrote. Master Humphrey refers to the child in the old shop as existing in "a kind of allegory," the allegorical source in both novels being Bunyan's *A Pilgrim's Progress*. Master Humphrey prefaces Nell's story by speculating what it would be like to "imagine her in her future life, holding her solitary way among a crowd of wild grotesque companions; the only pure, fresh, youthful object in the throng." Like Oliver, Nell has to escape from the City of Destruction by fleeing to the country, but even here the journey is beset with snares and dangers; the country is not the idyllic, innocent world of the Romantics after all. She meets this crowd of grotesque companions with unswerving compassion and kindness and is rewarded with duplicity and deceit from some, kindness and support from others.

Whereas Oliver was completely alone until reunited with his relatives, Little Nell, like many of Dickens's later child characters, is saddled with a childish adult, her grandfather, for whom she has to take responsibility. He even steals from her to support his gambling addiction, in a futile attempt to provide for her. Undoubtedly, Dickens's resentment at having to leave the sheltered realm of childhood to work in the blacking factory because of his father's fecklessness was the basis for Dickens's sympathy with children in this position. Dickens shared this regret at the child's loss of innocence with the Romantics, but it was essentially his Christianity that inspired the sympathy. Dickens constantly reiterated Christ's support of the child in answer to the puritanical doctrine of original sin, which preached the sins of the fathers being visited on the child.

Little Nell is the victim also of her selfish brother, Fred, who, like most brothers of Dickens's heroines, tries to take advantage of her good nature; he wants her to marry his friend Dick Swiveller so that they can both share the inheritance he assumes she will be receiving. Thus, the male relatives who should be her support are actually enemies to her integrity and well-being; Little Dorrit will be similarly cast in the role of moral center for a weak-willed and selfish family.

Little Nell's death was not planned; in fact, Dickens worried about whether she should or should not die. But his friend John Forster felt it was essential, given the course of the story, and Dickens reluctantly agreed. Her death affected him deeply, as it did his many loyal readers, who wrote to him begging him to spare her. American fans are said to have shouted out, "Is Little Nell dead?" when the ship carrying the latest issue of *Master Humphrey's Clock* docked in New York. Part of the poignancy of her death lies in the vitality of her life; she is not marked out from the beginning as a child who will not survive, like Paul Dombey. Whereas Oliver Twist is a passive "principle of Good," who often falls asleep at critical points in his dangerous journey (but is spared death), Little Nell is a much more active figure who survives with resourcefulness and spunk the journey through Pilgrim's allegorical traps and snares as well as contemporary England's hostile places. Her death comes as a warning to all adults who would kill the spirit of a child through neglect, child labor, or just weak-mindedness.

The setting of *The Old Curiosity Shop* is both symbolic and actual, with the red and black smoke-caked brick of *Hard Times*'s Coketown entering the story through a Chartist[1] torchlight march of desperate, unemployed men. Nell finds herself in northern cities where "on every side, and far as the eye could see into the heavy distance, tall chimneys, crowding on each other, and presenting that endless repetition of the same dull, ugly form, which is the horror of oppressive dreams, poured out their plague of smoke, obscured the light, and made foul the melancholy air" (346). The sounds of engines "screeching and turning" and the "interminable perspective of brick towers, never ceasing in their black vomit, blasting all things living or inanimate, shutting out the face of day," tended by wild and savage people foreshadow *Hard Times* and *A Tale of Two Cities*, where such deprivation did indeed lead to revolution, as the Chartist marches threatened. So the child is endangered not just by individual devils like Quilp, but also by the contemporary hell of industrial life. The headmistress of a genteel boarding school foreshadows Mr. Gradgrind's theories of education when she tells Nell that, as a poor child, she should not be working in a wax-works; rather, she should be "assisting, to the extent of your infant powers, the manufactures of your country . . . [and] improving your mind by the constant contemplation of the steam engine" (242–43). Even the fairground people cannot escape the poverty of the times. Whereas the circus performers in *Hard Times* are a loving community of kind people, the travelling showmen whom Little Nell encounters are forced, through want, into jealousy of each other and grasping meanness.

Besides Little Nell herself, the novel offers many minor characters who provide humor and emotional warmth, such as Kit Nubbles, a young Joe Gargery figure who covers himself in ink when he tries to write and whose devotion to Nell brings on the wrath of Quilp. Kit is rescued by the kindly Garlands, flowery antidotes to the metallic partnership of Sally Brass and her brother Sampson, Quilp's lawyer. Most memorable of all are Dick Swiveller and the Marchioness. Dick (always a propitious name in Dickens's fiction) undergoes a change of heart when the Brasses' little servant girl (nicknamed the Marchioness by Dick) nurses him back to health after a fever and encourages him to help Kit. Dick, a relative of Sam Weller in the Dickens world, is famous for many expressions including his sage advice to Fred: "fan the sinking flame of hilarity with the wing of friendship: and pass the rosy wine!"

BARNABY RUDGE (1841)

Barnaby Rudge immediately followed *The Old Curiosity Shop* in the pages of *Master Humphrey's Clock*, appearing there weekly from February to November 1841. It was Dickens's first historical novel, and one he had been thinking about as early as 1836, when he had promised a novel entitled *Gabriel Varden, the Locksmith of London*, to the publisher John Macrone. The historical backdrop to the story is the Gordon Riots of 1780, an anti-Catholic movement led by Lord George Gordon, who appears in the novel. Gordon was violently opposed to the Catholic Relief Act of 1778, which had brought some lessening of the harsh restrictions imposed on Catholics by the protestant King William III.

Like Dickens's other historical novel, *A Tale of Two Cities*, *Barnaby Rudge* brings together private and public worlds by focussing on characters caught up in an historical event that involved ordinary people. In both novels, the effect of the mob mentality is central to Dickens's depiction of how individual conscience and action can become lost in group madness. *The Pickwick Papers* had made comic reference to this tendency at the Eatanswill election, when Mr. Pickwick advises his friends to do what the mob does:

> "But suppose there are two mobs?" suggested Mr. Snodgrass.
>
> "Shout with the largest," replied Mr. Pickwick.
>
> Volumes could not have said more. (145)

Dickens's model was partly Sir Walter Scott's portrayal of riot scenes, but he was also concerned to depict the danger of mob violence in the wake of the Chartist marches and the unrest in the country in the late 1830s.

At the heart of *Barnaby Rudge* is Dickens's fascination with states of mind, especially the criminal and abnormal mind. Some of his early stories in *Sketches by Boz* and *The Pickwick Papers* had dealt with murderers and madmen, as had two stories that he wrote for *Master Humphrey's Clock* before it became dedicated to *The Old Curiosity Shop*. A murder story and the murderer's guilty conscience underlie *Barnaby Rudge*, the details of which are concealed until the end of the novel. Barnaby Rudge is a half-witted boy whose father killed Reuben Haredale, his employer and the owner of a large house, The Warren, the day before Barnaby was born. To cover his tracks, Rudge also murders the gardener, whose remains are later found and presumed to be Rudge's, who has actually disappeared. He reappears at the beginning of the novel as a mysterious stranger who (like Aunt Betsey's husband in *David Copperfield*) extorts money from his wife.

The present owners of The Warren are a Catholic family, Reuben's brother, Geoffrey Haredale, and Reuben's daughter, Emma. Emma is in love with Edward Chester, whose father, Sir John Chester, a Protestant, is violently opposed to the marriage because he has quarrelled with Haredale, an old school friend. Dickens based his portrait of Chester—a polished, urbane, but brutally cold and selfish man—on the Earl of Chesterfield. Chester breaks up his son's love affair and dismisses his son when he refuses to marry a rich heiress to prop up the family fortunes.

The story also revolves around the Maypole Inn, where John Willet is another misguided, stubborn, and opinionated father. His son Joe, who is in love with Dolly Varden, rebels against his father's treatment of him and enlists in the army to fight against the Americans in the War of Independence. The groom of the Maypole is Hugh, a brutal man whose savage nature is tempered by his love for his dog and for Barnaby Rudge. He also has designs on Dolly. Hugh turns out to be the illegitimate child of Sir John Chester.

Dolly belongs to the third setting, her father Gabriel Varden's locksmith's shop. One of Dickens's many pretty flirts (all based on his own painfully flirtatious young girlfriend, Maria Beadnell), Dolly is kind-hearted but spoiled and rejects Joe's advances out of whim rather than conviction. She is also pursued by her father's apprentice, Simon Tappertit, a small, bony, scheming, and treacherously vain fellow who is the captain of a group of London apprentices and resentful of his kind-hearted master.

The three houses and groups of characters come together through the Gordon Riots, when Simon Tappertit joins the rioters with his "knights" and Barnaby is dragged into the riot without understanding anything about it. Ned Dennis, the public hangman (based on the real one in the Gordon Riots), and Hugh are ringleaders of the riots, partly because of their anti-Catholic feelings but mostly because of their brutal liking for violence. The rioters head for The Warren, looting the Maypole on the way and leaving John Willet tied up and permanently stupefied. Dolly and Emma (now friends) are kidnapped; Barnaby is arrested and imprisoned in Newgate Prison, which the rioters storm, in a scene that will reappear in the attack on the Bastille in *A Tale of Two Cities*. Barnaby's father is also in Newgate, having been seized by Geoffrey Haredale when he is irrevocably drawn back by his guilty conscience to the scene of his crime, The Warren.

The overturning of the natural order is everywhere in the novel, from the murder twenty-two years earlier to the closing scenes, where Hugh, Dennis, and Mr. Rudge are all hanged, Simon Tappertit loses both legs, and even Joe Willet has lost an arm fighting in America. Sir John Chester, who refuses to acknowledge his son Hugh, is killed by Geoffrey Haredale. The riot scenes are vivid and horrifyingly realistic depictions of people turned into wild animals. As they frantically scoop up the burning liquor that flows in a torrent from the ruins of a vintner's house, the rioters are a wilder, cruder mob than the Parisians who scoop up the spilled wine and smear their faces into tigerish grins in *A Tale of Two Cities*.

Barnaby Rudge is an unusual hero, and yet his perceptive madness is closer to the characters and interests of Master Humphrey and his visionary, unusual storytelling friends than is Gabriel Varden, the sensible locksmith who was to have been the hero of the novel as Dickens originally intended it. John Willet's pig-headedness and Sir John Chester's destructive rationalism are both countered by Barnaby's fanciful half-wittedness, which is often eerily perceptive. He tells Sir John:

Why, how much better to be silly, than as wise as you! You don't see shadowy people there, like those that live in sleep—not you. Nor eyes in the knotted panes of glass, nor swift ghosts when it blows hard, nor do you hear voices in the air, nor see men stalking in the sky—not you! I lead a merrier life than you, with all your cleverness. You're the dull men. We're the bright ones. (Penguin 133)

In the disordered midnight world of London, *Barnaby Rudge* enacts the unleashing of violence and brutality, but it also gives credit to the imaginative flights of fancy, dreams, and perceptions of a simple-minded boy.

THE LIFE AND ADVENTURES OF MARTIN CHUZZLEWIT (1844)

Between the writing of *Barnaby Rudge* and *Martin Chuzzlewit*, Dickens had taken a welcome year's break from his hectic publishing schedule (five novels completed in four years). A six-month tour of America with his wife allowed him to take stock of his writing career and design his next work more purposefully. Running in monthly issues from January 1843 to July 1844, *Martin Chuzzlewit* had a central theme: to exhibit selfishness in all its many forms. Here, Dickens was following his eighteenth-century master, Henry Fielding, whose novels focused on a particular human vice such as hypocrisy or vanity. Dickens also admired Ben Jonson, who embodied single vices and virtues in his characters; in 1845 he chose Jonson's *Every Man in his Humour*, a study of jealousy, for the amateur theatricals of Dickens and his friends.

Dickens told his readers in a Preface that having this central theme in mind helped him to "keep a steadier eye upon the general purpose and design" and "resist the temptation" to let his creativity loose in the individual monthly installments. Despite this central controlling idea, *Martin Chuzzlewit* did, in fact, veer off in a completely new direction—to America—at the end of the fifth monthly number, when sales were flagging and a new interest was required. But while unplanned, the American chapters sustained the theme and expanded on it; his visit to America may well have inspired his choice of theme.

There are two Martin Chuzzlewits: Old Martin is a wealthy miser whose relatives he suspects are waiting impatiently for their inheritances; Young Martin, his grandson, is the hero of the book and at first is seemingly as selfish as the grandfather who has raised him. Even worse are Old Martin's brother Anthony and his son Jonas, whose character is so nasty that Dickens defended the truth of it in an 1849 Preface, noting that Jonas had inherited the vices of cunning, treachery, and avarice, had been shown them daily in the character of his father, and had been praised for developing them himself. Hardly surprising, then, that he would turn out as he did.

Young Martin has not inherited his grandfather's selfish nature, and the old man is testing him to see if he is more worthy than the other grasping relatives. Actually, the boy's nature "was a frank and generous one," but he had "unconsciously reasoned as a child" that the only way to combat his grandfather's selfishness was to look out for his own interests himself. "So he had grown selfish." He is reminded of his own frank and generous nature by tending to his friend Mark Tapley when he falls ill in America; for the first time, he reflects on his character and compares it to that of Mark, who has had few advantages but is a much more likeable person. The conversion of a selfish miser back to a better, more generous nature was the subject of *A Christmas Carol*, whose writing Dickens managed to combine with *Chuzzlewit* during October and November 1843. Young Martin's conversion at Mark's bedside is almost as rapid as Scrooge's but without the intervention of ghosts. He returns to England and wins the hand of Mary Graham, Old Martin's young companion and another of the "young, beautiful and good" Marys in Dickens's novels (such as Madeline Bray) who were inspired by Mary Hogarth.

Dickens's decision to revisit America through his fiction was partly a response to the outraged criticism that met *American Notes*, his series of essays about his visit. His battle with the American press over international copyright laws was also still very heated, and his disappointment in finding America not the Utopia he had hoped for is evident in his satirical attack in the novel. Mark and Martin buy a piece of land in "Eden," a midwest settlement that is advertised as a thriving community but that turns out to be a disease-infested swamp that has killed off most of the inhabitants. Dickens's satire of America is barbed and extensive, the attack ranging from simple lack of manners and pretentiousness to racism, arrogance, and snobbery. It was a one-sided portrait; other than Mr. Bevan, a kind physician, there are no Americans in the book who resemble Dickens's many friends who treated him with great generosity and with whom he remained close all his life.

Dickens's portrait of the English in *Martin Chuzzlewit* is equally unflattering of course, and his central design of uncovering selfishness in all its manifestations makes the novel less genial than usual. There are kindly characters, but they are few. Even the gentle and thoughtful brother and sister, Tom and Ruth Pinch, are given a name that suggests selfishness rather than generosity, so unlike the names Cheeryble or Garland. Dickens attacks self-interest in most of his novels, but it is usually an attack on the philosopher Jeremy Bentham's belief that we are motivated only by self-interest, which he is at pains to show is *not* the norm of human behavior. Here, selfishness does seem to be widespread, although Martin's reversion to his innately unselfish nature denies Bentham's theory, and Old Martin also rises to generosity at the end. Kindliness exists also at Mrs. Todgers's boarding house, where gravy (always associated with generosity in Dickens) flows freely, despite the trouble it causes the harassed Mrs. Todgers.

Martin Chuzzlewit is memorable for two wholly Dickensian creations. Mr. Pecksniff, an architect and cousin of Old Martin, embodies hypocrisy in every fiber of his being and appearance. "He was a most exemplary man: fuller of virtuous precept than a copy-book. Some people likened him to a direction-post, which is always telling the way to a place, and never goes there; but these were his enemies" (Everyman 13). Even his throat is moral and seems to say on his behalf, "There is no deception, ladies and gentlemen, all is peace, a holy calm pervades me" (14). His daughters Charity and Mercy are the very opposite of their names, the former's humor being "of a sharp and acid quality, as though an extra lemon (figuratively speaking) had been squeezed into the nectar of her disposition, and had rather damaged its flavour."

Sarah Gamp is a midwife and nurse whose dialogue is Dickens at his most comic and inventive. Sairey likes her clients to leave a bottle on the chimney-piece, "and don't ask me to take none, but let me put my lips to it when I am so dispoged." Sairey has an imaginary friend, Mrs. Harris, to whom she frequently refers but whose existence is doubted by her colleague Betsey Prig, an equally disreputable and incompetent nurse.

Dickens's fascination with murderers, evident in *Oliver Twist* and *Barnaby Rudge*, is vividly realized in the portrait of Mercy's husband Jonas Chuzzlewit, a brutal man who contemplates murdering his father and ends up murdering his associate in the Anglo-Bengalee Disinterested Loan and Life Assurance Company, Montague Tigg, who has been blackmailing him. Jonas suffers agonies of fear and dread that he will be discovered, his emotions embodied in his small and enclosed bedroom. Jonas poisons himself before he can be brought to trial, a suitable end for a thoroughly poisonous villain.

Dickens considered *Martin Chuzzlewit* by far the best of his novels thus far, and in many ways, it was. The central design is carefully worked out in the parallel stories of young Martin and his cousin Jonas, with Pecksniff an exuberant variation on the theme who weaves in and out of both plots. Stylistically, the novel is a tour de force of invention that exhibits a huge range of styles, voices, and diction. In Dickens's attention to design and theme and his mastery of language, the novel is usually considered the bridge between the loosely plotted novels of his early career and the richly symbolic and carefully constructed works that were to follow.

NOTE

1. Chartism was a political movement of the late 1830s and 1840s that lobbied for electoral reform. It was named for the People's Charter, a list of demands submitted to Parliament in 1837–1838.

4

Oliver Twist
(1838)

HISTORICAL BACKGROUND

When *Oliver Twist* first began in serialized form in the monthly magazine *Bentley's Miscellany* in 1837, its subtitle was "The Parish Boy's Progress." For the first few installments, Dickens's intention was to describe for his readers what it was like to be a "parish boy" in the years following the passing of the new Poor Law Amendment Act of 1834. Dickens would have seen the bill being hotly debated when he was a parliamentary reporter for the *Morning Chronicle*, and he would continue to attack it in his fiction and journalism for the rest of his life.

Prior to 1834, poor workers were given a tiny sum, or "dole," by their parish to keep them from starvation on their fixed agricultural wages. It was intended as emergency funds to tide people over until they could get on their feet again. The infirm and unemployable were also the responsibility of each parish. While there were many problems in the old system that the new legislation was intended to redress, many people felt that the cure was much worse than the disease. The new act, designed to prevent idle people from living off the community, grouped parishes together into "poor law unions" and established "workhouses" (which became known as "unions"); here, people with no other home or means of support were housed and put to work for the parish.

To discourage the poor from taking advantage of this social assistance, the workhouses were deliberately made as unappealing as possible. The Royal

Commission that recommended the new system specifically stated that conditions in the workhouse must be less appealing than those of the poorest laborers. Forced to leave their homes and sell their possessions, many families found themselves unable to get out of the workhouse once they were in it (and they were separated, with husbands, wives, and children sent to different places). All aspects of life in the workhouse were strictly governed by rules, including the subsistence-level food allowed to the inmates. In March 1838, Oliver's famous request on behalf of his fellow inmates for "more" was taken up by real-life workhouse paupers in a petition to the House of Lords. No wonder the workhouses soon became known as Bastilles, after the infamous French prison and symbol of the oppression of the poor.

When Oliver is "farmed" out to Mrs. Mann's house with "twenty or thirty other juvenile offenders against the poor-laws" (3), Dickens is referring to the accepted practice of the time. Pauper children were sent to "baby farms" where all kinds of abuses took place because nobody in authority considered the children anything other than a burden. To the Mrs. Manns who ran the farms, they were purely a source of income, and the less they ate, the better. Dickens's description gave the system some publicity, but nothing was changed until after 1848, when an outbreak of cholera at a baby farm at Tooting brought the system national attention. Drouet's farm housed 1,400 children in appalling conditions of neglect and overcrowding; when many of them died, Drouet was charged with manslaughter, and the Poor Law guardians and commissioners were also found liable. In 1849 Dickens wrote about the Tooting orphanage for the *Examiner*, where he called it "brutally conducted, vilely kept, preposterously inspected, dishonestly defended, a disgrace to a Christian community, and a stain upon a civilized land."

According to Marcus Stone, the illustrator of *Our Mutual Friend*, Dickens's description of the pauper's funeral in Chapter Five was also historically accurate. Stone recounts that while they were walking together in Cooling, near Rochester, Dickens pointed out the church where he had seen "the pauper's funeral in *Oliver Twist* exactly as it is written in the book." Dickens told Stone that when the minister of the church disputed the portrait of the uncaring clergyman, who arrives an hour late and then compresses the burial service into four minutes, Dickens replied that the minister was that clergyman.[1]

In his rendering of Fagin's gang and their surroundings, Dickens intended a realism that he felt was lacking in the popular crime fiction of the time, the so-called "Newgate Novels." In his Preface to the third edition of *Oliver Twist*, Dickens explained that he wanted to portray the criminals realistically because he wished to show how easily young homeless children could be dragged into the net of crime that could only lead to their transportation or death. Such realism had not been attempted before in a novel like *Oliver Twist* (although Daniel Defoe's grimly realistic story of the prostitute in *Moll Flanders* has similarities with Dickens's portrayal of Fagin and his gang). Dickens complains in the Preface that many criminals in literature are attractive people like Macheath in *The Beggar's Opera*. The highroads and hostelries they inhabit are exciting places that would inspire rather than deter the young audience. And deterrence was his aim, as he explains:

It appeared to me that to draw a knot of such associates in crime as really do exist; to paint them in all their deformity, in all their wretchedness, in all the squalid poverty of their lives; to shew them as they really are, for ever skulking uneasily through the dirtiest paths of life, with the great, black, ghastly gallows closing up their prospect, turn them where they may; it appeared to me that to do this, would be to attempt a something which was greatly needed, and which would be a service to society. And therefore I did it as I best could.

While some readers criticized Dickens for his sordid portrait (and the dramatic version of the novel was banned for some years), others defended Dickens's moral purpose in depicting criminal life. Gangs such as Fagin's were rife in London at that time, and his contemporary readers recognized the authenticity of the account.

Also taken from life was the portrait of the magistrate Fang, who was based on a particularly unsympathetic magistrate in London. A friend who worked in the court smuggled Dickens in so that he could describe the magistrate's appearance accurately. Dickens intended him to be immediately recognizable; he wanted "a magistrate whose harshness and insolence would render him a fit subject to be 'shewn up' . . . " (*Letters* 1.267). Allan Stewart Laing, Mr. Fang's prototype, was removed from the bench for conduct unbecoming a magistrate, not long after Dickens's portrait of him appeared.

PLOT DEVELOPMENT

Oliver Twist opens with the birth of the hero and the death of his mother in a miserable workhouse. After suffering many cruelties at the hands of the parish authorities and villagers for whom he is put to work, Oliver runs away to London, where he is befriended by the jovial Jack Dawkins (the Artful Dodger) and lured into a gang of pickpockets run by the evil Fagin. We learn later that Monks, Oliver's evil half-brother, has discovered Oliver's whereabouts and is using Fagin to try to turn the boy into a criminal so that he cannot inherit the legacy left to him by their father. Oliver makes a brief escape from them when he is taken in by the kindly Mr. Brownlow, whose pocket he has been accused of picking but who accepts Oliver's innocence. Back in the clutches of Fagin, he is involved in a housebreaking with Fagin's accomplice, Bill Sikes, but the burglary is foiled and, again, Oliver's innocence is championed by the owner of the house, Mrs. Maylie.

Oliver's fortunes continue to vacillate between the evil underworld of Fagin's den and the good, loving home of Mrs. Maylie, whose beautiful young ward, Rose, turns out to be Oliver's aunt. Dickens brings together these allegorical extremes through Nancy, the prostitute who tries to protect Oliver from the plottings of Monks and Fagin and loses her life as a result. Her murderer, Bill Sikes, is pursued and accidentally hangs himself when he falls from a roof, while Fagin is convicted and condemned to death. Oliver's identity is proven, and he is restored to his family and Mr. Brownlow, his father's devoted old friend.

CHARACTER DEVELOPMENT

Looking back on the novel in his Preface for the third edition in 1841, Dickens saw it as an allegory in the manner of Bunyan's *The Pilgrim's Progress*: "I wished to shew, in little Oliver, the principle of Good surviving through every adverse circumstance, and triumphing at last; and when I considered among what companions I could try him best, having regard to that kind of men into whose hands he would most naturally fall; I bethought myself of those who figure in these volumes." The characters are thus chosen to exemplify goodness and evil, and Oliver himself is largely a pawn in the game that plays out around him. Dickens's first villains are those officially entrusted with the care of orphan children: Mr. Bumble the beadle, a petty official in the village; the members of the local Board of Guardians who were appointed to administer the Poor Law; and the various adults such as Mrs. Mann who profited from the orphans. Dickens refers to the administrators as philosophers because their treatment of Oliver, a "systematic course of treachery and deception" (3), was justified by the writings of the political economists and social scientists of the day. Thomas Malthus, whose 1803 essay on population had denied those without income or support the right to exist, was the authority for those officials who self-righteously patted themselves on the back for any help they offered to paupers and orphans, however inadequate. Dickens attacks such smugness relentlessly in the opening pages, when those who pretend to be acting charitably and selflessly are clearly out for their own gain, from Mrs. Mann, who "farms" orphans for the money she is paid for their upkeep, to the "well fed philosopher" (25), who might learn something from seeing Oliver voraciously eating the dog's leftover food.

Mr. Bumble the beadle was actually a part of the old Poor Law system, and as such, he represents the pompous, stupidly arrogant petty official with whom his name has become synonymous. In the orphan's search for family, Mr. Bumble is one of many inadequate fathers; he is responsible for naming the child, which he does according to an alphabetical system, and for finding him employment. But "Bumble" suggests fumbling incompetence rather than the more deliberate and heartless policies of the "philosophers," and Dickens grants Mr. Bumble some natural sympathy when Oliver appeals to him as his only source of kindness. Bumble is reintroduced to help uncover the mystery of Oliver's birth, by which time, Dickens has altered his role from the symbol of parish authority to a more traditional comic figure: the henpecked husband. Mr. Bumble marries Mrs. Corney, the matron of the workhouse, for her position and her money, so he gets what he deserves when she turns out to be very different from the submissive housewife he had courted. But the reader is allowed to feel a little sympathy for Bumble once Oliver is free from his clutches. The Bumbles are both dismissed from their parochial office because Mrs. Corney, who has come into possession of Oliver's mother's locket and gold ring, sells them to Monks, who wants to destroy this proof of Oliver's identity. Although it was Mrs. Corney's doing, Mr. Bumble is also guilty because, as Mr. Brownlow tells him, "the law supposes that your wife acts under your direction." In a frequently misquoted statement, Bumble replies, "If the law supposes that . . . the law is a ass—a idiot" (335).

If the village characters represent the legislated cruelty of the Poor Law administrators, the criminals of London reveal Dickens's developing interest in personality and motivation. These scenes are powerfully created, with Dickens's imagination coming to life among the byways that he inhabited as a young worker at Warren's blacking factory. That he remembered those days when he was writing the novel is evident in his choice of Fagin for the name of the devilish man into whose clutches Oliver repeatedly falls. Bob Fagin was one of the boys with whom Dickens worked at Warren's, and just as Fagin acts as Oliver's first "teacher," having the boys demonstrate how to earn a living as a pickpocket, so on the first day of work, Bob Fagin had taught Dickens how to wrap and tie the labels on the bottles of blacking.

Dickens had been reading Daniel Defoe's *History of the Devil* while he was writing *Oliver Twist*, and his portrayal of Fagin is devilishly convincing if somewhat stereotypical. Repulsive but powerfully persuasive, Fagin is the personification of evil, like his counterpart Long John Silver in Stevenson's *Treasure Island*, a similar book about a father figure's demoniacal hold over a young boy. Fagin inhabits the darkest room in the darkest house in the very center of the labyrinthine city. Oliver gropes his way up the "dark and broken stairs" into a room whose walls and ceiling are "perfectly black, with age and dirt" (50) as well as with crime and corruption, where the perversion of boys into "middle-aged men" and girls into "fallen women," or prostitutes, takes place. That

Fagin preys on his "boys" sexually as well as financially is hinted at in Dickens's description of den life.

There is humor, though, in Dickens's portrayal of the street boys with whom he rubbed shoulders as he padded about the streets, a solitary working boy, in the blacking factory days. The Artful Dodger, living off his wits and always watching out for number one, is one of Dickens's most memorable Londoners, a realistic and unsentimentalized young ruffian whose impudent self-confidence has made his name a household word. His real name, Jack Dawkins, is no doubt a reference to the clever thieving bird, the jackdaw.

When he was pondering his villain's demise, Dickens wrote that Fagin was "such an out and outer that I don't know what to make of him" (*Letters* 1.441). Fagin's trial and death sentence are brilliant early examples of Dickens's skill at depicting the human mind under stress. As Fagin waits for the jury's verdict, he is both consumed with fear but also strangely detached, his mind fixing on the irrelevant details on which his eyes happen to fall. His final hours alone in his cell, waiting for the sentence to be carried out are also convincingly described, although less powerfully than Charles Darnay's interior monologue in the condemned cell in *A Tale of Two Cities*.

In a story where many characters are either black or white, one of the more complex characters is Nancy, the prostitute whose heart is touched by Oliver's innocence. Because the writer Thackeray and others found her portrayal sentimental, Dickens defended the apparent contradictions in her behavior in the Preface to the third edition: "It is useless to discuss whether the conduct and character of the girl seems natural or unnatural, probable or improbable, right or wrong. IT IS TRUE." Dickens was referring here not just to Nancy's fatal attraction and loyalty to Sikes, but also to her sympathy with Oliver, which springs from her remembrance of her own deprived childhood. Her murder affected Dickens greatly. He wrote to John Forster in October 1838, "Hard at work still. —Nancy is no more. I shewed what I have done to Kate last night who was in an unspeakable '*state*,' from which and my own impression I augur well. When I have sent Sikes to the Devil, I must have yours" (*Letters* 1.439). Two years before he died, Dickens started to include the murder of Nancy in his public readings, and although he was warned that reading this passage was dangerous to his health, he could not resist the tremendous impression it made on his audiences. Unfortunately, it distressed him as much as it did his audience; his pulse rate rose from 72 to 124 during the reading, and he would have to rest for ten minutes before going out on stage again. He died of a stroke three months after his last public performance of it, but according to a friend, he re-enacted the death once again in his own garden just two days before he died.[2]

Equally powerful, and an early instance of Dickens's fascination with the guilty mind of the criminal, is his description of Sikes after the murder, relentlessly pursued by the vision of Nancy's face. Sikes attempts to block out the sight by throwing himself into the fighting of a fearful fire, a vivid representation of the turmoil raging inside the desperate man who has killed his lover. If Nancy is irresistibly attracted to Sikes, even though she knows her life is in danger, Sikes discovers himself to be equally in the power of Nancy. In his Preface, Dickens answers the objection that Sikes has no glimmering of human feeling by arguing that there are such men: "Whether every gentler human feeling is dead within such bosoms, or the proper chord to strike has rusted and is hard to find, I do not know; but that the fact is so, I am sure." In Sikes's guilty conscience, though, Dickens does reveal Sikes as far from impervious: His rusty chord has been manipulated by Fagin, but it is a chord all the same. In this, Sikes is a much more interesting and plausible character than Monks, who speaks the language of the stock stage villain and whose banal real name, Edward Leeford, is typical of the unimaginative names Dickens sometimes used for characters who never really come to life. (His assumed name connects him to the Gothic horror tale *The Monk*.) Dickens would return to the Monks figure often, however, in the villain's dogged attempt to pursue Oliver and destroy him.

THEMATIC ISSUES

Dickens explores many themes in *Oliver Twist*, but in having an orphan child as hero, the novel's main focus (new for the novel genre) is the psychology of the child and the responsibilities that both parents and society in general have to their children. If parents are absent or negligent and the "guardians" appointed by the state are governed by a Utilitarian system, what future will the child face? Dickens had felt abandoned by his own family when his father was imprisoned and his mother wished to keep him working in the blacking warehouse. He saw all hopes of becoming an educated man extinguished, and he even feared for his moral growth. Oliver's plight at the beginning of the novel is caused not just by his father's enforced marriage to an older and immoral woman, but by his parents' moral weakness in conceiving a child, Oliver, out of wedlock. Agnes's death in childbirth is clearly the result of the neglect incurred by her unmarried state. If society is partly to blame for ostracizing her as a "fallen woman," the novel also makes clear that the responsibility belongs to Agnes and Oliver's father as well. In their absence, who will become his protector?

On her deathbed, Oliver's mother prays that God will "raise up some friends" (150) for her abandoned child, and that is what the novel does, not just in the Maylies, but also in more humble encounters such as the old lady who feeds him when he is half-dead on the road to London: She "took pity upon the poor orphan; and gave him what little she could afford—and more—with such kind and gentle words, and such tears of sympathy and compassion, that they sank deeper into Oliver's soul, than all the sufferings he had ever undergone" (46). Dickens invokes the story of the Good Samaritan many times in the novel to remind his readers what must be done for the orphan and the outcast, and to draw attention to the parish authorities who profess to be charitable but who are anything but. On his beadle's official coat, Mr. Bumble has elegant brass buttons decorated with a picture of the Good Samaritan "healing the sick and bruised man" (22). Bumble remembers that he was given the coat to attend the inquest of a poor tradesman who had died in a doorway.

Oliver Twist is often criticized for taking up two themes without integrating them: the abuses of the new Poor Law system in the village, and the evils of the criminal world in London. But these disparate worlds have much in common in Dickens's story of a vulnerable child, the clearest link being the philosopher Jeremy Bentham's belief that self-interest is our chief motivation. The Poor Law "system" of parish relief operates according to Bentham's code, but Dickens specifically refers to the same doctrine of self-interest when he describes how the Artful Dodger and Charley Bates ran away after picking Mr. Brownlow's pocket, leaving Oliver to be charged with the theft. The narrator satirically notes that their running away should win the admiration of Englishmen because "their anxiety for their own preservation and safety, goes to corroborate and confirm the little code of laws which certain profound and sound-judging philosophers have laid down as the mainspring of all Nature's deeds and actions: the said philosophers very wisely reducing the good lady's proceedings to matters of maxim and theory . . . putting entirely out of sight any considerations of heart, or generous impulse and feeling" (73). Later in the same passage, the narrator attacks Bentham's theory of morality (that the greatest happiness of the greatest number is the measure of right and wrong), noting that "to do a great right, you may do a little wrong; and you may take any means which the end to be attained will justify; the amount of the right, or the amount of the wrong, or indeed the distinction between the two, being left entirely to the philosopher concerned." Thus, the "every man for himself" doctrine that sustains the subculture of Fagin's den embodies the theory of human behavior spelled out in Benthamism and incorporated into the operation of the New Poor Laws. Oliver's treatment in the parish is truly criminal.

In Hard Times, Dickens dramatizes the effects of Benthamism on the development of the child, and his conclusions there expand on the view that he offers in Oliver Twist. While Noah Claypole, the village charity boy, acts solely out of self-interest and thus quickly takes his place among the criminals of London, other boys brought up in the parish system remain honest and compassionate. Both novels make clear that it is a very dangerous system, likely to produce selfish adults such as Bitzer and Tom Gradgrind, but Dickens was also anxious to show that Bentham's blanket theory of self-interest is wrong. The novel suggests that we are all born with different tendencies and natures, and some are more inclined to selfishness than others. Deprivation will cause many pauper children, such as Noah Claypole, to become self-serving criminals, while others, such as Oliver and little Dick, will have a natural inner moral sense that will respond to kindness. "Nature or inheritance had implanted a good sturdy spirit in Oliver's breast" (4), but even so, Dickens fears that such a sensitive nature "was in a fair way of being reduced, for life, to a state of brutal stupidity and sullenness by the ill-usage he had received" (23). Even good and gentle natures such as Oliver's can be hardened by cruelty or neglect, and thus the novel emphasizes the need for kindness and compassion, especially in our treatment of children. Oliver's mother's prayer enacts God's mercy in providing friends for the orphan: Good Samaritans, like the old lady, who defy Bentham's dictum that self-interest is our only motivation. Little Dick's blessing on Oliver when he leaves the village provides another source of the divine providence that makes possible Oliver's rescue from the evil world that ensnares him. Although Oliver does not develop very fully as a character, remaining rather the "principle of Good," Dickens does make clear the importance of kindness and sympathy in the boy's moral growth. The old lady's compassion sank "deeper into his soul" than his sufferings; as Madame Defarge learns in *A Tale of Two Cities*, love is always stronger than hate.

Also uniting the two worlds of parish and criminal den are the various attempts of both adult communities to either deny the orphan his identity or attempt to give him a new one. In the statistical world of Utilitarianism, that identity is not human. The narrator ironically first refers to Oliver as an "item of mortality," adopting the view of the political economists who find it easier to deal with people if they are numbers rather than individuals. In his first reference to the use of clothes to brand and ostracize the social outcast, Dickens describes Oliver as being an "excellent example of the power of dress." When Oliver was wrapped in a blanket, he was anonymous and could have been the child of a nobleman. "But now that he was enveloped in the old calico robes which had grown yellow in the same service, he was badged and ticketed, and fell into his place at once—a parish child—the orphan of a workhouse—the humble half-starved drudge" (3). "Work'us" becomes his generic name.

To be identified as a workhouse boy without family means that Oliver is now regarded as a criminal, even when he is acting out of the purest motives. He is also an illegitimate child, and according to the old doctrine that the sins of the fathers shall be visited on the sons, the villagers cast him out as "born bad." Whenever Oliver has the courage to assert himself, his reputation as a parish child prevents him from being seen as he really is. When Oliver, on behalf of the starving boys in the workhouse, asks for more, the illustration by George Cruikshank for the first edition vividly catches the stares of disbelief on the faces of the master and his servants. But equally condemning are the stares of the boys who put him up to asking for them. Their blank, open-mouthed faces see not Oliver, but a troublemaker whose life is already decided: "That boy will be hung," asserts the gentleman in the white waistcoat. Later, when Oliver fights Noah to defend his mother's good name, he is immediately punished as the workhouse boy who not only attacks the innocent Noah, but who, in the words of Charlotte, the maid, is one of "these dreadful creeturs, that are born to be murderers and robbers from their very cradle" (39). So easily, Dickens says, do children become singled out and found guilty. Is it any wonder that they sometimes fulfil Charlotte's prophecy?

Just as the parish identifies the workhouse child as a born criminal, the criminals themselves set about to destroy Oliver's nature and turn him, by slow degrees, into one of them. In this perverted underworld school where boys look and act like middle-aged men, Fagin is a "merry old gentleman," their "play" is picking pockets, and Oliver is "educated" into becoming a criminal through isolation, example, and training. Even his textbook is a perversion: Instead of a boy's school book Fagin gives him the *Newgate Calendar*, a hair-raising account of the lives of notorious criminals. Through these means, Fagin "was now slowly instilling into his soul the poison which he hoped would blacken it, and change its hue forever" (115).

Oliver's education in Fagin's den is not very different from the education he would have received in the village from another perverted father, the chimney sweep Gamfield, who takes Oliver "off the hands of the parish" (13) to work for him. Gamfield considers his business "a light pleasant trade" and defends the charge that boys are smoked out of chimneys with the argument that if the fire is properly blazing, "it's humane too, gen'lmen, acause, even if they've stuck in the chimbley, roastin' their feet makes 'em struggle to hextricate theirselves" (15). In both trades, the legal one of chimney sweeping and the illegal ones of picking pockets and housebreaking, the adult preys on very small children by putting them into positions of danger. Gamfield had "bruised three or four boys to death already" (16), but he regards his trade as morally edifying; like the good father, he is concerned for their moral upbringing. His boys are cured of faults such as obstinacy and laziness. Whereas Dickens's later child heroes are acutely aware of the injustices that surround them and the hypocrisy of the adults who pretend to be acting in the child's interest, Oliver is often too innocent or too afraid to see through the adults' mask of benevolence. The narrator thus takes on the role of ironic commentator. Oliver mistakes Fagin's disciplining of his "boys" as "the stern morality of the old gentleman's character." Not yet realizing that the "game" they play is pickpocketing, Oliver also does not know that Fagin disciplines his boys by knocking them downstairs; the narrator comments, "but this was carrying out his virtuous precepts to an unusual extent" (59).

Oliver is rescued from the identities that would be forced upon him by encountering people who see the human face behind the labelled clothing, whether workhouse calico robe or prison stripes. The first person to look at Oliver directly is, ironically, the half-blind and half-childish magistrate who is to indenture him as a chimney sweep to the villainous Mr. Gamfield. As he looks around for the inkstand, "his gaze encountered the pale and terrified face of Oliver Twist" (18). This sudden recognition that the "item of mortality" is actually a heartsick child inspires the magistrate to cancel the indentures and tell Mr. Bumble to take him back to the workhouse and treat him kindly. Systems of philosophy may inspire legislated cruelty, but more often, it is simply short-sightedness, a lack of imagination that is symbolized by the empty, unnoticing stare. It is Oliver's face, so like the portrait of his mother, that will identify him as the missing child and restore him to his rightful identity.

If Oliver is a passive hero, often dropping into sleep when circumstances become too troubling, in two central and linked scenes, Dickens explores the semiconscious state between waking and sleeping that will feature in many of his novels. In the first, Oliver half wakes in Fagin's den and, while still dreaming, incorporates into his dream the scene acted out in front of his half-closed eyes. He sees Fagin open a small box ("his eyes glistened as he raised the lid") and pore over the contents: watches, rings, brooches, and other jewelery. In a parallel scene, Oliver again catches Fagin unawares, but now Fagin is watching him. Dozing at the window of the Maylies' house in the country, and again suspended between sleeping and waking, Oliver suddenly senses that he is both in the flower-laden safety of the little room and back in the "close and confined" atmosphere of Fagin's den; he sees Fagin and another man and hears their whispered conversation identifying Oliver. When Oliver raises the alarm and rushes out with Harry, Giles, and Mr. Losberne, there is no sign of Fagin and his friend; not even a footprint indicates that they have been there, so their presence is dismissed as a dream. The implication is that Fagin, the embodiment of evil, is ever-present and ever-vigilant, and the mingling of his consciousness with Oliver's in these scenes suggests an interplay of goodness and evil that makes the novel more complex than just the "principle of Good surviving through every adverse circumstance."

STYLISTIC AND LITERARY DEVICES

In *Oliver Twist*, we see Dickens's style developing in the use of distinct voices to intensify different elements of the story. The biting satire in the opening attack on Bumbledom shows the influence of Jonathan Swift's essay "A Modest Proposal," which is hardly surprising, as both essay and novel bitterly condemn the abuse of children by mechanical systems that purport to be reasonable. Dickens is less subtle than Swift, who seldom allows his own voice to penetrate the voice of the political economist whose solution to Ireland's overpopulation and lack of food is to eat the babies of the poor. Swift's subversive attack on his narrator is made through the use of words that have an economic or literal meaning but also a moral or emotional one. Thus, when Swift's narrator talks about "poor" people, he means financially indigent, whereas the reader understands Swift's meaning, which, of course, is worthy of pity. The word "good" can mean simply "very" or it can have the moral overtones that Swift and Dickens wish the reader to adopt. Thus, Swift refers to a "good fat child," who will feed the gentleman paying ten shillings for him. Dickens similarly refers to the children's stipend of sevenpence-halfpenny as being enough to provide a "good round diet," but Mrs. Mann "had a very accurate perception of what was good for herself" (3–4) and so appropriates most of the fee. Both Swift and Dickens draw attention to the premise underlying the attitudes of the political economists and the Poor Law administrators: If children are regarded as animals, then they may be treated as such, even to being eaten. Oliver is "farmed" to a barnlike place where he and his fellow orphans "rolled about the floor all day" like little piglets.

The title of Chapter Two, "Treats of Oliver Twist's Growth, Education, and Board," draws attention to the discrepancy between the expected progress of a child and the progress of an orphan in early Victorian England where growth was stunted by malnutrition, education was nonexistent, and "board," or food and lodging, was administered by a "board" with as much human compassion as a piece of lumber. When Oliver is taken before the commissioners, he confuses them with the table: " 'Bow to the board,' said Bumble. Oliver brushed away two or three tears that were lingering in his eyes; and seeing no board but the table, fortunately bowed to that" (8).

This satirical tone gives way to other voices when Oliver leaves for London and Dickens's interest in psychological states takes over from overt social criticism. Graham Greene referred to this new voice as "the tone of Dickens's secret prose, that sense of a mind speaking to itself with no one there to listen, as we find it in *Great Expectations*."[3] This voice takes the reader from present-day Bumbledom into the world of memory, of the past impinging on the present in Mr. Brownlow's sense that Oliver's face recalls faces long dead, and in Oliver's sense of a past that, as an orphan, he needs to recover. He has only a glimmering of that past, but that glimmer gives rise to a poetic style that will become more pervasive in the later novels. Asleep and tended gently by Rose Maylie, Oliver stirs, "as though these marks of pity and compassion had awakened some pleasant dream of a love and affection he had never known; as a strain of gentle music, or the rippling of water in a silent place, or the odour of a flower, or even the mention of a familiar word, will sometimes call up sudden dim remembrances of scenes that never were, in this life; which vanish like a breath; and which some brief memory of a happier existence, long gone by, would seem to have awakened, for no voluntary exertion of the mind can ever recall them" (183–84). In this and many passages in the later novels, Dickens is clearly influenced by the Romantic poets, especially William Wordsworth. In its juxtaposition of the Maylies' idyllic country home with the London of Fagin and its defense of the innocent child, *Oliver Twist* is one of Dickens's most Romantic novels.

A FEMINIST READING OF *OLIVER TWIST*

Feminist criticism of the last thirty years has brought different approaches to the reading of literature. French feminists have been primarily interested in language and in establishing whether there is such a thing as feminine language, as opposed to the dominant masculine discourse. Other feminists have concentrated on rediscovering unknown works by women or reconsidering the works of famous women writers. A third interest has been the reexamination of works by male writers from a perspective that focuses on the portrayal of women in their works. These critics are concerned with such issues as male power, domination, and oppression in the literature of a patriarchal society. Thus, they focus on the female characters and look at the story from their point of view.

Dickens is often viewed as offering stereotypical views of women as domineering shrews (Mrs. Corney, after she becomes Mrs. Bumble in *Oliver Twist*) or "angels in the house," as the domestically and morally perfect wife came to be known after Coventry Patmore's sequence of poems of that title in the 1850s and '60s. Many female readers resent the Victorian male desire to turn them into angels responsible for the moral education of the men and children in their well-regulated households and therefore prohibited from the complexities of moral behavior that make up the human condition. Certainly Dickens frequently placed angels in his fictional houses, but they were based, not on an idealized philosophical theory, but on a real woman: his sister-in-law Mary Hogarth. Dickens's letters reveal that he truly believed Mary to be perfectly good; she died at the age of seventeen, too early for his devout faith in her to be shaken. (It is important to note, though, that Dickens was not alone in considering Mary Hogarth in this light: Her family all regarded her as an angel.) That she died suddenly during the writing of *Oliver Twist* could not help but influence the portrait of Rose Maylie. Rose and her dead sister, Oliver's mother, merge into one figure that stands for Mary: one lost, the other remaining as a guardian angel to Oliver, much as Dickens had regarded Mary while she lived. But the novel also offers more complex views of women and their place in Victorian society, and Dickens's sympathetic view of their position is often at odds with that of the accepted mores of the day. His intention in the novel was to defend women against prejudice and remove the stigma of the so-called fallen woman who could come from any class, as Agnes, Oliver's well-born mother, and Nancy, the working-class prostitute, demonstrate.

The New Poor Law that Dickens attacks on many counts absolved the fathers of illegitimate children from any financial obligation for them; the unmarried mother, like Oliver's, was held fully responsible for her child's maintenance. This new regulation was hotly debated at the time, with its proponents arguing that it would discourage women from licentious behavior. This prejudice was based on the story of Eve's temptation in the Garden of Eden as told in the Bible and was firmly held by a large segment of nineteenth-century society. Make the woman solely responsible, they said, and she would be less likely to act in a manner that would "tempt" men to seduce her. But others recognized the double standard in the legislation and even feared that it would lead to infanticide on the part of desperate women, financially and physically unable to feed their children.

Dickens clearly opposed the new regulation. When at Oliver's birth the doctor sympathetically refers to Oliver's mother's unmarried status as "the old story," he means the seduction of a young woman by a more powerful or calculating man. Agnes's story is different: Oliver's father intended to marry her but is trapped in a disastrous marriage to Monks' mother (the marriage selfishly arranged by his father, Edwin Leeford, his mother having died). Their affair is described as weakness, morally wrong only because of the suffering it brings to the offspring, Oliver, born, in society's view, with the stain of illegitimacy on him. When Monks, Oliver's evil half-brother, refers to Oliver as a bastard, Mr. Brownlow rebukes him roundly.

That Agnes and Nancy are both outcasts from their society because of their "fallen" status is important to Dickens's view that both are deserving of understanding and support, regardless of class. Nancy acts as a sister to Oliver by attempting to protect him from Monks and Fagin and restore him to his lost family, thus taking the place of his dead mother who is unable to shield her child. Oliver regards his Aunt Rose as a sister also, and Dickens intended the reader to see Nancy and Rose as counterparts: "I hope to do great things with Nancy. If I can only work out the idea I have formed of her, and of the female who is to contrast with her, I think I may defy Mr. Hayward [an early critic of Dickens] and all his works" (*Letters* 1.328). Nancy and Rose are drawn to each other by their maternal interest in the child, just as Mrs. Bedwin, Mr. Brownlow's housekeeper and symbol of the good mother, recognizes that Bumble is lying when he tries to blacken Oliver's name: She knows "what children are, sir; and have done these forty years; and people who can't say the same, shouldn't say anything about them. That's my opinion!" (108–9). Female intuition is shown to be accurate and valuable, in contrast to Mr. Brownlow's absurd old friend Mr. Grimwig's blind prejudice against Oliver.

Both Nancy and Agnes die because they are sexually attracted to men who fail them: Oliver's father is already married, and Sikes brutally kills Nancy to protect himself and Fagin. Dickens denies their "fallen" status, emphasizing, instead, their moral worth in their mutual concern for the child Oliver's welfare. In Nancy, he dramatizes a complex woman whose goodness is not that of an "angel in the house" at all, but of a woman who has not allowed her better nature to be totally destroyed by the exploitation of Fagin and Sikes.

NOTES

1. "Some Recollections of Dickens," *The Dickensian* 6 (1910), 61–64.

2. Charles Dickens, *Sikes and Nancy and Other Public Readings*, ed. Philip Collins, World's Classics edition (Oxford: Oxford University Press, 1983), 231.

3. "The Young Dickens" in *The Lost Childhood and Other Essays* (1951). Reprinted in *The Dickens Critics*, ed. George H. Ford and Lauriat Lane, Jr. (Ithaca, NY: Cornell University Press, 1961), 246–47.

those who are at the mercy of heartless philosophical systems and selfish attitudes.

Christmas in England had not been widely celebrated since the Puritan ban on any type of Christmas festivities during the Interregnum (1649–1660), when the monarchy was overthrown and a commonwealth was established under Oliver Cromwell. It would have been celebrated mainly by the gentry, the old country families such as the Wardles in Dickens's *The Pickwick Papers*, but the new industrial, urban population resulting from the Industrial Revolution would not have had Christmas traditions. Dickens wanted to bring such a celebration to his poor city readers through the writing of *A Christmas Carol*, and the book coincided with other signs that by the 1840s, Christmas was once again becoming more widely celebrated. In 1841, Prince Albert had made popular the German tradition of the Christmas tree, first introduced from the Continent a few years earlier. Christmas cards were first designed in the 1840s, often with the intention of inspiring charitable thoughts in the manner of *A Christmas Carol*, although it was some years before they became commercially popular. But it was Dickens's book that truly revived the celebrating of Christmas for the urban poor, not just for the rural gentry.

In the few spare hours left to him during the writing of *Martin Chuzzlewit*, Dickens threw himself into his Christmas parable, telling his friend C. C. Felton that he "wept, and laughed, and wept again, and excited himself in a most extraordinary manner, in the composition; and thinking whereof, he walked about the black streets of London, fifteen and twenty miles, many a night when all the sober folks had gone to bed" (*Letters* 4.2). It took just six weeks to write. At its conclusion he "broke out like a Madman" (*Letters* 4.3) and threw himself into making it a uniquely attractive book for Christmas gift-giving: It had hand-colored prints by the famous artist John Leech and a reddish-brown cover with gold lettering. Unfortunately, Dickens's arrangement with his publisher Chapman and Hall meant that he paid for the expensive production, so even though it sold out its first run of 6,000 copies in the first few days, he made little financial profit from it.

In more important ways, though, it was an unqualified success. He told Felton how "by every post, all manner of strangers write all manner of letters to him about their homes and hearths, and how this same Carol is read aloud there, and kept on a very little shelf by itself. Indeed it is the greatest success as I am told, that this Ruffian and Rascal has ever achieved." Even gruff literary critics were moved. Thomas Carlyle, Dickens's friend but a notoriously unsentimental Scot, rushed out to buy a turkey with which to entertain his friends. The novelist William Makepeace Thackeray perhaps summed up the universal love of the book best, when, in *Fraser's Magazine* (February 1844), he called it

The Christmas Books
and Christmas Stories
(1843–1867)

A CHRISTMAS CAROL (1843)

Christmas was Dickens's favorite celebration, and the one with wh
most often associated because of the abiding popularity of his 1843 C
book, *A Christmas Carol*. A well-known story recounts how a barro
Covent Garden market exclaimed, on hearing of Dickens's death, "I
Father Christmas die too?" We do not know if the story is true, but sin
Dickens has been a part of Christmas wherever in the world it is ce
Scrooge's transformation from miserable miser to benevolent master I
versal appeal in an increasingly fragmented and Utilitarian world. Wh
Claus (or Father Christmas to the barrow girl) and his gift-giving have
tarnished by the commercialism of the twentieth-century Christmas,
mas Carol is often welcomed as an antidote that keeps alive the real sig
of the celebration. It is sometimes criticized for glorifying a secular and
nevolence that is easily packed away with the Christmas decorations
ary. Dickens, however, stressed that *A Christmas Carol* and the succee
Christmas books cannot "be separated from the exemplification of tl
tian virtues and the inculcation of the Christian precepts. In every on
books there is an express text preached on, and the text is always taken
lips of Christ" (*Letters* 9.557). Dickens had in mind Christ's Serm
Mount in the books' defense of the meek, the poor, the lame, and the

"a national benefit, and to every man and woman who reads it a personal kindness."

In his joyful "carol" (divided into Staves rather than chapters as though it were indeed a song), Dickens set out to show how selfishness and greed had become the dominant spirit of the age. Juxtaposed against Scrooge, the miser engaged in the lonely pursuit of gain, is his nephew, Fred, and his clerk, Bob Cratchit: Both celebrate Christmas not just as the keeping alive of old rituals and entertainments (although party games and family activities do play a large part in *A Christmas Carol*), but as a reminder of Christ's teachings. For Fred, Christmas is "a kind, forgiving, charitable, pleasant time: the only time I know of, in the long calendar of the year, when men and women seem by one consent to open their shut-up hearts freely" (9).

Scrooge's conversion is brought about by supernatural means, and Dickens acknowledges the usefulness of this device, in plotting the short Christmas books, in his Preface to the first collected edition of *A Christmas Carol* and the four books that succeeded it: "The narrow space within which it was necessary to confine these Christmas Stories when they were originally published, rendered their construction a matter of some difficulty, and almost necessitated what is peculiar in their machinery. I could not attempt great elaboration of detail, in the working out of character within such limits. My chief purpose was, in a whimsical kind of masque which the good humour of the season justified, to awaken some loving and forbearing thoughts, never out of season in a Christian land." But while the supernatural "machinery" allowed Dickens to telescope time into a very brief span (Scrooge's conversion takes place in only one night), the psychological implications of the conversion are valid. Scrooge is first touched by memory. The ghost of Christmas Past is actually the ghost of Scrooge's past, who shows him the sympathetic and loving child that he once was and can recover. Scrooge is shown a vision of himself as a young boy left alone in a schoolroom at Christmas time, and in remembering his early reading—the stories that had kept alive Dickens's own imagination (such as *Robinson Crusoe*)—Scrooge pities the boy who sang a carol at his keyhole and regrets that he had given him nothing.

The shifting scenes of Scrooge's past remind him of his first employer's kindness to him, and how Mr. Fezziwig had the power to make him happy or unhappy, just as Scrooge now wields this power over Bob Cratchit and his family. He is reminded also of his early love for a young girl, and he sees how his misanthropy grew in a nature not innately selfish. The girl admonishes him, "You fear the world too much. . . . All your other hopes have merged into the hope of being beyond the chance of its sordid reproach. I have seen your nobler aspirations fall off one by one, until the master-passion, Gain, engrosses you" (38–39). Although Scrooge blames his avarice on the expectations of society ("this is the even-handed dealing of the world! . . . There is nothing on which it is so hard as poverty; and there is nothing it professes to condemn with such severity as the pursuit of wealth!"), the responsibility for Scrooge's miserable state is clearly his own. The fetters that prevented his partner Jacob Marley from being able to help his fellow men had been forged of his own free will, and Scrooge chose money rather than love. Even his face had shown "where the shadow of the growing tree would fall" (38).

In the prevention of that fall lies the characteristic of the Christmas books that sets them apart from Dickens's later novels and accounts for their optimism and suitability for Christmas. Having reforged his link with humanity through his chain of past remembrances, Scrooge, who in fear of self-examination, had drawn back from the ghost of his past, now goes forward to meet the ghost of Christmas Present and share in the experiences of other men. Shown the physical isolation of miners, sailors, and lighthouse keepers, he can now comprehend the bonds that make each man a part of humanity, capable of sympathy and compassion and thus active for good.

The ghost of Scrooge's future brings him back to his own life, but he cannot accept that the dead body he sees is his own until he is faced with his grave. Scrooge must journey to the underworld of his own death to be redeemed, and although the supernatural machinery makes the transformation immediate by bringing the past and future into the present, Scrooge's redemption is essentially performed by the timeless device of the dream or vision. He comes back from the grave a new man, reborn as an infant who can fulfil Christ's injunction to "become as little children." Scrooge wakes on Christmas morning with the excited cry, "I don't know anything. I'm quite a baby. Never mind. I don't care. I'd rather be a baby."

The effects of Scrooge's selfishness are shown to have consequences for society: Ignorance and Want are the children born to the world out of individual lack of concern, and in Scrooge's Utilitarian world, Tiny Tim has no place. When Scrooge tells the charitable gentlemen that the poor would be better to die and "decrease the surplus population," Dickens was responding to the political economists of the time whose systems were partially based on the writings of Thomas Malthus. In his *Essay on the Principle of Population* (1803), Malthus had argued that anyone who could not be supported by his parents and could not provide labor that society requires "has no claim of *right* to the smallest portion of food, and, in fact, has no business to be where he is."[1] *A Christmas Carol* reminded Dickens's readers that, although the tenets of Christianity were being eroded by the new society, the human heart is essentially compassionate, and business can co-exist with kindness.

Artistically, *A Christmas Carol* is of great importance in Dickens's development as a writer. For the first time, he was able to plan the whole story before writing it, and he recognized its cohesiveness at once, telling a friend that he could see "the effect of such a little *whole* as that, on those for whom I care" (*Letters* 3.605). Stylistically also, *A Christmas Carol* bursts with energy and wit, ensuring its worldwide popularity as a reading, a play, and a film. From Scrooge's growling response to Marley's ghost that he is just suffering from indigestion ("There's more of gravy than of grave about you, whatever you are!") to his closing instructions to his clerk ("Make up the fires, and buy another coal-scuttle before you dot another i, Bob Cratchit!") the book never falters in its rapid pace and exuberant evocation of the Christmas season.

THE CHIMES (1844)

Encouraged by the tremendous success of *A Christmas Carol*, Dickens wrote a companion book the next year entitled *The Chimes*, which was to be an even more savage attack on Utilitarianism and laissez-faire economics. He was living in Italy in the autumn of 1844, and the supernatural device of goblins in a bell tower was suggested to him by the church bells of Genoa. He wrote to John Forster in a quotation from Shakespeare: "We have heard THE CHIMES at midnight, Master Shallow!" (*Letters* 4.199). Aware that jolly Christmas descriptions could become very tiresome (and the Christmas scenes from *A Christmas Carol* were to be repeated endlessly by other writers, egged on by Victorian publishers), Dickens set the next book in January, and his vivid portrait of a chill and foggy London betrays no hint that it was written in sunny Italy. He intended the book to make

a great blow for the poor. Something powerful, I think I can do, but I want to be tender too, and cheerful; as like the *Carol* in that respect as may be, and as unlike it as such a thing can be. The duration of the action will resemble it a little, but I trust to the novelty of the machinery to carry that off; and if my design be anything at all, it has a grip upon the very throat of the time. (*Letters* 4.200)

Dickens wrote the book in October 1844, and it held a grip on him during the writing. He told Forster, "I am in regular, ferocious excitement with the *Chimes*; get up at seven; have a cold bath before breakfast; and blaze away, wrathful and red-hot, until three o'clock or so: when I usually knock off (unless it rains) for the day. . . . I am fierce to finish in a spirit bearing some affinity to those of truth and mercy, and to shame the cruel and the canting" (*Letters* 4.201). "Cant" was a favorite word of Thomas Carlyle, Dickens's main influence in his writings against contemporary Utilitarian philosophy and economic theory. Both writers meant by it the hypocritical and self-serving members of the ruling classes who prided themselves on their apparent concern for the poor. *The Chimes* abounds with such hypocrites, most of them based on recognizable dignitaries of the time.

All of the Christmas books tell the story of a man who has lost faith in human goodness or has become hardened or cynical. By remembering the past and seeing a possible future (in four of the books, made possible by supernatural means), the hero is restored to trust in other people and leaves behind his isolation and fear. In *The Chimes*, Toby Veck, the poor little ticket porter (or messenger), has become so accustomed to the ruling classes telling him that the poor have only themselves to blame for their plight that he begins to believe it. Mr. Filer, a political economist, "proves" by statistics that Toby is taking food out of the mouth of widows and orphans when he eats his meager lunch. When John Forster read the manuscript of the book, he recommended that Dickens tone down the attack, but Dickens was reluctant to alter too much, remembering how the *Westminster Review*, Jeremy Bentham's utilitarian journal, had criticized *A Christmas Carol* because "who went without turkey and punch in order that Bob Cratchit might get them . . . is a disagreeable reflection kept wholly out of sight" (June 1844). Dickens gave Forster permission to make corrections to the manuscript; Forster could "file away at Filer," but should "bear in mind that the *Westminster Review* considered Scrooge's presentation of the turkey to Bob Cratchit as grossly incompatible with political economy" (*Letters* 4.209).

In a horrifying dream, brought about by the goblins that live among the church bells, Toby is shown the results of his loss of faith in the goodness of his own class. He dreams that his beloved daughter, Meg, is driven by poverty to attempt drowning herself and her baby, a scene that Dickens based on the case of Mary Furley, who in April 1844, was tried for infanticide and sentenced to death when her attempted drowning resulted in the death of her child. In Alderman Cute, Dickens fiercely satirized the Middlesex magistrate Sir Peter Laurie (1778–1861), who liked to think that he knew how to speak colloquially to the poor but whose harsh treatment of desperate suicidal women he defended on religious grounds.

The Chimes also takes up the plight of the country worker in Will Fern, who was forced to seek work in London and was accused of being a revolutionary. The source of his misery is Sir Joseph Bowley, who was based on the wealthy country squire and member of parliament Lord Brougham, who prided himself on supporting philanthropic causes and being the "poor man's friend." Another object of Dickens's attack was the Young England movement, a group of Conservative aristocrats led by Benjamin Disraeli who extolled the "good old days" and longed for a return to feudal times. Dickens removed most of his satire on the movement but retained a reference to landowners playing skittles with their tenants, a barb directed at the movement's suggestion that feudal games could restore a right relationship between aristocracy and worker. Meanwhile, Will Fern and his niece would have starved had Toby Veck not given up his own supper for them.

The Chimes has been less successful than *A Christmas Carol* because the frightening dream vision is given to the innocent ticket porter rather than to the misanthropic Scrooge, while the cruel and canting political economists remain unpunished in the book. Even though Toby awakes from his nightmare just as Meg is about to drown and celebrates, instead, his daughter's joyful New Year's Day marriage breakfast, the shadow cast by the dream vision is not wholly dispelled at the end of the book. As social criticism, though, *The Chimes* remains with *Hard Times* one of Dickens's most accurate portrayals of the prevalent attitudes of many powerful Victorians, and it was recognized as such at the time. If it offers no solutions for Toby and his class other than to ignore Alderman Cute and believe in each other, it does contrast the unimaginative, sterile, and mechanical world of the political economist with the emotional and rich world of the ticket porter and his friends. Stylistically, *The Chimes* owes much to Thomas Carlyle, whose strident rhetoric is sometimes at odds with the simple little ticket porter. Toby's passionate words, spoken "in some inspiration," look forward to the central sea metaphor that Dickens borrowed from Carlyle to describe the French Revolution in *A Tale of Two Cities*: "I know there is a sea of Time to rise one day, before which all who wrong us or oppress us will be swept away like leaves. I see it, on the flow!" (178).

THE CRICKET ON THE HEARTH (1845)

For the 1845 Christmas book, *The Cricket on the Hearth*, Dickens left behind the political satire of *A Christmas Carol* and *The Chimes* to return to the more cheerful notion of the Christmas book as "a whimsical kind of masque." Commenting on Dickens's lifelong love of fairy tales, John Forster notes that "he had a secret delight in feeling that he was here only giving them a higher form" (Forster 1.301). In *The Cricket on the Hearth*, which is subtitled "A Fairy Tale of Home," Dickens re-creates a domestic ideal of hearth and comfort that was warmly received by his Victorian readers but that many today find sentimental. Like all fairy tales, the simple, stylized tale of deceptions and revelations, of ogres and fairies, is actually concerned with very serious adult issues that Dickens would return to again in *David Copperfield*.

In 1845, Dickens wrote to John Forster proposing a new periodical to be called "The Cricket." It would contain "*Carol* philosophy, cheerful views . . . and a vein of glowing, hearty, generous, mirthful, beaming reference in everything to Home, and Fireside" (*Letters* 4.328). When Forster was unenthusiastic, Dickens decided to retain the idea of the cricket, an insect whose cheerful chirping was thought to bring good luck to the house, for the Christmas book where "it would be a delicate and beautiful fancy ... making the Cricket a little household god—silent in the wrong and sorrow of the tale, and loud again when all went well and happy" (*Letters* 4.337). A real cricket chirps on the hearth in the story, symbolizing the warmth and security of home, but fairy crickets are the supernatural machinery that bring about the Christmas-book transformation.

Within this fantasy world, Dickens explores two interrelated themes: January/May marriages, and deception and blindness. The Christmas-book protagonist, John Peerybingle, suspects that his young wife, Dot, is in love with an apparently more suitable man, a mysterious stranger who is clearly a young man in disguise. John is on the point of killing his rival when he is suddenly halted by the fairy crickets, who remind him of his wife's goodness and truth. But while Scrooge and Toby are forced to realize the value of what they had distrusted, John is led by the fairies not to believe in his wife's fidelity, but to accept her apparent desire for a more suitable husband. He begins to see his marriage as a selfish one, and he resolves to set Dot free from a union that cannot be fair to a wife so much younger than himself. The reader shares John's suspicion that Dot may be contemplating an affair with the mysterious house guest, but John's sacrifice turns out to be unnecessary when the supposed lover, who had been disguised as an old man, is revealed to be the long-lost son of Caleb Plummer and suitor of Dot's friend, May.

In a parallel plot, Dickens considers disparate marriages from another point of view. May has been forced into an engagement to the old misanthropic toymaker Tackleton, Caleb Plummer's employer, a relationship that she clearly dreads. But a third young woman, Caleb's blind daughter Bertha, is in love with Tackleton because her father, in a well-meaning attempt to make her dismal world happier, has built a false world around her. Besides pretending that their poor little house is lavish and comfortable, Caleb has pretended that Tackleton is only pretending to be a curmudgeon as a joke.

Dickens drew upon Chaucer's "The Merchant's Tale," which tells the story of May, a young woman who takes advantage of the blindness of her old husband, January, to have an affair. But while Chaucer makes fun of the old husband, Dickens, in the Christmas book and in *David Copperfield*, leads the reader to sympathize with the young wife's attraction to a man her own age but then affirms her fidelity to the older husband. In *David Copperfield*, the "unsuitability of mind and purpose" occurs not in the marriage between and elderly Doctor Strong and his young wife Annie, but in the marriage of David to Dora. Like the Christmas book, the novel also incorporates the motif of deception and blindness in David's marriage to Dora, made explicit when his aunt comments "Blind, blind!"

Deception, especially self-deception, can be dangerous. The fantasy world of Caleb (which is vividly paralleled by the toy world he creates), comes crashing down when his daughter realizes that her "truths" have all been lies. Only when Dot tells her of her father's selfless devotion is her "sight" restored: "I have been blind, and now my eyes are open. I never knew him! To think I might have died, and never truly seen the father who has been so loving to me!" (264)

Deception is the stuff of fairy tales, as are magical transformations. To ensure a happy ending for all, Dickens unexpectedly converts Tackleton the misanthrope into a jovial benefactor without any of Scrooge's complex motivation. The reader can only echo Dickens's query, "what had the fairies been doing with him, to have effected such a change!" (276). As in the pantomimes of the day, such transformations were expected of a Christmas book. It was an immediate hit, with dramatic versions running in seventeen theaters simultaneously during the 1845 Christmas season. On New Year's Day, Dickens proclaimed it "a most tremendous success. It has beaten my two other Carols out of the field, and is going still, like Wildfire" (*Letters* 4.464).

THE BATTLE OF LIFE (1846)

In 1846, Dickens was back in Switzerland and working on *Dombey and Son* when he devised "a pretty story, with some delicate notions in it agreeably presented, and with a good human Christmas groundwork" (*Letters* 4.623). *The Battle of Life* is a tale about personal heroism, the "quiet victories and struggles, great sacrifices of self, and noble acts of heroism ... done every day in nooks and corners, and in little households, and in men's and women's hearts" (297). The Christmas-book conversion takes place in the heart of Doctor Jeddler, a jovial but cynical father of two daughters who finds life a joke and human cares and sufferings trivial. His change of heart is brought about not by supernatural means, but by the example of his daughters who both hide their own love for their mutual friend Alfred so that he will turn to the other.

Unfortunately, working out the story within the scope of the Christmas book and without supernatural means proved to be a mistake, as Dickens realized too late. Ill and overwhelmed with working on *Dombey and Son* as well, he even considered abandoning the book until the following year. He was pleased with the battlefield motif that opens the story, but without the advantage of dream visions to bring back the past or foretell the future, the plot became impossible to manage, the most glaring improbability being one sister's exile to her aunt's house for six years while her family thinks she has eloped.

The Battle of Life was very successful despite its flaws, selling 23,000 copies on the first day and outselling by far its predecessors by the end of January. It was very popular on the stage also, with the famous acting partnership of Robert Keeley and his wife playing the strongest characters in the book, the comic but kind-hearted maid Clemency Newcome (developed later as Peggotty in *David Copperfield*) and her abrasive but loving husband Benjamin Britain. Dickens told his friend Edward Bulwer-Lytton that he would like to rework the book, which he did thirteen years later in *A Tale of Two Cities*, where the love triangle involves one woman and two men and the idea of self-sacrifice is successfully realized in the character of Sydney Carton.

THE HAUNTED MAN (1848)

The strain of writing *The Battle of Life* discouraged Dickens from writing a Christmas book for 1847, when *Dombey and Son* was still in progress, even though he had conceived "a very ghostly and wild idea" for it in 1846 and had made a start. He was "very loath to lose the money. And still more so to leave any gap at Christmas firesides which I ought to fill" (*Letters* 5.165), but the book was postponed until 1848, when in *The Haunted Man* he returned to the themes, rhetoric, and structure of *A Christmas Carol* if not to its cheerfulness. The hero, like Scrooge, is haunted by a ghostly double who is a part of himself; the Cratchit family reappears as the Tetterbys; and the allegorical children Ignorance and Want are fleshed out in "a baby savage, a young monster, a child who had never been a child" (397). And once again, memory is found to be the source of all compassion and imagination.

Like Scrooge, the chemist Mr. Redlaw is a solitary and morose man, embittered not by the pursuit of wealth, but by regrets and the constant memory of past injustices. When a ghost appears, offering him the gift of forgetfulness, Redlaw accepts eagerly, not realizing the significance of relinquishing the "intertwisted chain of feelings and associations, each in its turn dependent on, and nourished by, the banished recollections" (395). To be free from hurtful memories seems like a blessing to him, but without the associated human emotions, Redlaw is unable to appreciate beauty or music or even human kindness. Worse still, the Phantom's gift demands that he will pass this curse on to everyone he meets. Only a neglected street child, devoid of emotion because of his deprivation, is unaffected by Redlaw's evil power and represents allegorically the enormity of Redlaw's emotionless condition. In metaphors from growth and the sea that Dickens will use to very powerful effect in *A Tale of Two Cities*, the Phantom reminds Redlaw that, while the waif's state is the result of someone else's neglect, Redlaw has brought the curse on himself. Both waif and man are dangerous: "There is not ... one of these—not one—but sows a harvest that mankind MUST reap. From every seed of evil in this boy, a field of ruin is grown that shall be gathered in, and garnered up, and sown again in many places in the world, until regions are overspread with wickedness enough to raise the waters of another Deluge. . . . He is the growth of man's indifference; you are the growth of man's presumption. The beneficent design of Heaven is, in each case, overthrown, and from the two poles of the immaterial world you come together" (448).

Dickens allows Redlaw a "saving clause" (*Letters* 5.443) that permits him to recognize his harmful influence, and his change of heart is also brought about by the example of Milly, a young woman whose compassion for those around her springs from her remembrance of losing her child. Like the other Christmas books, *The Haunted Man* teaches us that memory is the source of compassion because it links us to our childhood and to our better natures. Good and evil are inextricably linked, and without the remembrance of suffering, there can be no joy. It was a solace that Dickens was particularly seeking that Christmas. His sister Fanny had died in September, and in the months preceding her death from consumption, he had visited her often and retrod with her the paths of their childhood.

The Haunted Man is starkly allegorical in its characterization and plot, but it is also powerfully suggestive in its creation of atmosphere. In the opening passages, Dickens sets the scene for his ghost story by establishing metaphors of light and shadow, appearance and reality. In one image, a child sits listening to his nurse's stories while the light from the hearth throws their shapes onto a wall behind them, the shapes taking on a shadowy and unearthly life in the transformation of the real figures before them. The shadows "fantastically mocked the shapes of household objects, making the nurse an ogress, the rocking-horse a monster, the wondering child, half-scared and half-amused, a stranger to itself" (377). Dickens is recalling his own "half-scared, half-amused" reaction to hearing frightening tales at his nurse's knee, but in transforming a "household" scene into a supernatural one, he is describing the work of the storyteller, and of the mind. The Phantom is the projection of Redlaw's thoughts, as the narrator explains at the end of the story: "Some people have said since, that he only thought what has been herein set down; others, that he read it in the fire, one winter night about the twilight time; others, that the Ghost was but the representation of his own gloomy thoughts, and Milly the embodiment of his better wisdom. *I* say nothing" (472). The book closes with light from a fire once again creating shadows that show the children "marvellous shapes and faces on the walls, and gradually changing what was real and familiar there, to what was wild and magical" (472). All five Christmas books—unique blends of fairy tale, social realism, and ghost story—perfected Dickens's characteristic heightening of the ordinary into the strange and mysterious, "the romantic side of familiar things" as Dickens said in a preface to *Bleak House*.

In the six years that Dickens had been writing Christmas books, the form had become very popular. Always an innovator, he decided to move on from it and search for some other form of writing that would "awaken some loving and forbearing thoughts," as he described the purpose of the books in the Preface to the collected edition. He saw Christmas as the time when he should return to the themes of selflessness, individual responsibility for others, and the innate goodness of man. His reason was not only for his own spiritual growth, but because he realized his power as a writer to influence people for the good. Writing after Dickens's death in 1871, Margaret Oliphant remembered how *A Christmas Carol* "moved us all in those days as if it had been a new gospel" (*Blackwood's Magazine* 109 [1871], 689–90). From 1850 to 1867, Dickens worked to make the Christmas story accessible to a wider audience, and the sombre tone of *The Haunted Man* was replaced by the gentler, personal voice of Dickens himself.

CHRISTMAS STORIES (1850–1867)

Dickens found his new Christmas format in the special Christmas numbers of his two weekly magazines, *Household Words* (1850–1859) and its successor *All the Year Round*. The numbers were unique experiments in journalism for Christmas, written in collaboration with other writers and taking many forms from autobiographical essay to ghost story to comic monologue. Dickens gave his own contributions to the Christmas numbers the title "Christmas Stories" when he edited them for separate publication in 1867, but they are best read as originally written, as parts of a whole number that, like Chaucer's *Canterbury Tales* or Dickens's favorite *The Arabian Nights*, surrounded a variety of tales with a unifying framework story.

Of the five Christmas books, only *A Christmas Carol* had been specifically about Christmas. In turning from the Christmas book to the annual Christmas number, Dickens intended to create for his readers not so much the trappings of the Christmas season as the moral lessons of the Christmas story, lessons that were central to all his work. In 1846, he had written to his friend John Forster that "good Christmas characters might be grown out of the idea of a man imprisoned for ten or fifteen years" (*Letters* 4.590). These Christmas characters were realized in two novels, *Little Dorrit* and *A Tale of Two Cities*. Dickens's "*Carol* philosophy," as he came to call his seasonal theme, was an appeal for greater compassion and understanding. In the Christmas books, Scrooge, Toby Veck, John Peerybingle, Doctor Jeddler, and Mr. Redlaw are rescued from isolation, doubt, and cynicism about the value of the human spirit by ghostly means or by example. Remembering past losses and regrets helped them regain a more open and childlike faith in the human condition, a faith that was founded on Dickens's belief in the purity of the human imagination and its power to inspire compassion and right action. According to his opening statement, the purpose of *Household Words* was to "tenderly cherish that light of Fancy which is inherent in the human breast; which, according to its nurture, burns with an inspiring flame, or sinks into a sullen glare, but which (or woe betide that day!) can never be extinguished." Later Christmas characters—acting without the intervention of a ghost—rely on their memories to recapture their earlier imaginative selves; throughout the Christmas Stories, memory is seen as essential to moral growth and redemption. The dangers of living alone, of living for ourselves and not for our fellow men, are reiterated in many forms throughout the Christmas stories. The lessons of the Sermon on the Mount rather than the celebration of Christ's birth are what makes a "Christmas Story" for Dickens, although as Scrooge's nephew says, "the veneration due to its sacred name and origin" can never be separate from the lessons of Christianity.

Dickens's own voice is one of the most appealing and characteristic aspects of the Christmas stories: Writing in the first person either for himself, as in "A Christmas Tree," or for a thinly disguised persona who relates events from his life, he filled his Christmas stories with his own strongly felt philosophy that was tied to his Christian faith. At the heart of his editing and writing for the Christmas numbers was a conviction that personal or autobiographical storytelling was morally and spiritually renewing; in reliving childhood memories, the adult storyteller can regain a sense of the wonderful that makes moral regeneration possible in a world of regret and loss.

Many of the Christmas numbers contained a story written by Dickens and sometimes his friend Wilkie Collins, which allowed the telling of other stories. At first, the device was just a round of stories at the Christmas fire, but each year, the device became more elaborate. *The Seven Poor Travellers* described a visit Dickens made with a friend to Watts's Charity in Rochester, where travellers could be fed and housed. The stories, written by Dickens and other contributors, were narrated by the visitors to the house and were linked to the framework. It was Dickens's intention that the stories should preferably be autobiographical, so that memory was a part of the narration and if not autobiographical, then at least they should be suited to the teller. For many years, Dickens tried to instill this vision in the minds of his contributors, with varying success, but his own contributions were rich in his memories of past events in his life: travels in Europe, ghost stories heard through the years, family connections, outings with friends, the places of his past that haunted the heroes of his mature novels as well.

Devising a storytelling setting was entertaining for Dickens in the early years of the numbers. Tales were told by the snowed-in guests at *The Holly-Tree Inn,* the survivors of *The Wreck of the Golden Mary,* the visitors to *The Haunted House,* and the observers of *A House to Let.* Dickens was the thinly disguised narrator of *Tom Tiddler's Ground,* which told of a visit to a misanthropic hermit. Wilkie Collins collaborated on the adventure numbers, when he and Dickens explored their mutual interest in heroism and male friendship, and sometimes they wrote the whole number together (*The Perils of Certain English Prisoners* and *No Thoroughfare*). But after several years of wrestling with the editing and trying to unite wildly differing stories and poems into a thematic whole, he made fun of the whole enterprise in the 1860s, writing, as he said, "in comic defiance" (*Nonesuch* 3.304) of the framed-tale (stories within a story) form, and producing, as a result, some brilliant character sketches and monologues.

Somebody's Luggage in 1861 is narrated by Christopher the waiter, who finds old manuscripts stuffed into the bits and pieces of luggage left behind by a former visitor to the hotel. The incongruity of the contributed stories is thus accounted for, as Christopher jokes that the visitor's "Boots was at least pairs—and no two of his writings can put any claim to be so regarded." Doctor Marigold the cheap-jack (a travelling hawker) describes the editing of the contributions, or "prescriptions," in his number as being "no play," but "when it come to my own article! There! I couldn't have believed the blotting, nor yet the buckling to at it, nor the patience over it. Which again is like the footboard. The public have no idea." He sells the prescriptions as a "general miscellaneous lot," which he knocks down from eight pounds to four pence, the price of Dickens's Christmas numbers in 1865. The 1863 and 1864 numbers are narrated by Mrs. Lirriper, the kindly but garrulous landlady whose "Lodgings" and "Legacy" are a return to the sparkling humor of Dickens's early novels. Modern stream-of-consciousness techniques owe much to Mrs. Lirriper's breathless narration.

In the later numbers, Dickens also makes fun of his own enthusiasm for giving public readings of his works. Many of the Christmas-story characters are public servants of some kind—waiters, landladies, street artists, entertainers, cheap jacks. In one of the most brilliant of the Christmas sketches, "Going into Society" from the 1858 number *A House to Let,* Toby Magsman, speaking for Dickens the entertainer, complains, "the Public will turn away, at any time, to look at anything in preference to the thing show'd 'em; and if you doubt it, get 'em together for any indiwidual purpose on the face of the earth, and send only two people in late, and see if the whole company an't far more interested in takin particular notice of them two than of you." Many readers have suggested that Dickens was not at his best in the short-story genre and that the scope was too confining for his characteristically expansive imagination. And yet it was a form that he particularly valued, stemming from his early love of ghost stories and fairy tales. In his later years, the Christmas stories freed him from the demands of the long novel and allowed him to experiment with monologues and confessional stories. Always a devotee of the ghost story, he produced his two finest contributions in the 1865 and 1866 Christmas numbers with "To Be Taken with a Grain of Salt" and "The Signal-Man."

Dickens reluctantly abandoned the Christmas numbers after the 1867 adventure story *No Thoroughfare* because he was tired of his writing being "swamped" by the inferior work of his contributors (*Nonesuch* 3.677). The difficulty of inventing a framework and editing the contributed stories year after year made him feel—he told his actor friend Charles Fechter—as though he had "murdered a Christmas number years ago (perhaps I did!) and its ghost perpetually haunted me" (*Nonesuch* 3.630). Still, in 1868, he worked for weeks to try to devise a new idea, but his best idea he felt was better suited to a novel and "could not in the least admit of even that shadowy approach to a congruous whole on the part of other contributors which they have ever achieved at the best" (*Nonesuch* 3.661). He even offered a large reward to anyone at his home, Gad's Hill, who could think of a good framework idea. When a month later he could think of nothing "which would do otherwise than reproduce the old string of old stories in the old inappropriate bungling way" (*Nonesuch* 3.662), he reluctantly laid the Christmas number to rest. The 28 November edition of *All the Year Round* announced the news to its readers:

The Extra Christmas Number has now been so extensively, and regularly, and often imitated, that it is in danger of becoming tiresome. I have therefore resolved (though I cannot add, willingly) to abolish it at the highest tide of its success.

While the Christmas numbers, like most journalism, have not retained that popularity, many of Dickens's contributions are still read and valued as "Christmas Stories." They will always be overshadowed, however, by the genius of his one true celebration of the season, *A Christmas Carol*.

NOTE

1. As quoted in Michael Slater's *Charles Dickens*, The Christmas Books (London: Penguin, 1976), I, 257.

6

David Copperfield
(1850)

In his 1867 Preface to the novel, Dickens called *David Copperfield* his "favourite child," and it has been a favorite with readers also in the 150 years since its publication. Lacking the controlling attack on contemporary society that is central to so many of Dickens's novels, *David Copperfield* adopts the gentler tone and more genial comedy that one would expect from an author writing his "favourite child." Written in the first person in 1849–1850 when Dickens was approaching forty, the novel is permeated with Dickens's memories of his childhood and youth, their disappointments and triumphs. The authenticity of those memories strikes a chord with many readers who have no experience of the Poor Laws of 1834 (so central to *Oliver Twist*) but who remember all too vividly their own sometimes traumatic, often comic, growth from childhood to maturity. Dickens had just completed the Christmas books with their emphasis on the restorative power of memory, and his sister Fanny had died in 1848, causing him to return to those early years and reassess them. The presence of Charles Dickens in the story of David Copperfield is both poignant in its portrayal of Dickens's early sufferings but also comic, too, in true Dickensian fashion. His initials are reversed in the hero's name (in *A Tale of Two Cities*, the connection between Charles Dickens and Charles Darnay is more obvious); and his other presence in the novel, Mr. Dick, is constantly trying to write but cannot keep King Charles's head out of his manuscripts (1849 was the bi-centenary of the beheading of Charles I,

Mr. Dick's obsession). When at the conclusion of the writing Dickens told Forster that he seemed "to be sending some part of [himself] into the Shadowy World" (*Letters* 6.195) he was acknowledging how much of Charles's head had found its way into David's story.

AUTOBIOGRAPHICAL BACKGROUND

In 1847, Dickens had written an account of his father's imprisonment for debt and his own days in Warren's blacking factory, a time in his young life that he had, until then, kept completely secret. His friend John Forster had asked him if he had worked there, having heard something about it from a mutual acquaintance, and Dickens wrote out his painful memories of that time for Forster to read. He quickly gave up on the notion of writing an autobiography, deciding to transmute his own life into fiction, instead, in his next novel, *David Copperfield*. The autobiographical fragment was not published until after Dickens's death when Forster included it in his biography, but the account of those grim days at Warren's entered, sometimes word for word, into Dickens's description of David Copperfield's employment at Murdstone and Grinby's wine bottle-washing factory in a rat-infested warehouse near the river. Uppermost in both accounts was Dickens's sense of being abandoned, of having, at the age of twelve, no adult who cared what became of him. In both accounts, Dickens uses these words to describe this feeling of loss: "I know that I lounged about the streets, insufficiently and unsatisfactorily fed. I know that, but for the mercy of God, I might easily have been, for any care that was taken of me, a little robber or a little vagabond" (157). As in *Oliver Twist*, Dickens emphasizes, in the novel and the autobiographical fragment, the injustice of a child's being deprived of his childhood, forced to take on the responsibilities of the adult world long before he is ready. The painfulness of recalling those days, so long a secret until revealed to John Forster in 1847, is evident in David Copperfield's retelling:

The two things clearest in my mind were, that a remoteness had come upon the old Blunderstone life—which seemed to lie in the haze of an immeasurable distance; and that a curtain had for ever fallen on my life at Murdstone and Grinby's. No one has ever raised that curtain since. I have lifted it for a moment, even in this narrative, with a reluctant hand, and dropped it gladly. The remembrance of that life is fraught with so much pain to me, with so much mental suffering and want of hope, that I have never had the courage even to examine how long I was doomed to lead it. Whether it lasted for a year, or more, or less, I do not know. I only know that it was, and ceased to be; and that I have written, and there I leave it. (210)

Dickens told Forster that he incorporated the autobiographical fragment into the novel "ingeniously, and with a very complicated interweaving of truth and fiction" (*Letters* 5.569).

Many other memories from Dickens's past found their way into *David Copperfield*. Mr. Micawber was based on Dickens's father, whose infuriating carelessness with money led to the miseries of Dickens's childhood and dogged his adult life until his father's death in 1851. The Micawber family's imprisonment for debt and Mr. Micawber's pride in having some authority among the other inmates came from Dickens's memory; and like Mr. Micawber, John Dickens was also a likeable, generous, and kind man whom Dickens regarded with great affection as well as annoyance. Equally charged with affection and irritation is Dickens's re-creation of his first love, Maria Beadnell, as Dora Spenlow. In 1855, Dickens wrote to Maria, now Mrs. Winter:

you may have seen in one of my books a faithful reflection of the passion I had for you, and may have thought that it was something to have been loved so well, and may have seen in little bits of "Dora" touches of your old self sometimes, and a grace here and there that may be revived in your little girls, years hence, for the bewilderment of some other young lover—though he will never be as terribly in earnest as I and David Copperfield were. (*Letters* 7.539)

Although this letter affirms that Dickens's comic and poignant description of David's infatuation with Dora was based on Dickens's own devoted attachment to Maria Beadnell, the sense of David and Dora's unsuitability and the lack of substance in their marriage seems to derive from Dickens's sense that his marriage to Catherine was increasingly unsatisfactory to both of them. David speaks of "the old unhappy loss or want of something" that had "some place" in his heart, though not to embitter it:

I did feel sometimes, for a little while, that I could have wished my wife had been my counsellor; had had more character and purpose, to sustain me and improve me by; had been endowed with power to fill up the void which somewhere seemed to be about me; but I felt as if this were an unearthly consummation of my happiness, that never had been meant to be, and never could have been. (629)

The "interweaving of truth and fiction" is most markedly evident in the reflective tone of the novel. *David Copperfield* is Dickens's "portrait of an artist"; like Dickens, David develops into a novelist through employment as a proctor in Doctor's Commons and as a shorthand reporter. But of central importance to both David and Dickens is the growth of the novelist's imagination. David's account of his voracious reading of the eighteenth-century novelists Smollett, Fielding, Defoe, and Goldsmith, as well as the picaresque novels of Cervantes and Le Sage and the stories of the Arabian Nights, was also taken directly from Dickens's autobiography. (Just before he began the novel, he named his eighth child Henry Fielding Dickens instead of Oliver Goldsmith Dickens "in a kind of homage to the style of work he was now so bent on beginning" [Forster 2.77].) These books connected David to his dead father (they were his books) and nurtured him when his new father, Mr. Murdstone, threatened to make him "sullen, dull, and dogged" through his callous Calvinistic treatment of the child. Imaginative literature, David says, "kept alive my fancy, and my hope of something beyond that place and time" (53), just as they sustained Dickens in Warren's blacking factory. And just as Dickens entertained the boys at Warren's by relating the stories he had read, so David gains the admiration of the powerful Steerforth in relating nightly those same stories in the dormitory of Salem House School. Like Scheherazade, who saves her own life by telling the Sultan the thousand and one tales of the Arabian Nights, Dickens and David survive through fostering the imagination.

The lesson of Dickens's Christmas books was that memories—especially hurtful ones—should not be repressed but should be used as an incentive to greater compassion. In recalling, through a fictional medium, the blacking warehouse days, his father's insolvency, his sense of abandonment and loss, and Maria Beadnell's rejection of him, Dickens was able to look at past events (which until then, he had deliberately kept to himself) without bitterness or blame. He was able to write about them with neither sentimentality nor cynicism, but with poignancy and humor. His mother, for whom he had the strongest sense of resentment because of her indifference to his education, is neither David's gentle but spineless mother nor the ebullient Mrs. Micawber. And Dickens's father, with all his faults that were so devastating to his children, is transformed in Mr. Micawber into one of the greatest comic characters in English literature.

PLOT DEVELOPMENT

Unlike many of Dickens's novels, *David Copperfield* does not rely on the revelation of secrets for its plot. There are no hidden wills, no secrets of parentage to be uncovered, as there are in Dickens's earlier novels and the eighteenth-century models that influenced them. There are secrets in the novel (such as Betsey Trotwood's mysterious visitor who turns out to be her reprobate husband), but the purpose of the plot is to delineate David's emotional growth; rather than the quest for identity or family, David's quest as he grows up is for love, an emotional relationship that is both nurturing and equal. Widowed before David's birth, his mother remarries while David is happily away with his nurse, Clara Peggotty, visiting her brother, who lives in an old boat on the shore at Yarmouth with his adopted niece and nephew, Little Em'ly and Ham. Returning to a very different household, David finds his mother dominated by her new husband, Mr. Murdstone, who sends David away to Salem House School, where he meets the charismatic James Steerforth. When David's mother dies, Mr. Murdstone dismisses David by sending him to London to work in a bottle-washing factory. In London, he lodges with the kind but perpetually bankrupt Micawber family.

David's search for love is punctuated by two poignant journeys that he makes alone. In the first, he runs away from London to Dover in search of his mysterious Aunt Betsey Trotwood, who takes in the footsore and ragged waif and restores his identity as a gentleman's son. She sends him to Doctor Strong's school in Canterbury, where he lodges with Mr. Wickfield, who is gradually falling into the clutches of his clerk, Uriah Heep. Mr. Wickfield's daughter, Agnes, becomes the "golden thread" of his life (as Dickens was to refer to Lucie Manette in *A Tale of Two Cities*), but David misunderstands her place as his soulmate or fails to recognize it until the end of the novel. Instead, he falls passionately in love with Dora Spenlow, the charming but childish daughter of a proctor in Doctors' Commons for whom David is now an articled clerk. They marry and David becomes a novelist, but Dora fails to grow into a wife and companion and is inept at housekeeping. David's recognition of their disparity is aided by a subplot in which Doctor Strong's young wife, Annie, appears to have fallen in love with her cousin, Jack Maldon. Also troubling is Uriah Heep's mastery of Mr. Wickfield's affairs, which results in the financial collapse of Betsey Trotwood.

In the other major thread of the novel, David has introduced Steerforth to the Peggotty family at Yarmouth. Little Em'ly is engaged to Ham, but she is lured away by Steerforth and elopes with him to the Continent. Her uncle Daniel pursues them, but Em'ly returns when Steerforth tires of her. In a brilliantly dramatic scene, David, whose beloved Dora has died in childbirth, witnesses a shipwreck at Yarmouth in which Steerforth (returning from the Continent) and Ham (attempting to help from the shore) are both drowned.

In the second solitary journey, David travels aimlessly and miserably on the Continent in search of solace and peace of mind. He returns to marry Agnes, whose father has been released from Uriah Heep's clutches by Mr. Micawber, who as the new clerk has uncovered Heep's villainy. At the end of the novel, the Micawber family emigrate to Australia with Little Em'ly and her uncle, who with Emily's friend Martha, a reformed prostitute, find a better life there.

CHARACTER DEVELOPMENT

David Copperfield, the first-person narrator of the novel, speculates in the first page whether he "shall turn out to be the hero" of his own life "or whether that station will be held by anybody else." The central characters in the novel all play vital roles in the formation of David's identity, fulfilling or failing to fulfil the question that Dickens later asked of his own life: "Why is it, that as with poor David, a sense comes always crushing on me now, when I fall into low spirits, as of one happiness I have missed in life, and one friend and companion I have never made?" (Forster 2.197). Failing to nurture and support him are his mother Clara and his wife Dora: childish, affectionate, devoted to him, also self-centered and subtly manipulative, both women are lacking in will and strength of character. Their relationships with David are complex and artistically convincing: David's mother fails him by marrying Murdstone and allowing David to be dominated by him and separated from her; Dora's silliness (although she understands more than she lets on, which makes her silliness even more annoying) appeals to David's emotional immaturity at first. Although he never ceases to love his "child-wife," her failure to grow and develop into a woman and his intellectual equal causes an inseparable gulf to grow between them. The deaths of Clara and Dora, both connected with childbirth, are expected because of their inability to move out of childhood themselves and their timidity and fear of confronting life as adults.

Much more tenacious and, therefore, helpful to David are his nurse Peggotty (also Clara, like his mother) and his aunt, Betsey Trotwood. Both are deliberately prickly in their appearance (Peggotty's cheeks and arms are "so hard and red that I wondered the birds didn't peck her in preference to apples" [12]) to contrast them with the delicately soft child-wives. But both provide David with loving affection as well as practical and sound advice and guidance. Betsey is David's fairy godmother, who appears out of the blue at his birth and disappears just as dramatically when he turns out not to be the girl she had been expecting. At this point, David describes her as "a discontented fairy" (12), the wicked visitor at Sleeping Beauty's birth who bestows a curse on the baby. But Betsey reveals herself as his fairy godmother when she makes possible his education and career. As an aunt, Betsey proves to be more helpful and practical than most of the mothers in the novel. Dickens saw that, as an aunt, she is free from the strongly emotional tie that leads so many of the parents in the novel to indulge their children, much to the detriment of the child's development.

One such disastrous mother/son relationship affects David's story dramatically. James Steerforth is the spoiled son of an indulgent mother whose inflated view of his merits understandably comes to be shared by James as well. And yet Steerforth is one of Dickens's most convincing and compelling characters. He is one of the many idle young "gentlemen" whom Dickens attacked in James Harthouse (*Hard Times*), Bentley Drummle (*Great Expectations*), and many others. But Steerforth is more than just a critique of Bentham's theory of self-interest or an example of Carlyle's "dilettantism." Raised to be self-indulgent and lacking a father's guidance (as Steerforth himself admits), he misuses his charm and talent with tragic results. David is particularly vulnerable to flattery from the older boy; to be the "favourite" of someone so admired by all is irresistible for a child who has suffered neglect and abandonment. The reader, however, is never in doubt about Steerforth's real character, and David's innocent defense of him is all the more poignant. The adult narrator also recognizes—with the benefit of hindsight—his youthful infatuation with Steerforth and his blindness to Steerforth's real motives, but he tells the story without bitterness and with pity for his genuine love of the older boy that would be so acutely betrayed.

One of the many attractions of *David Copperfield* is the abundance of colorful and memorable characters, all of whom are vitally connected to the story of David's emotional growth. In their relationships with David, and with the other characters in the novel, each contributes to Dickens's exploration of the influence we exert over each other or of our failure to provide the right kind of support and love in our connections with other people. The misuse of power and the equally dangerous misuse of weakness surface in many of the characters. The name Uriah Heep has become synonymous with all hypocritical, fawning employees who, like Milton's corrupt clergymen, "for their bellies' sake, creep and intrude and climb into the fold." Like Chaucer, Dickens excelled in revealing the inner man through his appearance, and Uriah is one of his most memorable villains: red-haired, but with hair closely cropped and scant facial hair; high-shouldered and bony, with a "long, lank, skeleton hand" that is perpetually damp; his "snaky twistings of his throat and body" align him with the devil. Uriah's method is to pretend to a subservient position while all the time working to take over the weak-willed Mr. Wickfield's business. The result leaves many people in financial ruin, including Betsey Trotwood. "Ever so 'umble" is Heep's catch phrase, and in one of Dickens's finest scenes, after Heep has been exposed by Mr. Micawber, his doting mother infuriates Uriah by trying to maintain their humble facade.

Uriah Heep and James Steerforth typify two very different manifestations of power, the one self-assured, proud, and handsome, the other self-effacing, snivelling, and repulsive. Power and dominance are also the hallmarks of the intellectual bullies Edward Murdstone, David's step-father, and Mr. Creakle, the weak-voiced but vicious headmaster of Salem House. Murdstone and his sister Jane (their name a compound of "murder" and "stone") are two of many such stony characters in Dickens. The antithesis (opposite) of compassion and

Christian love, they represent the rigid Calvinistic beliefs of many evangelical protestants of the time. Like Mr. Brocklehurst in Charlotte Bronte's *Jane Eyre* (another first-person narrative of the growth of the personality, published two years before Dickens began *David Copperfield*), Mr. Murdstone prides himself on his rigid discipline of the young, which amounts to nothing more than mental and physical cruelty. Both Brocklehurst and Murdstone appear to the children as black pillars; both humiliate them and separate them from their fellow students. (Jane is accused of lying and is set apart on a stool while David is made to wear a sign warning that he bites.) In both novels, the child is punished for daring to retaliate against oppressors whose unjust and humiliating treatment drives them, like hunted animals, into self-defense. Both children are locked away in small rooms: Jane, for fighting back when her cousin throws a book at her, and David, for biting Murdstone's hand.

To counter those with power, the novel also abounds in gentle, childlike characters whose childishness is very different from the ineffectual immaturity of Clara and Dora. Mr. Dick, Betsey Trotwood's companion, is mentally below average but is a giant in compassion and innocent good sense, a wonderful foil to Betsey's impetuous and often misguided notions. David first meets him when he arrives at his aunt's cottage, footsore and bedraggled, after walking from London to Dover. Unsure what to do with him, Aunt Betsey asks Mr. Dick's advice, and receives the sensible reply "I should wash him!" Mr. Dick continues to be the wise fool in Betsey's eyes, but he also represents the many people in the world who are easily victimized by the powerful, if they are not protected and valued by open-hearted people such as Betsey Trotwood. While his literary efforts are a torment to him, Mr. Dick achieves peace and fulfilment in the flying of a kite made from his ill-fated manuscript.

Not mentally deficient but equally innocent and child-like are Ham and Daniel Peggotty, heroic in kindness, generosity, and compassion, the victims of Steerforth's callous assumption that a "gentleman" may do what he likes with the family of the working poor. Like Stephen Blackpool in *Hard Times*, Ham does not understand why the privileged classes would prey on working families, and like Stephen, he blames himself for his lack of understanding, telling David, "you han't no call to be afeerd of me: but I'm kiender muddled" (446). Ham is also like Joe Gargery in *Great Expectations* in having "the soul of a gentleman" (430), a natural sense of justice, honor, and loyalty that was thought by many to belong only to those with privilege and education. Ham's self-sacrificing death while attempting to rescue the victims of a shipwreck is strongly contrasted with Steerforth's death as one of the wrecked, although there is a poignancy in Steerforth's death too—the waste of a life that could have held much promise.

Agnes, David's "good angel," is first described as being like a stained-glass window in a church, and she remains an idealization, founded on Dickens's beloved sister-in-law Mary Hogarth, who had died in 1837. Their marriage is also idealized, a union of mind and heart but one that seems unfortunately dull. More appealing is Tommy and Sophy Traddles's exuberant household, where the high jinks of Sophy's visiting sisters accentuate the liveliness of the marriage.

Unrequited love is the dangerous motivation of Rosa Dartle, whose self-destructive personality fascinated Dickens (he would dramatize it again in Miss Wade in *Little Dorrit.*) If openness and connection are the keys to healthy growth (as Dickens reiterates throughout his work, Scrooge being the model), then Rosa's disease is clearly derived from her failure to free herself from her own intense passions. Rosa bears a scar caused when Steerforth hurled a hammer at her; he has disfigured her and continues to hold her in his power as her unrequited passion for him finds no outlet except in slowly destroying her. She is black-haired and unnaturally thin, "the effect of some wasting fire within her, which found a vent in her gaunt eyes" (285). But Rosa has her own power, too, a vindictive method of controlling the conversation through questioning and pretending ignorance. Just as the scar will "start forth like the old writing on the wall" (288), a vivid sign of her sexual frustration, she later abandons her rhetorical cleverness to excoriate the two women who were rivals for Steerforth's affection: his mother and Little Emily. While Rosa's outbursts are melodramatic, her repressed passion is a valid counterpoint to Steerforth's unemotional callousness.

In the abundance of characters in the novel, Dickens also includes the physically disabled in Miss Moucher, Steerforth's dwarf manicurist and hairdresser. Dickens originally intended her to be malicious, helping Steerforth in his seduction of Little Emily, but when his neighbor on whom the character was partially based threatened a libel suit he made her sympathetic instead.

THEMATIC ISSUES

The themes of the novel derive from the growth of David Copperfield from infancy to maturity. What are the formative relationships in our young lives? How are we affected by either weak or domineering parents? How do we choose our marriage partners, and what is a healthy marriage? Most importantly, why do some people seek power over others, and what effect does such power have on the timid or the easily influenced? How do we achieve a balance between weakly acquiescing to the demands of other people and asserting our own will and independence of mind? Dickens dramatizes these relationships through a vast range of parents and children, husbands and wives, friends and business partners, all of whom touch David's life and affect his own development as he searches for, and finds, the "one happiness . . . and one friend and companion" that eluded Dickens himself but that he grants to his fictional hero.

David undergoes no radical change of heart, as so many of Dickens's heroes do; rather, his heart becomes "disciplined" and his mind strengthened through his experiences. The novel encapsulates many Victorian ideals in its confirmation of what Betsey Trotwood calls "strength of character": hard work, earnestness, self-reliance, and self-discipline, qualities that come with age, experience, and wise training, and that the amiable but childish characters (such as David's parents, Dora, and Mr. Micawber) never achieve. Equally lacking in these ideals, but from a different background, are the idle young gentlemen James Steerforth and Jack Maldon. Both pride themselves on their lack of these qualities, affecting a disdain for conventional life and a cynicism about human affairs, especially the affairs of the poorer classes. David, the narrator, writing about Jack Maldon, comments that this dangerous lack of discipline is becoming more prevalent in Victorian society:

A display of indifference to all the actions and passions of mankind was not supposed to be such a distinguished quality at that time, I think, as I have observed it to be considered since. I have known it very fashionable indeed. I have seen it displayed with such success, that I have encountered some fine ladies and gentlemen who might as well have been born caterpillars. (510)

Lack of discipline and self-reliance dogs the financial fortunes of many characters in the novel, most notably Mr. Micawber, whose cheerfully optimistic belief that "something will turn up" usually results in someone else providing for him. Dickens suffered from his father's perpetual failure to provide for his family, both as a child (when his father's debts forced Dickens to work in the blacking factory) and as an adult, when his father would even apply to Dickens's publishers for handouts. In 1842, Dickens complained of his father, "how long he is, growing up," and in the novel, Dickens clearly distinguishes between adults like Mr. Dickens who are dangerously childish in their failure to take on the responsibilities of the adult world (especially as husbands, wives, and parents) and the adults who are childlike: spontaneous, clear-seeing, and naturally kind, like the simple Mr. Dick. David and Dora are two babies, according to Aunt Betsey, beset by financial problems because they are as easily the prey of shopkeepers as was the waif David. Their servants are hopelessly inept because, as David recognizes, he and Dora fail to train them. Even Jip the dog frequently has the upper hand in the household.

David Copperfield explores the reasons why some children fail to grow up, and one of the keynotes of the novel's theme is the name of Mr. Peggotty's local pub, "The Willing Mind." As David grows and matures, he learns through experience and through the example of others what it is to have a mind that is strong enough to survive the disappointments and hardships of life, but without dominating and destroying the minds of others. A "willing mind" can be victimized by bullies such as Creakle, who dismisses the gentle Mr. Mell, and Uriah Heep, who has no difficulty undermining Agnes's well-meaning but weak-willed alcoholic father. Mr. Murdstone effectively kills Clara and reduces his second wife to "a state of imbecility." David escapes from Murdstone's domination only because he has a strong enough mind to resist, but he is bullied and swindled by numerous waiters and vagabonds on his way to Canterbury.

In her education of David, Betsey Trotwood stresses the need to train the young mind so that it is not foolishly "willing." She particularly advises him to be firm, in the sense of mastering his own will, not bending others to it (as Murdstone defines the word): "But what I want you to be, Trot . . . is, a firm fellow. A fine firm fellow, with a will of your own. With resolution. . . . With determination. With character, Trot—with strength of character that is not to be influenced, except on good reason, by anybody, or by anything" (268).

In the battle of wills, Betsey Trotwood recognizes that while Murdstone's severity destroys the personality, spoiling children is equally destructive in failing to discipline the mind. David's father, she says, was weak-willed himself and spoiled his wife by overprotecting her, making her unfit for real life. Dora, like Clara, is also spoiled. In his working notes for the novel, Dickens reminds himself to stress that "Poor little Dora," daughter of a foolish and indulgent father, was "not bred for a working life" (882). The indulged child fails to cope with adult life and becomes childishly manipulative, like David's mother, and Dora, who wheedles and coaxes David into letting her have her way. He acknowledges to himself that just as her aunts treat her like a plaything, so does he, but his own mind is too "willing" to resist. Like her dog Jip, Dora has been "trained" to be decorative and affectionate, but impractical. David realizes his own guilt in encouraging the childishness that had first captivated him.

If Steerforth lacks moral fiber because of his mother's blind devotion to him, Little Em'ly also suffers from being "wayward . . . a little spoiled." Mr. Omer tells David that she "didn't know her own mind quite" (297) and thus was a prey to Steerforth's influence, as David was. Emily, an orphan, is raised and indulged by her Uncle Dan, whom his sister Peggotty regards affectionately as a baby, one of many adult babies in the novel who fail to raise self-disciplined children. Betsey Trotwood recognizes that nurture can sometimes help to overcome inherited weakness of character (Dickens saw his father's fecklessness in several of his own sons), and she notes that the grandniece she had been expecting would need to be "well brought up, and well guarded" (7) so that she would rise above her parents' weak characters.

David is fortunate in having Betsey as his guardian, for despite her eccentricities, she educates him well and finds him employment as a proctor. Aunt Betsey's assurance that this position would make him "firm and self-reliant" (346) proves to be overconfident, however. In the next chapter, David throws his first dinner party and becomes hopelessly drunk. Dickens's description of every young man's first days of independence is both accurate and hilarious, as is his account of young love in David's rapturous infatuation with Dora. The development of David's mind is far from complete, but Aunt Betsey is an admirable guide, advising him, "Never . . . be mean in anything; never be false; never be cruel" (218). She deliberately keeps from him the fact that they are not completely ruined financially in order to test his self-reliance and perseverance (recognizing that, like Pip in *Great Expectations*, as well as Jack Maldon and Steerforth, David is in danger of becoming feckless through not needing to earn his living). He passes the test and proves the wisdom of her training. That Betsey herself is not always firm is evident, however, in her using David's mother as her vehicle for praise or emotion. Just as she silently expresses her sympathy with Clara by gently touching her hair (a recollection of David's mother that gives him the courage to seek out his otherwise formidable-sounding aunt), she expresses her pride in David through Clara:

"It's a mercy that poor dear baby of a mother of yours didn't live," said my aunt, looking at me approvingly, "or she'd have been so vain of her boy by this time, that her soft little head would have been completely turned, if there was anything of it left to turn." (My aunt always excused any weakness of her own in my behalf, by transferring it in this way to my poor mother.) (268)

Dickens accurately recognizes the struggle many Victorian parents felt when wanting to praise but not wanting to spoil or encourage vanity. Betsey also uses Mr. Dick as an outlet for her instinctual good sense, in a comic counterpart to Dora's father Mr. Spenlow, who always attributes his own objections to the firmness of his partner, Mr. Jorkins.

If the "willing mind" is often too easily led and fails to learn self-reliance and practical good sense, another kind of "willing mind" in the novel is the mind that exerts its powerful will over others. Dickens is ambivalent about this kind of will, aware as he must have been of his own dominant and forceful personality and the contrast between his mind and that of his wife, which he described as "compliant." He could not help being affected by the influence of his writings on his readers, especially when he read in public. Although he had not yet started the readings that were to give him such a strong sense of his power to move people, he had read *The Chimes* to his friends in 1844 and reduced them to tears. David's new-found authority over the boys in his nightly storytelling in the school dormitory echoes this feeling.

Even more compelling evidence of the power of Dickens's own mind was his experiments with mesmerism. His successful hypnotism of his wife led to his treatment of Madame de la Rue, an acquaintance of the Dickenses in Italy, for a mental disorder. He was often called to her bedside in the middle of the night, and the effectiveness of his power over her mind was undoubtedly very flattering. Dickens translated such power into his portrayal of Steerforth, and parallels can be seen between his power and that of other dark-haired, handsome, and sexually powerful men in his short stories. Like Dickens, the mesmerist—most mesmerists were men and their patients were younger women—these men are able to "will" the woman to do their bidding. In one story, the young bride is even willed to die. Steerforth's hold over Emily is not just the lure of making her a lady; her ambivalence about going with him demonstrates a weak mind overpowered by a stronger one. When he visits the old barge, David describes how they were all brought "by degrees, into a charmed circle" (307–8). Little Emily, her eyes fastened on Steerforth all the time, keeps her distance from him, both fascinated and frightened by his power. While part of her motivation may be the desire to be a "lady" and raise her family out of their humble life, Emily clearly finds Steerforth's handsome sexuality irresistible.

David refers to the "kind of enchantment" that Steerforth's voice, manner, handsome face, and bearing cast over almost everyone: He "carried a spell with him to which it was a natural weakness to yield, and which not many persons could withstand" (99). That Steerforth's charm is deliberate—the result of art not nature—is evident in David's description of his power over Rosa Dartle. David sees her "struggle against the fascinating influence of his delightful art—delightful nature I thought it then. . . . I saw her try, more and more faintly, but always angrily, as if she condemned a weakness in herself, to resist the captivating power that he possessed" (422). Rosa is always won over by Steerforth's "art." Dickens's ambivalence about his own power to control minds makes this portrayal of James Steerforth particularly complex. The novel clearly censures Steerforth, but David's attraction to him is undeniable, and their unequal friendship is true to the experience of many young men who worship older, more "worldly" companions. David feels young beside Steerforth and knows that Miss Moucher and Littimer are as conscious as he is of the difference between his own lack of whiskers and Steerforth's exuberant growth of hair. (Dickens once had a moustache-growing contest with his friends and was delighted to be the clear winner.)

The "willing mind" thus has several manifestations: It encompasses not only the mind that exerts its will over weaker ones (Steerforth over David, Rosa, and Emily; Uriah Heep over Mr. Wickfield; Murdstone over his wives), but also the mind that is "willing" to be dominated by a more fascinating and powerful one, as David is dominated by Dora and Steerforth. A humorous comment on the "willing mind" is made by Barkis, Peggotty's husband, whose famous declaration to David that "Barkis is willin'" serves as his proposal of marriage to Peggotty. In marriage—and there are many in the novel—a willing mind, in the best sense, brings happiness to an equal partnership, where both husband and wife are equally willing to love and support each other. From Mrs. Micawber's constant avowal that she will "never desert" her husband to Annie Strong's declaration that "there can be no disparity in marriage like unsuitability of mind and purpose" (643), David learns that adult love is based upon a willing partnership of equal minds.

STYLISTIC AND LITERARY DEVICES

The language and style of *David Copperfield* show Dickens at the height of his powers, midway between the exuberant but sometimes derivative style of *Pickwick Papers* and the more serious, often declamatory tone of the novels of the 1850s and 1860s. It shares with *Great Expectations*, Dickens's only other first-person narrative, a blending of irony, reflection, and humor as the adult narrator looks back with combined affection and dismay at his youthful follies and errors. Pip, however, has greater errors to account for, so the tone of *David Copperfield* is generally gentler and more sympathetic. The sometimes wistful quality of the prose is set apart in chapters entitled "Retrospects," where David switches to the present tense as he recalls pivotal events in his life. As well as adding immediacy to the narrative, these interludes intensify the sense of memory at work and allow the narrator to distance himself from his past: "Let me stand aside, to see the phantoms of those days go by me, accompanying the shadow of myself, in dim procession" (609).

David Copperfield is famous for the range of its characters' distinctive speech, from "Barkis is willin'" to Mrs. Gummidge's "I'm a lone lorn creetur' . . . and everything goes contrary with me." Dickens was careful to reflect the speech of his Yarmouth characters accurately, and he incorporated suggestions from readers who knew the Norfolk dialect and wrote to him during the publication of the novel. Mr. Micawber's convoluted and prosy speeches and letters, usually terminating in an abrupt "in short," wonderfully demonstrate his untroubled and speedy transitions from the depths of despair to the heights of contentment. If he could only adhere to his own dictum on economics:

Annual income twenty pounds, annual expenditure nineteen nineteen six, result happiness. Annual income twenty pounds, annual expenditure twenty pounds ought and six, result misery. The blossom is blighted, the leaf is withered, the God of day goes down upon the dreary scene, and—and in short you are for ever floored. As I am! (169)

Central to the style of *David Copperfield* is its reliance on the fairy tale for many of its central metaphors. As a novel that dramatizes the relationship between childhood and adulthood, it uses fairy-tale imagery to depict the child's highly charged view of the world, a view that David gradually allows to give way to a more mundane but realistic adult vision. Like *Jane Eyre*, with which it has many similarities, *David Copperfield* explores the dangers of letting romanticism govern one's perceptions. The child's imagination is vividly represented on the road to Dover when David wishes to sell his jacket to a hideously ugly little man in a dirty den of a shop. The half-human creature terrifies the child, uttering "Oh, goroo, goroo!" and lunges at him as though he would eat him. This transference of the real into the fantastic also occurs in David's other relationships, and the adult David recognizes that his fatal infatuation with both Steerforth and Dora derived from a romantic view of them that blinded him to other aspects of their characters. What was necessary and nurturing to the child (as in both David and Jane's delight in imaginative literature) can be dangerous when carried into the adult world, if it feeds a detachment from the truth.

The blending of fairy tale and naturalism is evident also in echoes from Shakespeare's play *The Tempest,* which, like the novel, centers around storm, drowning, and rebirth, and uses the sea as the dominant leitmotif. Dickens wrote part of the novel, including the chapter "Tempest," which recounts the storm and shipwreck scene, at his favorite summer retreat of Broadstairs, where his room looked out over what was often a very stormy and wild sea. He told a friend that he was "writing to the Music of the sea" (*Letters* 6.183). On the opening page, David tells us that he was born with a caul and, therefore, according to superstition, will never drown. The turbulent and disturbing subplot that culminates in the tempest and in Steerforth's death is always connected to the sea through the old boat at Yarmouth, scene of young David's most vividly romantic dreams. The destruction of the old barge in the tempest, as well as the deaths of Ham and Steerforth, signals the death of David's youthful romanticism.

A PSYCHOANALYTICAL READING OF *DAVID COPPERFIELD*

Psychoanalytic readings of literature began with the psychology of Sigmund Freud and his theories concerning the unconscious mind. According to Freud, the human psyche consists of the rational, orderly, and conscious part, which he called the *ego*, or "I," and the irrational, unknown, and unconscious part, which he called the *id*, or "it." Freud also recognized a *superego*, which operates as a kind of conscience, guiding us to moral actions such as self-sacrifice. Freud saw the superego as a projection of the ego but external to it because it is influenced by institutions such as church or school.

Central to the application of Freudian psychology to literary interpretation is the idea of repression. Conscious thoughts that we do not wish to face are forced into the unconscious mind, but they reappear in dreams, in language (what we call "Freudian slips"), and in literary or artistic expression. Thus, works of literature will often contain the repressed desires or fears of the author. According to Freud, most of these desires are sexual taboos, the most famous being the "Oedipus complex," named for the Greek drama in which the hero's fate acts out the unconscious desire of the young boy to kill his father and marry his mother. Because such desires are condemned by most societies, we repress these urges that Freud considered natural aspects of the human psyche, as evidenced by their prevalence in myths and fairy tales.

David Copperfield lends itself to psychoanalytical readings because of its autobiographical basis, its use of universal symbols such as drowning, and its many dreams. As a novel that explores the growth of David's psyche, it is likely to project that psyche on to characters, events, and objects in David's life, the most central projection being the double, who represents unconscious aspects of David's mind, or the *id*. Uriah Heep can be seen to embody the darker side of David's character in Uriah's overtly sexual pursuit of Agnes. As such, he is a threat to David in the plot and in the subconscious. A psychoanalytic reading would examine Heep's appearance in David's dreams and his connection with water, which is traditionally associated with sex. David finds him both repulsive and fascinating and admits to being attracted to his very repulsiveness. The third male figure in the novel who is closely associated with David and his sexual life is, of course, Steerforth, who can be seen as representing another aspect of David's psyche. Steerforth represents and acts out a less repulsive but still dangerous side of David's sexual desires.

Uriah Heep is first identified as David's *id* when David dreams about him after their first meeting, when Uriah has accused David of wishing to take Uriah's place in Mr. Wickfield's business. In the dream, Uriah launches Mr. Peggotty's boat home on a piratical expedition with the intention of drowning

David and Little Emily. Uriah, or David's baser instincts, captains the ship and drives David to a future with Emily that in his conscious mind he now finds unacceptable (because he is a gentleman and she a fisherman's daughter). Steerforth fulfils this role in the novel when he elopes across the Channel with Emily and is drowned. Because in the dream David replaces Steerforth as the seducer of Emily, Steerforth represents David's repressed desires.

The psychoanalytical relationship between David and Steerforth can be seen in David's fascination with Rosa Dartle's scar, caused by Steerforth's flinging a hammer at her. That the scar is linked to sexual passion is clear; David is haunted by the way it flares up when Rosa is aroused to anger or to passion by Steerforth. In his mind, David adds the scar to the picture of Rosa in his bedroom, suggesting that David wishes to share in Steerforth's violation of Rosa.

David (whose surname suggests land, as does Agnes Wickfield's) is protected from drowning by the caul with which he is born. But he is also protected from disastrous sexual drownings by the enactment of his desires and inclinations through surrogate figures, Uriah Heep and James Steerforth.

7

Hard Times
(1854)

Utilitarianism, a system of philosophy first expounded by Jeremy Bentham at the end of the eighteenth century, was the object of Dickens's contempt throughout his life. He attacked it in *Oliver Twist* and in *A Christmas Carol*, but his most sustained and focussed blasts against it resounded in the 1844 Christmas book *The Chimes* and in *Hard Times*. The novel was dedicated to Thomas Carlyle, whose attacks on Utilitarianism had been equally consistent and prolonged. When asking Carlyle for his permission to make the dedication, Dickens told him, "It contains what I do devoutly hope will shake some people in a terrible mistake of these days, when so presented. I know it contains nothing in which you do not think with me, for no man knows your books better than I" (*Letters* 7.367).

The "terrible mistake," in Dickens's view, was Bentham's theory of utility, which had two main components: First, Bentham believed that self-interest is the basis of all human action, and that laws must provide strong sanctions to induce the individual to put the interests of the community first because he will not naturally do so. Second, Bentham believed that the rightness or wrongness of an action can be measured by how much pain or pleasure it causes, pain and pleasure being the "sovereign masters" governing our behavior. Pain and pleasure can be measured according to their intensity, duration, certainty, and other quantifiable aspects. Thus the greatest happiness of the greatest number is the measure of how right or wrong an action is, and questions of morality become a matter of expediency rather than principle. Many

Victorians such as Dickens saw their society increasingly accept Bentham's theory of self-interest as justification for greed and self-indulgence.

Bentham's theories also led to a reliance on statistics and the application of statistical methods to human affairs; statistics could be used to "prove" almost anything, and the results were often absurd. In 1854, when writing about his purpose in *Hard Times*, Dickens pointed out to a friend how soldiers froze in the Crimean War because the government averaged the winter temperatures there and dressed the troops for that temperature, forgetting that any one night could be many degrees colder. In *The Chimes*, Mr. Filer, the statistician, "proves" by figures that Toby Veck is taking food out of the mouths of widows and orphans when he eats his meager lunch.

Bentham's theory of utility extended into the arts as well. Painting and music were valuable only if they led to important social ends. Followers of Utilitarianism, in the Department of Practical Art, disapproved of flowers or other decorations on carpets that took away from the carpet's flatness, and they adhered to strict rules of taste in wallpaper and design. Bentham considered poetry misrepresentation: Words were perverted when they were used for uttering anything but precise, logical truth, or facts. This view of literature was pervasive in the nineteenth century and dangerous, in Dickens's view, because it failed to nurture the imagination. The deprivation of the classroom and nursery in *Hard Times* dramatizes the factual and didactic emphasis of much of the literature written for children prior to Dickens's own *Holiday Romance* (1868) and Lewis Carroll's *Alice's Adventures in Wonderland* (1865). In an 1853 essay for *Household Words*, Dickens took issue with the artist George Cruikshank for using the fairy tale to promote temperance; in 1869, one of his "Uncommercial Traveller" essays in *All the Year Round* made fun of Mr. Barlow, the pedantic tutor in the standard children's textbook of the day, Thomas Day's *The History of Sandford and Merton*. In true Benthamistic spirit, Mr. Barlow would have trimmed Aladdin's lamp while lecturing on the qualities of sperm oil and whale fisheries; he would have proved geographically that Casgar and Tartary did not exist; he would have demonstrated scientifically the impossibility of lowering a hunchback down an eastern chimney on a cord.

Bentham's theories were firmly entrenched in Victorian life by 1854. They were central to the reform movement in English politics, and Dickens had already come to blows with the leading proponents of Utilitarianism when their journal, the *Westminster Review*, criticized *A Christmas Carol* for ignoring the principles of political economy. Dickens was a reformer himself, of course, and he was in sympathy with many of the improvements that were encouraged by the Utilitarian movement, such as universal schooling. But he was adamantly and unswervingly opposed to the statistical view of human nature and human relations that was central to Bentham's doctrine. The idea of weighing and measuring human emotions, of refusing to acknowledge intuition, perception, or religious belief (the latter was pure superstition to Bentham), and of discounting imaginative literature was to Dickens the most dangerous of philosophies. He had the real-life example of John Stuart Mill as confirmation of this opposition: Mill suffered a severe mental breakdown as a result of his Utilitarian training and recovered through the agency of imaginative literature, particularly Wordsworth's poetry.

Dickens explained his intention for writing *Hard Times* in a letter to a friend: "My satire is against those who see figures and averages, and nothing else—the representatives of the wickedest and most enormous vice of this time—the men who, through long years to come, will do more to damage the real useful truths of political economy, than I could do (if I tried) in my whole life" (*Letters* 7.492).

PLOT DEVELOPMENT

Like *The Old Curiosity Shop* and *Barnaby Rudge*, *Hard Times* was written in weekly installments, this time for Dickens's own publication, *Household Words*, where it ran from 1 April to 12 August 1854. Shorter than most of his novels, it is also the most dedicated to a "purpose" that it shared with *Household Words* as well: the exposure of the dangers of Utilitarian thinking, the championing of imaginative and vital human experience, and the depiction of the life of the factory worker at mid-century. The topics of the novel overlapped with articles that appeared concurrently in the journal and also with Elizabeth Gaskell's novel about industrial life in Manchester, *North and South*, which followed *Hard Times* in *Household Words*.

Dickens found the difficulties of managing the small weekly sections "CRUSHING. Nobody can have an idea of it who has not had an experience of patient fiction-writing with some elbow-room always, and open places in perspective. In this form, with any kind of regard to the current number, there is absolutely no such thing" (*Letters* 7.282). He overcame the restriction partly by thinking of the novel in terms of monthly numbers (installments) and by dividing it into three parts, as he was to do again with *A Tale of Two Cities*.

The story takes place entirely in Coketown, a northern mill town dominated by Thomas Gradgrind, retired businessman and later member of parliament, and by his friend and banker, Josiah Bounderby. Mr. Gradgrind's two older children are Louisa and Tom, whose dull lives at Stone Lodge are brightened when their father takes in Sissy Jupe, a young circus performer whose father deserts her when the circus is visiting the town. Stunted by their father's Utilitarian views, Louisa does not have the will to resist him and enters a loveless marriage with Mr. Bounderby, encouraged by her self-serving brother, Tom, who is employed in Bounderby's bank.

Stephen Blackpool, one of the weavers, is trapped in a disastrous marriage to a drunken woman who returns from time to time. He is supported by Rachael, another mill worker, and wishes to marry her, but divorce is too expensive for a working man. At her request, he does not join the worker's union and is ostracized as a result. Then Tom Gradgrind robs the bank and contrives to throw suspicion on to Stephen, who has left town looking for other work. On his way back to clear his name, Stephen falls down an unused mine shaft and dies soon after being rescued.

Mr. Gradgrind's children are both found to be marred by their education. Louisa has been courted by James Harthouse, a handsome young politician, and she appears to be planning to elope with him, but, instead, she flees to her father's house, where Sissy again supports her. Tom, his theft from the bank now revealed, seeks sanctuary in the circus, where he is found by his father and Bitzer, the star pupil of Gradgrind's system of education. Bitzer is anxious to turn Tom in, but Mr. Sleary, the owner of the circus, helps Tom escape. Mr. Gradgrind is left to ponder the ruin of both his children.

CHARACTER DEVELOPMENT

The "hard times" suffered by the characters in the novel are the result of the "terrible mistake" of Utilitarianism as propagated by Thomas Gradgrind, retired hardware merchant and now Member of Parliament for Coketown, and his friend Josiah Bounderby, banker and manufacturer. Between them, they bring misery to almost everyone raised in their system: Gradgrind, through his role as father and school reformer; Bounderby, through his role as mill owner and husband to Louisa Gradgrind. Attempting to reverse the harm done are the circus performers.

The novel opens with a satire on Utilitarian schooling (based closely on many schools in Victorian England), which demonstrates the education of four very different children: Louisa and Tom Gradgrind; Sissy Jupe, the circus performer's daughter; and Bitzer, who grows into the epitome of Bentham's theory of self-interest. Sissy, vital and morally alive but a failure in the Gradgrindian hard-facts system, and Bitzer, an empty shell but the star pupil, are perfectly contrasted by a ray of sunlight that glances across both of them. While Sissy becomes more lustrous and deeply colored by the sun, Bitzer is merely made even whiter and colder than he already is: "he looked as though, if he were cut, he would bleed white" (5). The deprivation of the school of hard facts is compounded at Tom and Louisa's home, where they are instructed never to wonder and so are kept away from imaginative literature of any kind.

The way out of grinding Utilitarian boredom is soon established in Chapter Three, "A Loophole," the loophole being a peephole that allows the Gradgrind children to discover forbidden knowledge, in this case, the world of imagination, a circus. The link between this imaginative and human world of "fancy" and the hard, mechanical world of Thomas Gradgrind's aptly named Stone Lodge is Sissy Jupe, who is taken in by Gradgrind when her father disappears. Gradgrind's sympathy with Sissy points to his capacity to temper his Utilitarian attitudes, and her influence on him and his family forms one of the crucial threads in the novel. When Sissy brings the sensibility of the circus into Stone Lodge, she becomes the "loophole" that allows some escape from the terrible mistake of Gradgrind's system. Louisa learns compassion from Sissy and gains the moral strength to resist her brutal husband and the temptation of adultery.

Mr. Gradgrind is presented from the beginning as a fool rather than a villain, wrong-headed rather than malicious, although his educational system almost destroys his model pupils and children, Tom and Louisa. Dickens early establishes that "his character was not unkind, all things considered; it might have been a very kind one indeed, if he had only made some round mistake in the arithmetic that balanced it, years ago" (35). In a letter, Dickens even goes so far as to say that "there is reason and good intention in much that [Mr. Gradgrind] does—in fact, in all that he does—but that he over-does it. Perhaps by dint of his going his way and my going mine, we shall meet at last at some halfway house where there are flowers on the carpets, and a little standing-room for Queen Mab's Chariot among the Steam Engines" (*Letters* 7.354).

Louisa's temptation is prepared for when her father finds her peeping at the circus. She is sullen, but her face also contains "a light with nothing to rest upon, a fire with nothing to burn, a starved imagination keeping life in itself somehow, which brightened its expression. Not with the brightness natural to cheerful youth, but with uncertain, eager, doubtful flashes, which had something painful in them . . . " (16). Fire becomes the symbol of Louisa's repressed emotion that her upbringing has forbidden her to acknowledge; when Mr. Bounderby, thirty years her senior, kisses her cheek, she rubs the place "until it was burning red" (27). She is comforted by staring into the fire and "wondering" about her future, but emotionally deprived and scarred, she is no match for her selfish brother and obtuse father, who marry her to Mr. Bounderby to further Tom's career in the bank. Louisa's emotional repression is vividly represented as fire when she is discussing Mr. Bounderby's marriage proposal with her father. Looking out of the window at the factory chimneys, she exclaims, "There seems to be nothing there but languid and monotonous smoke. Yet when the night comes, Fire bursts out, father!" It is a warning to Gradgrind of what will happen to her if she marries Bounderby, but, of course, he fails to recognize it and replies, "I do not see the application of the remark" (132). Mr.

Gradgrind almost allows himself to understand Louisa's inner turmoil, but he is unable to overcome the "artificial barriers he had for many years been erecting, between himself and all those subtle essences of humanity which will elude the utmost cunning of algebra . . . " (132); sensitive always to regret (the "one happiness" he felt he had missed in his own life), Dickens comments poignantly that "the moment shot away into the plumbless depths of the past, to mingle with all the lost opportunities that are drowned there."

While Mr. Gradgrind is capable of human feeling, his friend Mr. Bounderby is not. Dickens's portrait of Bounderby is richly satirical: While Mr. Gradgrind's hair "bristled on the skirts of his bald head, a plantation of firs to keep the wind from its shining surface" (1–2), Bounderby's has mostly been talked off, the remaining tufts "all standing up in disorder . . . from being constantly blown about by his windy boastfulness" (18–19). Bounderby's boast is that he is a self-made man, the Victorian middle-class answer to good birth. In the new cities such as Coketown that were built on "new" money from the Industrial Revolution, it was possible for enterprising men to become wealthy and take on the possessions and social standing that had once been the sole reserve of the old gentry. Eventually, the two classes intermarried, but during the century, the old families continued to look down upon the manufacturers, despite their wealth. While boasting of his humble beginnings, Bounderby delights in casting his housekeeper Mrs. Sparsit as fallen gentry (her great-aunt is Lady Scadgers, and her late husband's mother had been "a Powler"); she is now beholden to him, an orphan boy who raised himself single-handed from a childhood of abject poverty and deprivation. A subplot uncovers Bounderby's story to be mere "windy boastfulness" when his timid mother reappears in Coketown and reveals his ordinary but far from deprived childhood.

James Harthouse is one of the many idle young dilettantes in Dickens's novels, a "thorough gentleman, made to the model of the time; weary of everything, and putting no more faith in anything than Lucifer" (158). Such idle cynicism is dangerous, especially since it is also attractive, not least to Gradgrind and Bounderby, who are also morally bankrupt and even imitate Harthouse's offhand and cynical manner: "They liked fine gentlemen; they pretended they did not, but they did. . . . they served out, with an enervated air, the little mouldy rations of political economy, on which they regaled their disciples" (164). Harthouse's danger lies in his smooth charm. Like the devil himself, he attracts because "he is trimmed, smoothed, and varnished, according to the mode . . . he is aweary of vice, and aweary of virtue." Bounderby is devilish in his "serving out of red tape" that destroys Stephen Blackpool; Harthouse is devilish in his "kindling of red fire" (239), which is Louisa's repressed sexuality and anger.

Harthouse's manipulation of Louisa and her selfish brother, Tom, is brilliantly described, the latter reminding the reader of Steerforth's power over David Copperfield. David's fault was an innocent desire to be loved, whereas Tom is a hypocrite, turned by Gradgrind's system into a monster of "grovelling sensualities" (175). Louisa, miserably married to Bounderby, is also vulnerable to Harthouse's charming London sophistication, and her gradual attraction to him is graphically depicted through Mrs. Sparsit's eyes. Jealous of Louisa for marrying Mr. Bounderby, which she had hoped to do herself, Mrs. Sparsit takes great delight in visualizing Louisa's attraction to Harthouse as a descent of a large staircase, which will lead her to abandon Mr. Bounderby to Mrs. Sparsit's care.

Mrs. Sparsit is one of Dickens's most memorable minor characters, her inner life emerging almost entirely through external signs. Her sexual frustration is evident in her constant working at netting (fancy needle work), with one foot in a stirrup of looped threads; the image also suggests the riding of a hobbyhorse, which is one aspect of mechanical thinking. Her intense jealousy of Louisa is graphically represented when, as Bounderby tells her of his engagement, she picks out holes in some fabric with the points of very sharp scissors, looking, with her bushy eyebrows and Roman nose, like "a hawk engaged upon the eyes of a tough little bird" (139). The viciousness implicit in this image leads to Mrs. Sparsit's deserved defeat; when she follows Louisa, calculating that she is secretly on her way to meet Harthouse, Mrs. Sparsit finds herself on a frustrating wild goose chase that leaves her dripping wet from a thunderstorm, bedraggled and finally defeated: "prickly things were in her shoes; caterpillars slung themselves, in hammocks of their own making, from various parts of her dress; rills ran from her bonnet, and her Roman nose. In such condition, Mrs. Sparsit stood hidden in the density of the shrubbery, considering what next" (283).

Uniting the Gradgrind house, Bounderby's menage, the circus, and the factory is Coketown itself, "the key-note," as Dickens calls it. His description has become, with Blake's "dark, satanic mills," the epitome of the new industrial towns that sprouted across the landscape of Victorian England in the middle of the nineteenth century. Here, Dickens joins the schoolroom to the factory in the effects of Utilitarianism on both child and factory worker, as he makes explicit:

Is it possible, I wonder, that there was any analogy between the case of the Coketown population and the case of the little Gradgrinds? Surely, none of us in our sober senses and acquainted with figures, are to be told at this time of day, that one of the foremost elements in the existence of the Coketown working-people had been for scores of years deliberately set at nought? That there was any Fancy in them demanding to be brought into healthy existence instead of struggling on in convulsions? That exactly in the ratio as they worked long and monotonously, the craving grew within them for some physical relief—some relaxation, encouraging good humour and good spirits, and giving them a vent . . . which craving must and would be satisfied aright, or must and would inevitably go wrong, until the laws of the Creation were repealed? (31–32)

Despite establishing this connection in depicting the plight of the workers, Dickens actually concentrates less on the deprivation of entertainment and fancy as on other problems. His hero is Stephen Blackpool, named after the first Christian martyr, who is certainly a martyr in every sense. Married to a drunkard and ostracized by his fellow weavers, he is driven out of town in search of other work, unaware that Tom Gradgrind has thrown suspicion on him for the bank robbery. Finally, he falls victim to management's carelessness when he dies after falling down an unused mine shaft. Stephen is supported in his miserable struggle by Rachael, a working woman who, like Stephen, exemplifies Dickens's belief that most people are not governed by self-interest. In the Bible, Rachael patiently waits for fourteen years before she is allowed to marry Jacob. In Dickens's story, Rachael is never rewarded with Stephen's hand, but she continues to support him and even care for his drunken wife. As the stars are to a candle, so was Rachael to "the common experiences of [Stephen's] life." In Bentham's theory of self-interest, how can one explain the Rachaels of the world?

THEMATIC ISSUES

None of Dickens's novels is more committed to a single theme than *Hard Times*. The exposure of Utilitarianism's petty and reductive meanness controls every aspect of the novel; using Coketown as the "keynote," Dickens offers a view of human nature and human relations that is open, vital, and compassionate. He strikes his keynote over and over again not just through the plot, language, and characterization, but through the narrator's direct comment. He draws attention to the contrast between machines (which can be weighed and measured) and the men who operate them (who cannot) when Stephen bends over his loom: "Never fear, good people of an anxious turn of mind, that Art will consign Nature to oblivion. Set anywhere, side by side, the work of GOD and the work of man; and the former, even though it be a troop of Hands of very small account, will gain in dignity from the comparison" (91). There is no mystery in the machine, he reminds us, but there is "an unfathomable mystery in the meanest of them, for ever.—Supposing we were to reserve our arithmetic for material objects, and to govern these awful unknown quantities by other means!" (92)

Dickens's answer to Bentham's mechanical view of human nature is Christianity, and he evokes biblical references throughout to destroy Bentham's reductionist system of philosophy. The three sections of the novel are entitled "Sowing," "Reaping," and "Garnering," an echo of the many references in the Bible to human development as organic and natural. Gradgrind tries to grow his children in the barren land of Stone Lodge, and Louisa later recognizes that the early springs of her imagination dried up under her father's harsh system: "Her remembrances of home and childhood were remembrances of the drying up of every spring and fountain in her young heart as it gushed out. The golden waters were not there. They were flowing for the fertilization of the land where grapes are gathered from thorns, and figs from thistles" (263). In the first paragraph, this metaphor of stunted growth is linked to the empirical view of education, according to which the child's mind is a blank slate on which experience imprints information. Mr. Gradgrind's governing principle is that "you can only form the minds of reasoning animals upon Facts: nothing else will ever be of any service to them." There is a chilling echo of Jonathan Swift's "A Modest Proposal" in this reference: Swift demonstrated how easy it is to advocate the eating of babies if they are no more than "reasoning animals."

Chapter One is entitled "The One Thing Needful," a reference to Christ's answer to Martha when she questioned whether Mary was doing enough for him when only Martha seemed to be busy with the housework. "The one thing needful" was love, a defense of the spirit over the more limited quality of usefulness. Further sharpening Dickens's view of the dangerousness of Benthamism is the title of Chapter Two, "Murdering the Innocents," a reference to Herod's decree to kill all children under the age of two because he had heard of the birth of Jesus. The phrase is not too strong for Dickens's outrage at the destruction of the child's imagination and moral sense by certain Victorian attitudes to schooling and imaginative literature.

Bentham's belief that self-interest governs all human behavior is countered by the Golden Rule, which is Sissy's innocent response to the question, what is the first principle of Political Economy? She replies, "To do unto others as I would that they should do unto me" (73). Sissy's moral sense is both natural and fostered by the circus, whereas Mr. Gradgrind has to gain it by the hard lesson of his children's destruction and by Sissy's good example. He continually tries to prove that "the Good Samaritan was a Bad Economist" (286), but by the end of the novel, he is "making his facts and figures subservient to Faith, Hope, and Charity; and no longer trying to grind that Heavenly trio in his dusty little mills" (395–96). Mr. Sleary is given the final word on Christian charity versus self-interest when he tells Mr. Gradgrind that "there ith a love in the world, not all Thelf-interetht after all, but thomething very different" (390).

The central corrective to Benthamism in the novel is the circus, considered by some critics to be a superficial or childish solution to the problem. But the circus is in many ways the perfect antidote to Gradgrindery because it embodies so many of the virtues that are lacking in Utilitarianism. First, of course, it is not "useful" in Bentham's interpretation of utility, but it nurtures the imagination through its artistry, color, music, and skill. The circus requires interdependence and trust among the performers, a mutual relationship that Dickens saw breaking down in the factory system when not only master and man were at odds, but man and man as well, when Stephen is ostracized for not joining the union. The keynote of the circus is not just kindness but a trust that allows the performers to build human pyramids, where fathers of families literally put themselves in each other's hands. How different, says Dickens, is this human family from the factory, where the master's only dealings with his men is to pay their wage.

Sissy goes to some trouble to buy nine oils for her father to treat his bruises and serves as a reminder that the circus represents fluidity, vitality, and compassion, the soft or open qualities suggested by oil in contrast to the metallic, stony metaphors that characterize Gradgrind and Bounderby. Dickens had thought to call the novel "Hard Heads and Soft Hearts," and the many references to Mr. Gradgrind's mill indicate the importance of the oil that makes compassion and spontaneity possible. Mr. Sleary, the circus manager, exemplifies fluidity also in speech and appearance: "a stout man . . . with one fixed eye, and one loose eye, a voice (if it can be called so) like the efforts of a broken old pair of bellows, a flabby surface, and a muddled head which was never sober and never drunk" (46). Sleary is no sentimentally idealized representative of goodness, but his superiority to Gradgrind and Bounderby is evident in his flexibility and kindness. At the end of the novel, Sleary talks about how mysterious love is and how it operates even in Sissy's father's dog, who somehow found his way, lame and blind, back to the circus in search of Sissy. In contrast to Gradgrind's view of children as "reasoning animals," the circus is willing to grant even animals the unfathomable qualities of love and devotion; even dogs are not always motivated by self-interest.

The circus saves Tom when he escapes prosecution for the robbery of the bank. Although some might question the rightness of Tom's avoiding punishment for his crime, his appearance, disguised behind a black face in the circus performance, represents the final and fitting defeat of Thomas Gradgrind's "model pupil."

Dickens raises many contemporary issues in his treatment of Stephen Blackpool. Just as in *The Chimes* (1844) he wanted to make a "great blow for the poor," so in *Hard Times* his purpose was to show that the English factory worker lived a life of grinding poverty and deprivation, shut out from amusement and relaxation by long working hours and restrictive laws. The English people, he asserts, "are as hard-worked as any people upon whom the sun shines" (83). His portrait of Coketown—the new model town—emphasizes the dullness of it, the sameness of the buildings, the drabness of the Utilitarian architecture, and the stunting effect such monotonous surroundings and occupation must have on the inhabitants of the miserable little houses. The chimneys, "built in an immense variety of stunted and crooked shapes" (83), are a sign of the people who are born into those houses. Treat people like machines, he warns, and they will turn into Bitzers.

Dickens has been criticized for not providing answers to the problems that beset the new industrial society. Stephen's word for them is "muddle," and he never attains a greater ability to articulate a solution, although he does achieve a heroic dignity at his death. Management's disregard for industrial safety is one of Dickens's subjects in the novel, but Stephen's descent into the "Old Hell Shaft" is also symbolic: Stephen may not achieve the enlightenment that usually accompanies the journey to the underworld, but his lack of understanding is central to Dickens's purpose in his story of Stephen the martyr. Uneducated working men have no chance in a world where the masters regard them as "hands" and men are pitted against men by unscrupulous union leaders such as Slackbridge. Stephen's dying words ask that "aw th' world may on'y coom together more, an' get a better unnerstand'in o' one another" (363). Elizabeth Gaskell was to make the same appeal in *North and South*. Both works exemplify Dickens's intention in the magazine: In the Preliminary Word, he tells his readers that he wishes to show the romance in everyday life and "teach the hardest workers at this whirling wheel of toil, that their lot is not necessarily a moody, brutal fact, excluded from the sympathies and graces of imagination; to bring the greater and the lesser in degree, together, upon that wide field, and mutually dispose them to a better acquaintance and a kinder understanding."

Louisa is brought to a "better acquaintance" with her Coketown neighbors when she visits Stephen and Rachael. Until then, she knows the working class only as "Hands": "she knew what results in work a given number of them would produce in a given space of time. She knew them in crowds passing to and from their nests, like ants or beetles. But she knew from her reading infinitely more of the ways of toiling insects than of these toiling men and women" (209). To James Harthouse, they are the "fluffy classes" and nothing more, a callous reference to the fluff in the factory air that poisoned Rachael's sister. To Josiah Bounderby, they are a greedy class who envy him his success and aspire only to being fed on turtle soup and venison.

It was important to Dickens's theme that he could show the middle-class characters—Harthouse, Tom Gradgrind, and Bitzer—made morally bankrupt by Utilitarianism, but he fiercely retains Stephen and Rachael's humanity despite their sufferings. While he feared the effects of deprivation and monotony on the working man, Dickens also believed that the human spirit was much stronger than any system that aimed to destroy it. There is a certain ambiguity in the novel as a result; the people who live in the identical houses are *not* "equally like one another" (28) after all. As the Industrial Revolution wore on and the factory system became a fact of life, Dickens turned away from his attack on the sameness of Coketown life and the monotony of the workers' day, realizing that such pessimism was not going to help the weaver who had no other means of earning a living. In his 1866 Christmas story *Mugby Junction*, he defends the factory worker against the criticism of writers like John Ruskin, who were harshly critical of the factory system and its effect on the workers' minds and spirits. Dickens wished to reassure them that their work would not destroy them, and actually had purpose:

How the many toiling people lived, and loved, and died; how wonderful it was to consider the various trainings of eye and hand, the nice distinctions of sight and touch, that separated them into classes of workers . . . of one complete whole which combined their many intelligences and forces, though of itself but some cheap object of use or ornament in common life; how good it was to know that such assembling in a multitude on their part, and such contribution of their several dexterities towards a civilizing end, did not deteriorate them as it was the fashion of the supercilious Mayflies of humanity to pretend, but engendered among them a self-respect and yet a modest desire to be much wiser than they were.

Stephen and Rachael's integrity and resilience under difficulties (in contrast to Harthouse's glib indifference) are emphasized in the scene in which Stephen drifts off to sleep while his wife (who has unexpectedly returned) lies nearby in a drunken stupor, a bottle of liniment (poisonous to swallow) at her side. Stephen dreams that he is being persecuted by false witnesses for breaking a commandment, just as his namesake in the Bible was stoned to death for apparent blasphemy. In his dream, Stephen is reviled and finally brought to his death when his loom turns into a noose to hang him. The implication is that Stephen was tempted to murder his wife and free himself from a marriage from which Bounderby had told him there was "no way out" for the working-class man. The dream mingles with reality when Stephen, somehow rescued from hanging, is ostracized by his community and pursued by the word "poison"; so strong is his sense of guilt that he may have contemplated ending his wife's life. He struggles awake to find his wife reaching for the poison, but Rachael intercedes and saves her.

The horror of this scene draws attention to the depth of suffering and human emotion that exists within the little boxes of Coketown, suffering that a

Benthamistic weighing and measuring of pleasure and pain can never account for. The waking dream that dramatizes Stephen's temptation and his salvation by Rachael enacts Dickens's earlier comment that "there is an unfathomable mystery in the meanest" of people, which must not be ignored.

Another issue is raised by the factory scenes in the depiction of Slackbridge, the union organizer who incites the men to ostracize Stephen when, due to a promise he made to Rachael, he will not join the union. Dickens had visited a strike in Preston early in 1854, and although he decided not to include a strike in the novel (Elizabeth Gaskell did have a strike in *North and South*), he based Slackbridge's empty rhetoric on the speeches he heard in Preston. While he sympathized with the lot of the men in their attempts to be heard by the masters, Dickens also recognized that many union leaders, such as Slackbridge, were bullies who did the workmen no benefit. The workers, victimized by their masters, are victimized again by their own leaders. Although the men know Stephen to be an honest worker, they are swayed by group pressure and afraid to stand up against it: "Private feeling must yield to the common cause" (190). The reader may feel that Stephen's promise to Rachael that he will not get involved with the union is a contrivance for the sake of the plot (she does not want to incite the workers to violence over her sister's death), but turning his own class against him was one of the common results of the early union movement, as Elizabeth Gaskell also realized. Mob action, for Dickens, was mechanical thinking again, and Slackbridge is portrayed as a robotic speaker whose gestures are always identical. The novel argues for the value of the individual over any system—whether it is Utilitarianism or a union movement—that dehumanizes people and sees them merely as statistics.

Dickens deliberately did not offer a solution to the problem of industrial relations, realizing that there was no easy one. Rather, he wanted to bring to the middle classes some idea of the attitudes that prevailed in their laissez-faire, statistical age. In the summer of 1854, he explained to a friend his purpose for writing fiction, and how he wished to avoid the extremism that made Bentham's blanket theory of self-interest so dangerous: "To interest and affect the general mind in behalf of anything that is clearly wrong—to stimulate and rouse the public soul to a compassionate or indignant feeling that it *must not be*—without obtruding any pet theory of cause or cure, and so throwing off allies as they spring up—I believe to be one of Fiction's highest uses. And this is the use to which I try to turn it" (*Letters* 7.405).

STYLISTIC AND LITERARY DEVICES

The language of *Hard Times*, like everything else in the novel, exemplifies Dickens's attack on Utilitarian thinking. Jeremy Bentham considered language valuable only to the extent that it was denotative: one word to signify one fact. Poetry or other allusive language was dishonest. Bentham's attitude is, of course, represented in the novel by Gradgrind and Bounderby, who insist on denotative meanings at all times. Sissy Jupe, daughter of a circus horse rider, is flummoxed by Mr. Gradgrind's request for a definition of a horse, which is given by Bitzer: "'Quadruped. Graminivorous. Forty teeth, namely twenty-four grinders, four eye-teeth, and twelve incisive. . . . Age known by marks in mouth.' Thus (and much more) Bitzer" (6). Sissy is told that now she knows what a horse is.

Mr. Bounderby also congratulates himself on insisting on a direct relation between object and name, telling the guests at his wedding that they "won't expect a speech from a man who, when he sees a Post, says 'that's a Post,' and when he sees a Pump, says 'that's a Pump,' and is not to be got to call a Post a Pump, or a Pump a Post, or either of them a Toothpick" (143).

Contrasting Utilitarian denotative language is the highly allusive language of the circus performers, epitomized in Mr. Sleary, whose lisp ("slurring" speech) makes his speech even more imprecise. The circus people stay at the Pegasus's Arms, whose sign depicts a winged horse (impossible in Utilitarian terms) inscribed with a flowing scroll and extended into the bar by another, more theatrical, representation of Pegasus, but a theatrical one "with real gauze let in for his wings, golden stars stuck on all over him, and his ethereal harness made of red silk" (36).

Dickens counters Utilitarian exactness of speech also in his use of alternative methods of communication to suggest different attitudes to language. Sissy and Rachael, the moral centers of the novel, rely largely on wordless communication, the language of the heart that reveals the importance of what is *not* said. When Sissy is told of Louisa's engagement to Bounderby, she says nothing, but looks "in wonder, in pity, in sorrow, in doubt, in a multitude of emotions, towards Louisa" (137), who understands (but resents) Sissy's compassion without having to look at her. Mr. Gradgrind, in his blind adherence to facts, fails to read his daughter's body language and cannot understand the nuances of her spoken words. When she tells him that he has trained her so well that she has "never dreamed a child's dream" nor had a "child's belief or a child's fear" (135), Gradgrind fails to hear the criticism in her tone and takes her comment as praise for his system.

The language of gesture—antithesis of denotative spoken language—is cleverly invoked in the scene in which Harthouse subtly wins over the whelp, Tom Gradgrind. Harthouse's disingenuous remarks usually appear in reported rather than direct speech in a kind of dramatic irony that is clear to the reader but not to the character. ("If anything could have exalted Jem's interest in Mr. Bounderby, it would have been this very circumstance. Or, so he told him"

[168]). The reader sees rather than hears Harthouse's duplicity. Tom fails to read Harthouse's body language when the older man lounges at the fireplace, smoking and plying Tom with drinks; but Harthouse and the reader read Tom's grovelling admiration for the suave visitor in Tom's attempts to be equally sophisticated:

Tom had by this time got both his legs on the sofa. If his second leg had not been already there when he was called a dear fellow, he would have put it up at that great stage of the conversation. Feeling it necessary to do something then, he stretched himself out at greater length, and, reclining with the back of his head on the end of the sofa, and smoking with an infinite assumption of negligence, turned his common face, and not too sober eyes, towards the face looking down upon him so carelessly yet so potently. (178)

Dickens's point in drawing attention to both the unspoken compassionate gestures of Rachael and Sissy and the unintentionally revealing body language of Tom is that the human psyche is complex and not subject to denotative measure; the subtleties of human motivation and communication cannot and must not be reduced to facts and figures.

Dickens has been criticized for lack of consistency in the use of language in the novel because he employs metaphor and imaginative language to describe the Utilitarians and the inhuman factories and looms of Coketown. Again, such description is clearly deliberate in revealing that even Utilitarians have unfathomable depths that can never be measured and imaginative cores that need to be nurtured. With Bitzer as a possible exception, the novel stresses that Utilitarianism twists the human out of shape but can never destroy it. So Gradgrind is immediately described in highly imaginative terms: His bald head is "covered with knobs, like the crust of a plum pie, as if the head had scarcely warehouse-room for the hard facts stored inside" (2). The image suggests that his head is ready to burst not just with facts, but with human potential. Throughout the novel, fancy constantly bursts through, like the fire that breaks out in the chimneys of Coketown and in Louisa's heart.

Dickens's characteristic use of metaphor and personification is also evident in the novel. Gradgrind's neckcloth is "trained to take him by the throat with an unaccommodating grasp, like a stubborn fact, as it was" (2). Coketown is evoked in vivid images connected with hell: unnatural red and black, serpents of smoke coiling from the chimneys, poisonous fumes that shut out the natural light of Heaven (as they do in John Ruskin's 1884 essay "The Storm-Cloud of the Nineteenth-Century"). The town and the factories are frequently described in fairy-tale metaphors because anywhere that human beings toil and suffer (as Stephen does) has the potential for transformation. In calling the factories "Fairy palaces" when they "burst into illumination" in the darkness be-fore dawn, and the pistons of the steam-engine "melancholy mad elephants" (91), Dickens is not inconsistent; rather, he is fulfilling the promise of his *Household Words* dictum that he will "teach the hardest workers at this whirling wheel of toil, that their lot is not necessarily a moody, brutal fact, excluded from the sympathies and graces of imagination." Denotative language is re-served for the Utilitarians when they attempt to reduce humanity to mechani-cal and measurable beings; thus, the workmen become "hands," recognized only for the part of them that does the work and ignoring their hearts and spir-its; schoolchildren become numbers in Mr. M'Choakumchild's classroom.

Mrs. Gradgrind's language reveals that she has been reduced to a shadow by some "weighty piece of fact" (19) constantly dropping upon her. She has no vi-tality, no human spark at all, and Dickens's simile for her is that she is like a transparency (or a picture painted on material) with too feeble a light behind it. The image recalls the shaft of sunlight that deepens Sissy's lustrous color but washes out Bitzer's whiteness even more. But Mrs. Gradgrind also reveals the human potential that Utilitarianism denies; she feebly fights her husband's sys-tem, but she lacks the physical strength to communicate by gesture and the mental strength to communicate by word. On her deathbed, she tries to tell Louisa that Mr. Gradgrind's system was not enough, that there was "some-thing—not an Ology at all—that your father has missed, or forgotten" (266), and she wants to name it and write it down because she has been led to believe that all knowledge is denotative and can be named. Mr. Gradgrind would have it so, but Dickens's use of fairy-tale imagery and metaphor, even for the least imaginative of the characters, is a deliberate rendering of the human potential in the most utilitarian of people. Mr. Gradgrind's head must burst open even-tually, however much he may try to contain and order it.

A MARXIST READING OF *HARD TIMES*

Marxist criticism is based on the doctrines of the German philosophers Karl Marx and Friedrich Engels, as they propounded in their *Communist Manifesto* in 1848. Marx and Engels both studied the effects of the Industrial Revolution on English society to formulate their theory that class division was the greatest social evil. They argued that the English struggle between the bourgeoisie (the capitalist factory-owning class) and the proletariat (the working class) was eco-nomic and would result, eventually, in the overthrow of the bourgeoisie. Both writers pointed to the alienation caused by capitalism and argued that religion and culture were derived from the class struggle. Marxist critics are concerned with the literary work in its relation to the class conflicts of its time. Many such critics regard Dickens as a radical who increasingly saw the need for revolution in England and who attacked bourgeois society through its institutions like the Circumlocution Office of *Little Dorrit* and the law courts of *Bleak House*. These critics naturally find *Hard Times* the most powerful, sustained example of Dickens's radical views in its relentless critique of industrial relations and capitalism and its focus on Coketown and the factory workers. Dickens's attack on Bounderby and Gradgrind, the new ruling class, can be seen as grimmer and more vicious than his earlier, often comic, portraits of the aristocracy because the aristocracy were no longer a threat, whereas the new ruling class of industrialists was very powerful. Stephen Blackpool is Dickens's strongest defense of the new industrial worker, and specific problems are addressed, such as safety: Stephen's loom is a "crashing, smashing, tearing piece of mechanism" (91) and in the manuscript, Rachael's sister is literally torn apart by such a machine.

Hard Times can be read as an attack on the Manchester School of economics, which supported laissez-faire and promoted Bentham's economic view of ethics. In *The Communist Manifesto*, Karl Marx condemns the new bourgeois society as having replaced the old feudal ties between people with cash payment. Gradgrind and Bounderby represent this new bourgeois view:

It was a fundamental principle of the Gradgrind philosophy that everything was to be paid for. Nobody was ever on any account to give anybody anything, or render anybody help without purchase. Gratitude was to be abolished, and the virtues springing from it were not to be. Every inch of the existence of mankind, from birth to death, was to be a bargain across a counter. And if we didn't get to Heaven that way, it was not a politico-economical place, and we had no business there. (384)

Marxist readers, though, would have to fault Dickens's presentation of the trade-union meeting, his portrait of Slackbridge, and the union members' treatment of Stephen. They would argue that, in this, Dickens just got it wrong, probably misled by using second-hand sources rather than his own observation, just as most artistic representations of trade-union activity is incorrect from a Marxist point of view. They would also agree that Dickens does not present any solutions to the problems of the capitalist society because there were none except revolution, a solution that the Marxist reader finds championed in *A Tale of Two Cities*.

8

A Tale of Two Cities
(1859)

After a disagreement with his publisher in 1859, Dickens closed his weekly magazine *Household Words* and began a new one, *All the Year Round*. Anxious to keep his old readers and attract new ones, he planned to open it with a new novel, and a stirring tale of the French Revolution was just what he needed. The return to weekly publication meant that, once again, he had the difficulty of condensing the story into short episodes that ended on a mildly suspenseful note. He was also concerned that readers were receiving too small a portion of this exciting story at a time (Thomas Carlyle called it "reading in teaspoons"), so he conceived what he considered the "rather original and bold idea" (Forster 2.280) of publishing the novel simultaneously in monthly numbers or install-ments, with two illustrations each: "This will give *All the Year Round* always the interest and precedence of a fresh weekly portion during the month; and will give me my old standing with my old public, and the advantage (very necessary in this story) of having numbers of people who read it in no portions smaller than a monthly part" (Forster 2.281). So the novel ran in weekly numbers from 30 April to 26 November 1859, and in monthly installments from June to De-cember 1859.

   The germ of *A Tale of Two Cities* had occurred to Dickens fourteen years be-fore he actually began the novel, while he was working on another story about self-sacrifice, his Christmas book *The Battle of Life*. He wrote to John Forster in July 1846 that he had "been thinking this last day or two that good Christmas characters might be grown out of the idea of a man imprisoned for ten or fifteen years: his imprisonment being the gap between the people and circumstances of the first part and the altered people and circumstances of the second, and his own changed mind" (Forster 1.419).

To this notion, which became the story of Doctor Manette's incarceration in the Bastille, Dickens added Sydney Carton's sacrifice of his life for that of his rival and double, Charles Darnay. While the substitution of one person for another at the guillotine was a well-known subject of plays and novels in the years following the French Revolution, Dickens's inspiration was more personal, as he explains in the Preface to the novel:

When I was acting, with my children and friends, in Mr. Wilkie Collins's drama of The Frozen Deep, I first conceived the main idea of this story. A strong desire was upon me then, to embody it in my own person; and I traced out in my fancy, the state of mind of which it would necessitate the presentation to an observant spectator, with particular care and interest.

As the idea became familiar to me, it gradually shaped itself into its present form. Throughout its execution, it has had the complete possession of me; I have so far verified what is done and suffered in these pages, as that I have certainly done and suffered it all myself.

Dickens helped to write *The Frozen Deep*, which was based on the loss of Sir John Franklin's expedition in search of the North West Passage in the 1840s. Franklin's close friend Sir John Richardson, a naturalist who had accompanied him on expeditions in the 1820s, led two unsuccessful parties to search for the missing expedition. The play transformed the Franklin-Richardson friendship into a rivalry over the love of one woman; Franklin became the good-hearted, noble Frank Aldersley, played by Wilkie Collins, and Richardson became Richard Wardour (played by Dickens), the morose and passionately jealous suitor whose beloved Clara Burnham has turned her attention to the deserving Frank. When the two men, members of an Arctic expedition, find themselves separated from the main party and stranded together, Wardour discovers that his companion is the hated rival on whom he has long ago sworn to take revenge. He could easily leave Frank to die, fulfilling the dream that he has brooded over for months. But when the time comes, he carries the dying Aldersley to safety at the expense of his own life. In a final scene that took Victorian playgoers—even Queen Victoria—by storm, Wardour (Dickens) staggered onto the stage, laid the rescued Aldersley at the feet of their mutual love, and then died—reassured by the real tears of the actress who wept over his body that he had done the right thing and had received his reward. So completely did Dickens identify with the heroic Wardour that he "terrified Aldersley to that degree by lungeing at him to carry him into the Cave, and the said Aldersley always shook like a mould of jelly, and muttered 'By G—this is an awful thing!'" (*Letters* 8.277). It was this experience, repeated night after night for a rapturous audience, and deepened by Dickens's love for the young actress who played Lucy Crayford in the play, that suggested a love triangle and the sacrifice of a dissolute and unlikable man, Sydney Carton.

HISTORICAL SETTING

It was the best of times, it was the worst of times, it was the age of wisdom, it was the age of foolishness . . . the period was so far like the present period, that some of its noisiest authorities insisted on its being received, for good or for evil, in the superlative degree of comparison only.

In his famous opening lines, Dickens makes clear that *A Tale of Two Cities* is as much about nineteenth-century England as it is about eighteenth-century France. The story takes place before and during the French Revolution—from 1757 to 1794—but Dickens recognized that the failure of the indolent French aristocracy to notice that an earthquake was building under their feet was an indifference shared by many of the ruling classes in Victorian England. Although, by the 1850s, the threat of revolution in England had waned a little, it had been a distinct possibility in the "hungry 40s," when rick (haystack) burning, hunger marches, and factory riots drew attention to the problems of the large and increasingly violent agricultural and factory workers. In the last chapter of the novel, Dickens issues a dire warning to his readers: "Crush humanity out of shape once more, under similar hammers, and it will twist itself into the same tortured forms. Sow the same seed of rapacious license and oppression over again, and it will surely yield the same fruit according to its kind" (459).

A Tale of Two Cities is an historical novel that combines fictional characters with factual ones who appear in historical events in the story. In his Preface to the novel, Dickens assures his readers of the accuracy of his historical sources: "Whenever any reference (however slight) is made here to the condition of the French people before or during the Revolution, it is truly made, on the faith of trustworthy witnesses. It has been one of my hopes to add something to the popular and picturesque means of understanding that terrible time, though no one can hope to add anything to the philosophy of Mr. CARLYLE'S wonderful book." This book was Thomas Carlyle's epic three-volume account, *The French Revolution*, which had appeared in 1837. After Dickens began *A Tale of Two Cities* in February 1859, he asked Carlyle to suggest background reading for him and received in return "two cartloads" of books from the London Library.[1]

The cartload included several books that Dickens told a friend he had used in portraying the *ancien régime*, or pre-revolutionary feudal system. Mercier's *Tableau de Paris*, an eyewitness account in twelve volumes published in 1782–1788, gave him many details about the Monseigneur, including the mowing down of Gaspard's child, for his picture of a decadent, callous, and self-serving aristocracy. Jean-Jacques Rousseau's autobiography *Confessions* (1782) was the source for a scene in which Madame Defarge's dying brother speaks of hiding meat in case the Marquis's men took it from him. Rousseau tells of dropping by a peasant's cottage to rest. The peasant gives him some simple food, but after a few minutes he produces a better meal. He explains to Rousseau that he had feared that his unknown visitor was an excise man, who would have charged him duty on the bread and wine. Guessing that Rousseau was an "honest man," the peasant happily shared what he had. According to Rousseau, this evidence of the poor man's generosity in the face of intolerable burdens of taxation and deprivation instilled in him a hatred for the aristocracy and a strong sense of the oppression of the poorer classes.

As Dickens tells us in his Preface, however, his main source of material for the factual events in the book was Carlyle's *The French Revolution*. Dickens joked that he had read it five hundred times, and he carried it around with him when he was writing the novel. He followed Carlyle closely, both in the chronology of the events of the Revolution and in his descriptions of the major historical scenes. He was selective, of course, in his portrayal of the Revolution, using only those scenes that supported his plot.

The storming of the Bastille is undoubtedly the most famous event of the Revolution; it is still celebrated in France on 14 July because it was the beginning of the wave that was to sweep away all the old ways. Although, as Dickens points out, only seven prisoners were released, the Bastille was the target of the first attack because for years it had housed innocent victims, such as Doctor Manette, incarcerated often for years by the *lettres de cachet* that had allowed aristocrats to imprison enemies without trial. In describing the fall of the Bastille and its immediate results, Dickens relied on Carlyle for the sequence of events, the layout of the prison, and many details of the action. He also employed Carlyle's extended metaphor of the mob as a "living sea" (263), a relentless and mindless force that, once set in motion, cannot be turned back.

In the murder of De Launay, the governor of the Bastille, Dickens follows Carlyle's account of the historical event, but makes his own character, Madame Defarge, the central actor in the drama. Carlyle describes De Launay's attempt to take his own life, his appeal that they kill him fast, his decapitation and the gruesome carrying of his head aloft on a pike through the streets. To the crowd's dogging of De Launay's footsteps, Dickens adds the grim picture of Madame Defarge remaining "immovable close" to him (Dickens repeats the phrase five times) so that she can be the one to hew off his head once he is down, using her foot to steady his body.

To the historical murder of Joseph-François Foulon, a Counsellor of State to Louis XVI, Dickens added the intervention of the Defarges, the Vengeance, and Jacques Three. According to Carlyle, Foulon was a treacherous man who had proposed harsh economic measures. To the question, "What will the people do?" he had replied publicly that they could eat grass. Dickens includes Foulon's capture, hanging, and decapitation, partly because it was a well-known event, but also because it was another instance of his "buried alive" theme. Fearing for his life, Foulon had faked his own death, mounting a lavish funeral (the body actually belonging to a servant), and going into hiding in the country. Like Roger Cly in the novel, Foulon hoped to free himself from his prior, and now dangerous, identity by literally burying it and coming to life as another person.

Despite Foulon's treachery and arrogance, Dickens and Carlyle were appalled by the brutality of the revenge against him. For both writers, this turning of the tables, when the people he had said could eat grass now stuff grass into his dead mouth, epitomized what was most disturbing about the course of the Revolution: The more oppressed a people are, the more violent and brutal will be their rebellion when it comes; and the injustices and wrongs that caused the revolution will be adopted by the new ruling class—the oppressed become the oppressors in their turn. Carlyle considered the revenge meted out to Foulon unjust, and in Dickens's account, a "kindly ray as of hope or protection" (274) shines down on the old man's head during his trial, incensing Madame Defarge and the others to sudden retribution. It was perhaps Foulon's age and infirmity that inspired a sort of sympathy in Dickens, who describes Madame Defarge's enjoyment of his long-drawn-out hanging as that of a cat playing with a mouse. When the rope eventually breaks, Dickens describes it as "merciful" (275).

Dickens deliberately set Darnay's return to Paris and arrest at the time of the September Massacres, a four-day execution of 1,089 prisoners from four Paris prisons who were condemned in minutes each by what Carlyle refers to as courts of wild justice. Again Dickens took the main details of his hellish description from Carlyle, who prefaces his horrific account with the comment that "there are depths in man that go the length of lowest Hell" (2.148).[2] Dickens's sympathy with the revolutionaries has all but disappeared by this scene, as he makes clear at the end of it, when he describes the "frenzied eyes" of the mad workers at the grindstone: "eyes which any unbrutalised beholder would have given twenty years of life, to petrify with a well-directed gun" (322).

In his dramatic depiction of the historic scenes of the novel, Dickens, like Carlyle, took a Romantic approach to history, bringing it to life for the reader in a way that was new to nineteenth-century readers. The historian Hedva Ben-Israel's assessment of this new approach describes exactly Dickens's success in the writing of history: "the Romantic movement aimed at a new history, narrative, live, picturesque, direct, full of particular detail and local colour, alive with the touch and the atmosphere of the past, populated by individual characters, a history which is artistically effective, written through artistic identification and creating a sense of emotional identification in the reader."[3] In all of these ways, Dickens built upon Carlyle's foundation, but he bound the historical scenes into his own dramatic story.

PLOT DEVELOPMENT

Chronologically, the story told in *A Tale of Two Cities* begins eighteen years before the opening of the novel, with the rape of a peasant girl (Madame Defarge's sister) and the murder of their brother by Charles Darnay's evil uncle, the Marquis St. Évrémonde. Doctor Manette, called to attend to the dying girl, was imprisoned in the Bastille to prevent his disclosure of the crimes. At the beginning of the novel, he has been released and his daughter Lucie and her trusted friend Mr. Lorry are on their way to Paris to bring him home.

Charles Darnay, who has renounced his French citizenship and is in England working as a tutor, is charged with being a spy. He is acquitted at his trial because Sydney Carton, a bright but degenerate lawyer, draws attention to their close resemblance and questions the reliability of eyewitness identification. Both young men befriend Lucie and her father, who is recovering from his long imprisonment but who is still subject to lapses when he will think himself back in the Bastille, working again as a shoemaker. When Lucie and Darnay become engaged, Carton promises to aid her and her family if they are ever in danger.

In Paris, events are building toward the Revolution. The Defarges' wine shop is the center of the movement, and Madame Defarge is knitting a register of aristocrats. When Charles's uncle is murdered, Charles is called back to France to help his tenants and is arrested. Lucie follows with her daughter and her father, whose long imprisonment at the hands of aristocrats has made him a hero of the revolutionaries. With his help, Darnay is acquitted briefly, but at a retrial Defarge produces a letter written by Doctor Manette in the Bastille in which he tells the story of the rape and condemns the race of Évrémondes to destruction. Thus, his beloved son-in-law is found guilty and sentenced to the guillotine.

With the help of Solomon Pross, an English spy then working in the prison under the name Barsad, Sydney Carton gains entry to the prison, drugs Darnay, and has him carried out in Carton's clothes, apparently overcome at having to part with his friend Darnay. Believing that the unconscious man in their coach is Carton, Lucie and her family flee hurriedly from France while the tumbril slowly carries Carton to the guillotine.

CHARACTER DEVELOPMENT

From the start, Dickens intended to focus on plot rather than on character, as he explained in a letter to John Forster:

I set myself the little task of making a *picturesque* story, rising in every chapter with characters true to nature, but whom the story itself should express, more than they should express themselves, by dialogue. I mean, in other words, that I fancied a story of incident might be written, in place of the bestiality that *is* written under that pretence, pounding the characters out in its own mortar, and beating their interests out of them. If you could have read the story all at once, I hope you wouldn't have stopped half way. (*Letters* 9.112–13)

Forster considered this new emphasis on incident a "hazardous" undertaking that "can hardly be called an entirely successful experiment" (Forster 2.282), a view shared by many later readers. The idiosyncratic and often comic characters that inhabit most of Dickens's novels are missing from *A Tale of Two Cities*. Jerry Cruncher has the potential to be comic, but as a wife-beating grave robber, he does not provide much humor, and his change of heart at the end is not entirely convincing. Jerry operates rather as a sometimes comic, sometimes sinister, counterpart to Sydney Carton.

Many of the characters in the novel are deliberately stylized because Dickens wanted to show how both the *ancien régime* and the Revolution dehumanized people. Citizens lost their individual identity, becoming just Jacques One, Two, or Three; Madame Defarge's friend is simply The Vengeance. The major characters operate to some extent as allegory, so Madame Defarge is pure evil and revenge, while Lucie, whose name means "light," exemplifies truth, purity, and goodness. Madame Defarge remains a memorable character, however, in her implacable and tiger-like hunting down of the Evrémonde family. In a letter to Edward Bulwer-Lytton on 5 June 1860, Dickens defended her accidental death in the struggle with Miss Pross as being the working out of divine justice; he also saw the rightness of giving her a "mean death—instead of a desperate one in the streets—which she wouldn't have minded," as a contrast to Carton's dignified and noble end (*Letters* 9.260).

Doctor Manette, Charles Darnay, and Sydney Carton are often seen as representing different aspects of Dickens himself. Doctor Manette is forty-five when he is rescued from his living grave; Dickens was forty-five when, in 1857, he acted the part of Richard Wardour and met the young actress Ellen Ternan.

For some years Dickens had felt "buried alive" in an unhappy marriage to Catherine. But Dickens had always been sympathetically drawn to the long-term prisoner: In *The Pickwick Papers* Mr. Pickwick meets the Chancery prisoner, who has been shut up in the Fleet Prison for twenty years, and is more skeleton than human. In Doctor Manette, as in Mr. Dorrit in the novel that preceded *A Tale of Two Cities*, Dickens convincingly explores the long-lasting effect of incarceration on the mind, even after release.

More clearly autobiographical are the rivals for Lucie's affection, Charles Darnay (who shares Dickens's first name and initials), and Darnay's alter ego and double, Sydney Carton. Lucie's features and mannerisms were based on Ellen Ternan, and Dickens particularly wanted Ellen to see the chapters in which Darnay and Carton declare their love for Lucie; he had the proofs of Chapters Ten to Thirteen sent to her. While Darnay is a bland and rather uninteresting hero, Carton is unconventional and at first unlikable, like his predecessor Richard Wardour from *The Frozen Deep*. In 1856, Dickens had complained to John Forster that the conventional British reader insisted on decent heroes who had "not even any of the experiences, trials, perplexities, and confusions inseparable from the making or unmaking of all men!" (Forster 2.267). A mysterious figure, always seemingly on the edge of the action but increasingly bound up in it, Carton is at first the indolent and uncaring young gentleman of so many of Dickens's later novels, but love inspires him to free himself from his dangerous cynicism and perform the ultimate sacrifice. He has become one of Dickens's most beloved heroes, well-known through the many film and stage versions of the novel. Dickens once wrote to a friend that he would like to have acted Carton, feeling he "could have done something with his life and death" (*Letters* 9.177).

THEMATIC ISSUES

From the balanced contrasts in the opening paragraph—"It was the best of times; it was the worst of times"— to the parallelism of Carton's closing words—"It is a far far better thing that I do, than I have ever done; it is a far, far better rest that I go to than I have ever known"—contrasts and parallels illuminate a novel based on two cities, two countries, and two heroes who look the same. Through these doublings (emphasized by the many linked chapters), Dickens reinforces the twofold nature of his vision of the French Revolution and its aftermath: the passage from humanity to bestiality that marked the *ancien régime* as well as the Terror, followed by the movement from darkness to light, and from destruction to rebirth.

Dickens thought of calling the novel *Buried Alive,* and although he rightly rejected that title as being "too grim" (Forster 2. 280), it certainly draws attention to one of the major themes. Doctor Manette has been "buried alive" in the Bastille for eighteen years, and the novel explores the damaging effects of such solitary confinement on the psyche. It was a subject that had haunted Dickens ever since his 1842 visit to a Philadelphia prison that practiced the "separate system," where prisoners were kept in total isolation, often for many years. Dickens described visiting those prisoners and regarding them "with the same awe as I should have looked at men who had been buried alive, and dug up again" (Forster 1.211-12). Manette's condition is prefigured in Dickens's description of the prisoners in *American Notes*: "I believe that very few men are capable of estimating the immense amount of torture and agony which this dreadful punishment, prolonged for years, inflicts upon the sufferers. . . . I hold this slow and daily tampering with the mysteries of the brain, to be immeasurably worse than any torture of the body" (Everyman 108).

Many of the characters in the novel have buried either an internal life (Carton's better nature, Manette's Bastille memories, Mr. Lorry's unbusinesslike gentle heart) or a separate identity: The highwaymen that prowl the Dover Road by night are City tradesmen by day; Jerry Cruncher is a resurrection man by night but a messenger by day; Solomon Pross is John Barsad the spy; Charles Darnay the teacher is Charles Evrémonde, with a family past that requires atonement; as Ernest's wife, Madame Defarge runs a wine shop but conceals her identity as the avenging sister of two murdered peasants. Old Foulon and Roger Cly even pretend to be dead, staging a mock funeral and burial and then being "reborn" under another name and identity. Because so many people lead a double life, the action of the novel is frought with spying and other attempts to unearth concealed lives.

Jerry Cruncher's secret occupation of removing bodies from the grave and selling them to doctors (a lucrative practice in the early part of the nineteenth century) runs through the novel as a chilling antithesis to Christian resurrection: man's rebirth after death into eternal life. This sacred resurrection surrounds Carton's last hours, of course, as his mind reiterates Christ's assurance of everlasting life: "I am the Resurrection and the Life, saith the Lord: he that believeth in me, though he were dead, yet shall he live: and whosoever liveth and believeth in me shall never die." Carton not only finds consolation in the words, but becomes a Christ-figure himself, sacrificing his own life for the life of Lucie and her family. Innocent of any wrong, he is put to death that others may live.

Jerry Cruncher has Christ's initials, and in his macabre second profession as an "honest tradesman," he carries on, under cover of darkness, a removal of bodies that mocks the discovery of Christ's empty grave after the Crucifixion. Jerry provides a counterpoint—sometimes comic, sometimes frightening—of the Christian themes underlying the novel, from his brutal treatment of his wife to his failure as a father. He even echoes Carton's rebirth into a better life at the end when he assures Mr. Lorry that he will give up grave-robbing and take up "flopping" (or praying) like his wife.

Dickens mulled over the idea of rebirth and how it relates to people as well as to plants, in a dialogue he wrote in his Memoranda Book in 1855:

"There is some virtue in him too."

"Virtue! Yes. So there is in any grain of seed in a seedsman's shop—but you must put it in the ground, before you can get any good out of it."

"Do you mean that *he* must be put in the ground before any good comes of *him*?"

"Indeed I do. You may call it burying him, or you may call it sowing him, as you like. You must set him in the earth, before you get any good of him." (*Memoranda* 4)

Most people are allowed their dark night of the soul, their setting in the earth, without actually losing their life. But Sydney Carton's final words reveal that his capacity for doing a "better thing" can be fulfilled only by his death. For Carton, "you must set him in the earth, before you get any good of him."

In the context of Carton's heroic self-sacrifice, Dickens reiterates the attack on Utilitarian thinking and the mechanical weighing and measuring of the human spirit that was so central to *Hard Times*. He shared Thomas Carlyle's concern with the dynamism of human life, the mysteries of man's spiritual nature and imaginative powers. *A Tale of Two Cities* emphasizes that "every human creature is constituted to be that profound secret and mystery to every other" (12) and how this secret inner life can inspire a person to true heroism. Set against such dynamism in the main duality of the book is the mechanism of both the *ancien régime* and the Revolutionaries, once their movement has taken hold. The stone chateau of the Marquis (like Stone Lodge, the home of Thomas Gradgrind in *Hard Times*) is immune to human emotion; the chateau, like its occupant, is a blind mask, incapable of expression until at last the fire and wind, "driving straight from the infernal regions" (283), wipe away the stone faces. The stony Marquis represents the inhumanity of the old order that treated people as though they were mere animals, and whose own society was an empty sham of fine clothes, frizzled hair, and artificial complexions, disfigured by "the leprosy of unreality" (126). In what could be called the thematic statement of the novel, Dickens reminds us of the causes of the Revolution: "Crush humanity out of shape once more, under similar hammers, and it will twist itself into the same tortured forms" (459).

The "tortured forms" of the revolutionaries become mechanistic in their turn, reiterating Jeremy Bentham's emphasis on the group rather than on the individual, in his doctrine of "the greatest happiness of the greatest number." The frenzy sweeps people up into a terrifying ocean, submerging individual thought and action in the tide of mob violence and blind sheeplike conformity. The road mender who had sympathized with Gaspard at the beginning of the book becomes an inhuman and callous observer of the Terror, one of the nameless "citizens" or "Jacques" who will sacrifice all for an institution, the Republic. We see this turning of people into mechanical followers of a cause throughout the novel, and Dickens shows how it can happen regardless of the cause or its value. At Roger Cly's funeral, for example, the crowd has no idea who is being buried, but at the suggestion that there are spies involved, "the idea was so acceptable in the prevalent absence of any idea, that the crowd caught it up with eagerness . . . " (187). Even more telling is when the mender of roads is taken to see the King and Queen by Madame Defarge, in order to whet his appetite against them and the aristocracy. But the simple peasant is so taken up by the pomp and ceremony of the royal procession and the fawning crowd around it that he "cried Long live the King, Long live the Queen, Long live everybody and everything! as if he had never heard of ubiquitous Jacques in his time" (210).

One of the most striking images of the contrast between vital, human love and its perverted revolutionary form occurs in Dickens's description of the Carmagnole, the mad dance associated with the Revolution. What should be a celebration of humanity's sense of music, harmony, rhythmic movement, and fellowship has become a travesty of all those qualities, a "fallen sport—a something, once innocent, delivered over to all devilry—a healthy pastime changed into a means of angering the blood, bewildering the senses, and steeling the heart. Such grace as was visible in it, made it the uglier, showing how warped and perverted all things good by nature were become" (342–43). Dickens juxtaposes natural, human love with this frightening perversion of love into lust and sensuality when, as the Carmagnole dancers sweep past Charles and Lucie, he "held her to his heart and turned her beautiful head between his face and the brawling crowd, so that his tears and her lips might come together unseen" (353). This picture of pure human love sheltering itself from the abased violence of the Carmagnole is repeated by Carton and the little seamstress, who are the counterparts of Darnay and Lucie, when they ride in the tumbril together: "He gently places her with her back to the crashing engine that constantly whirrs up and falls, and she looks into his face and thanks him" (462–63).

In these two images of a man and a woman united in love against the violence and degradation of the Terror, Dickens expresses his main hope for the human race. By using dualities to work out his "tale" and its themes, he counters mob destruction with personal heroism, public irresponsibility with private integrity. Even though he asks, "what private solicitude could rear itself against the deluge of the Year One of Liberty" (335), the private life, as demonstrated by Lucie's golden thread and Carton's secretive sacrifice, is seen to exemplify what is best in human affairs. While the mob is fickle and changeable, Lucie, in particular, demonstrates loyalty and faithfulness to the death. While the mob acts irrationally, driven, ostensibly, by a cause but acting often out of blind fury, the honest individual acts out of a sense of duty and honor. Such a sense draws Darnay back to Paris, shamed into a sense of his own duties to his tenants by the knowledge that his servant Gabelle is threatened with the guillotine because of his fidelity to his master Darnay. Duty sustains Lucie when Darnay is in prison, just as it gives Miss Pross the strength to overcome Madame Defarge. It is a sense of duty to Lucie that gives Carton his new interest in life and allows him to overcome his inertia and take over the initiative when Doctor Manette fails.

From its opening statement, "It was the best of times; it was the worst of times," *A Tale of Two Cities* moves the reader through a world of paradox and contradiction, of people being "buried alive," of a dissolute, wasted man performing a sublime action, until at the end, the great Christian paradox of the Resurrection is realized with Sydney Carton's victory of love over Madame Defarge's implacable hate. In the working out of these paradoxes, *A Tale of Two Cities* is perhaps the most Romantic of Dickens's novels and exemplifies the attitudes of the Romantic writers who were so influenced by the French Revolution. Like the generation of writers who preceded him, Dickens sees the need for revolution, but he recognizes the dangers of mass action. Like the Romantics, he sees a new world and a new vision coming about through the spiritual revolution of the individual. Carton's prophetic vision of "a beautiful city and a brilliant people rising from this abyss" (465) echoes the prophetic writing of Blake, Coleridge, and Wordsworth, who also saw the fallen world being reborn not through revolution but through the individual imagination, and the individual's capacity for love.

STYLISTIC AND LITERARY DEVICES

Dickens's purpose in *A Tale of Two Cities* was dramatic. He wished to re-create for the reader the storm of emotion that swept Paris during the French Revolution while at the same time re-creating the emotion that he suffered as he lay on the stage acting out Richard Wardour's heroic sacrifice in *The Frozen Deep*. For the emotions of the Revolution, he used Thomas Carlyle's account and took up the metaphor of a violent sea to describe the tide of revolutionaries that swept through the Bastille, carrying all in its wake. To this he added images of deluge and storm, lightning, earthquake, and flood to give the novel a sweeping sense of cataclysmic change.

These elemental images form the religious framework of the novel by tying together Christian belief and the natural cycle of death and rebirth. The novel abounds with biblical references, but the most striking are those connected with water, wine and blood. The spilt cask of wine in the first French scene is a brilliant depiction of the transformation of water into wine, and wine into blood. As the gutters flow with wine rather than rain, the starving peasants frantically lap it up as it streams through the cobblestones. (Dickens had described such a scene before in *Barnaby Rudge*, when the rioters set fire to a vintner's house and drink themselves to death as the spirits pour down the street.) Then, in a grim foreshadowing of the blood that is soon to flow over those same cobblestones, Gaspard writes the word "BLOOD" in wine on the wall. The reference, of course, is to the Christian sacrament of Communion, which re-creates Christ's invitation to his disciples at the Last Supper to drink the wine in the cup because it is his blood, shed for mankind. The crazed drinking of the wine among the cobbles becomes the even-more-crazed violence of the Terror as the wine stains become blood stains. But in the final reenactment of Christ's sacrifice, Sydney Carton's blood is shed that another may live. Death has been turned into life.

The transubstantiation, or the changing of one substance into another, is reversed for Madame Defarge, whose feet are met by water from a broken basin when she confronts Miss Pross and her own imminent death. The peasants who drank the spilled wine at the beginning "had acquired a tigerish smear about the mouth" (34), a smear transformed by the Terror into the grim figure of Madame Defarge, whom "opportunity had developed . . . into a tigress" (447). Madame Defarge is figuratively swept away by the water that had swirled in a maelstrom around her wine shop, the victim of her own violence. And in that washing away of Madame Defarge, Paris is purged of one of its most vicious citizens.

Dickens repeatedly casts the human action in the elemental terms of flood, rain, seas, and storm, because he wants to emphasize that the enormity of the Revolution's destruction will wash away the old evils and give rebirth to a new order. Such is Carton's vision as he steps up to the guillotine, and his death is a baptism. As he takes his last steps, "the murmuring of many voices, the upturning of many faces, the pressing on of many footsteps in the outskirts of the crowd, so that it swells forward in a mass, like one great heave of water, all flashes away" (464).

In contrast to the elemental images that suggest the sweeping away of the old and a rebirth of the new, the metaphors Dickens employs for the destruction of the individual within the larger historic process come from mechanical, man-made sources such as anvils, furnaces, and the forming of metal. The faces of the revolutionaries are "hardened in the furnaces of suffering until the touch of pity could make no mark on them" (268). Madame Defarge's customers pay for their wine with "battered small coins . . . as much defaced and beaten out of their original impress as the small coinage of humanity from whose ragged pockets they had come" (199). Even Saint Antoine itself, personification of its residents, is changed, its face distorted because "the image had been hammering into this for hundreds of years, and the last finishing blows had told mightily on the expression" (271). The contrast between soul-destroying machine and malleable humanity is constantly reiterated in such metaphors and is reinforced by the frighteningly graphic machines of death: the grindstone and the guillotine.

Other recurring images are important in linking the two plots, the two countries, the past and the present: Footsteps, raindrops, and especially shadows build up a pervasive sense of lives overlapping, past actions impinging on the present, and secrets waiting for their inevitable revelation.

Stylistically, *A Tale of Two Cities* has been criticized for its melodramatic language, and, certainly at times, its genesis in a stage play is evident in the dialogue, as in Doctor Manette's first meeting with Lucie. Also somewhat unconvincing is Dickens's use of "franglais," where the French characters speak in French idiom but use English words, such as, "That's well," "How goes it?" and "Behold the manner of it." Often, though, Dickens's use of repetition and other rhetorical devices is highly effective and memorable, as in the contrast between the relentless, mechanical prose that describes Sydney Carton's final journey through the streets of Paris and the breathless, jerky rhythms that describe (in the present tense) the Manettes' flight to England. Equally memorable is the opening description of the stagecoach lumbering through a clammy mist on Shooter's Hill on the way to Dover, taking Mr. Lorry on his mysterious errand. Charles Darnay's last night in his cell, counting the hours before the tumbril will come for him, is vividly realized, as is Sydney Carton's actual journey in that tumbril. The strength of the narrative and the power of the descriptions of the French Revolution have made *A Tale of Two Cities* one of Dickens's most memorable and best-loved novels.

A FEMINIST READING OF *A TALE OF TWO CITIES*

Chapter four in this book outlines the general purposes of feminist criticism, whose concern with the depiction of women in works by male writers is of particular interest for *A Tale of Two Cities*. Women are central to Dickens's portrayal of the French Revolution, the evils that caused it, and the cruelties it inspired. In a novel that depends on incident and metaphor, with stylized rather than individual characters who are often doubled, Dickens sets Lucie

Manette and her "golden thread" against Madame Defarge and her deadly knitting needles.

Lucie Manette is often criticized as being a bloodless heroine, a typically Victorian "angel in the house" (see discussion p. 53), who exemplifies the domestic ideal but is not allowed to think and act on her own. But in her actions, Lucie exemplifies the heroic women of another recent war, the Indian Mutiny of 1857, whom Dickens honored in his Christmas story *The Perils of Certain English Prisoners* (which also features a love triangle involving a man called Carton). While she is not as physically courageous as Lizzie Hexam in *Our Mutual Friend*, whose skill at the oars allows her to pull a drowning man to safety, Lucie exemplifies the determined and patient courage that is another kind of heroism. She supports her mentally crippled father, braves the dangerous streets of Paris to stand beneath the walls that emprison her husband, and provides a moral center from which the people surrounding her draw their strength.

Dickens focusses on the female characters to dramatize the degradation of human life that characterized both the suffering of the people during the *ancien régime* and the behavior of the revolutionaries during the Terror. The rape of Madame Defarge's sister begins the story and dramatizes the brutal oppression of the peasant class by a callous aristocracy. The perversion of humanity he dramatizes most vividly in the women, whose vicious fingers tear into old Foulon because he told them their babies "might suck grass, when these breasts were dry with want!" (273). The *ancien régime* deprived these women of their most basic instinct, the need to feed their children. In doing so, it "laid a dreadfully disfiguring hand" (447) upon them and turned them into wild beasts, the most dreadful of all being the tigerish Madame Defarge. The perversion of womanhood caused by ill-treatment and suffering is symbolized by the juxtaposition of useful, creative domestic work (Lucie's golden thread and the work of the little seamstress who goes to the guillotine with Carton) and the knitting of Madame Defarge's deadly register and the other revolutionary women, whose knitting needles turn into knives.

Not all the strong, powerful women in the novel have turned their strength to violence. Miss Pross is a counterpart to Madame Defarge; at first, like Mr. Lorry, she is just a comic example of British nationalism, but as the Terror in France grows, they both become symbols of loyalty, common sense, and reason. Her confrontation with Madame Defarge makes clear the tragedy of Madame Defarge's bitter and blind desire for revenge. Miss Pross is no angel in the house, but as she and Madame Defarge grapple to the death, she overcomes the tiger through "the vigorous tenacity of love, always so much stronger than hate" (455).

Dickens is sometimes accused of promoting the ideal marriage as relying on a devoted and submissive wife, but in the novel, he offers several different types of marriage, which argue against this stereotype. Lucie is certainly lovingly devoted to Charles, but her devotion is returned; their marriage is based on mutual love and respect. That a submissive wife is neither required nor beneficial is made clear in Dickens's condemnation of unequal marriages in all social classes. The bullying lawyer Stryver wants to marry Lucie so that he will have a home to go to when he feels like it and a wife who "will always do [him] credit" (169). Jerry Cruncher heaps physical and mental abuse on his gentle and honest wife because she does not conform to his standards of a dutiful wife and mother.

Another important woman makes a brief appearance in the novel when as Carton goes to the guillotine he is compared to the heroic Madame Roland, a real-life victim of the Terror. Like Carton she went to her death without flinching, and when her request for a pen and paper was refused she uttered a now-famous phrase to the Statue of Liberty, which stood beside the guillotine: "O Liberty, what crimes are committed in thy name!" This comparison, made at the climax of the novel, draws attention to the importance of women in the novel. Dickens chose Madame Defarge as the leader of the revolutionaries because he considered the cruelty of the women to be the most unnatural aspect of a revolution characterized by the overturning of human decency and reason. Lucie holds the golden thread that, in English law, refers to the tenet that we are innocent until proven guilty. Without the golden thread, no other virtue can survive. If it was a stereotype to consider women more naturally just and compassionate than men, it was a stereotype that Dickens believed to be true.

NOTES

1. Charles Dickens the Younger (Dickens's son) in his Introduction to the Macmillan edition of *A Tale of Two Cities* (1902); quoted by Andrew Sanders in " 'Cartloads of Books': Some Sources for *A Tale of Two Cities*," in *Dickens and Other Victorians*, ed. Joanne Shattock (London: Macmillan, 1988), 40.

2. Thomas Carlyle, *The French Revolution* (London: Oxford University Press, 1989).

3. Hedva Ben-Israel, *English Historians on the French Revolution* (Cambridge: Cambridge University Press, 1968), 111.

9

Great Expectations (1861)

The story of Pip and Magwitch came to Dickens while he was writing a series of articles for his magazine *All the Year Round* under the title "The Uncommercial Traveller." Seeing the potential of the new idea, he considered building it into a twenty-number novel like *David Copperfield*, as he explained to John Forster: "For a little piece I have been writing—or am writing; for I hope to finish it today—such a very fine, new, and grotesque idea has opened upon me, that I begin to doubt whether I had not better cancel the little paper, and reserve the notion for a new book. You shall judge as soon as I get it printed. But it so opens out before *me* that I can see the whole of a serial revolving on it, in a most singular and comic manner" (*Letters* 9.310). As sales of *All the Year Round* were down, however, he decided that he would follow up the success of *A Tale of Two Cities* by writing the new work as a novel in weekly installments for the magazine instead. It appeared there between 1 December 1860 and 3 August 1861.

Dickens considered it a sacrifice to reduce the planned long novel to a much shorter one, and he regretted that his contemporary readers could not read the whole last part at one sitting, when "its purpose would be much more apparent" (*Letters* 9.403). He found planning the weekly installments very difficult also, because the novel had to fall naturally into both the small weekly numbers of one or two chapters, each ending on a mild note of suspense, as well as into three long sections. These sections he called "Stages," to emphasize that the story is essentially a *Bildungsroman*, the journey of a young hero from childhood to maturity. The sections of a long and often difficult journey across rough roads in a stagecoach were known as stages, so Dickens is also reminding his readers that *Great Expectations* takes place in the 1810s and 1820s, forty or more years before the writing of the novel and several years before the railway transformed not just travel, but a whole way of life. Although the novel finishes in the 1820s, Pip's journey takes him from the settled, rural life of the early part of the century into a new urban world that is both frightening and challenging, like the Industrial Revolution itself.

PLOT DEVELOPMENT

Philip Pirrip, or Pip, as he names himself, lives with his sister and her husband, the blacksmith Joe Gargery. In one of the finest opening scenes in literature, Pip encounters, in a graveyard on Christmas Eve, a "fearful man, all in coarse grey, with a great iron on his leg." The convict Magwitch, escaped from the nearby prison ship, turns him upside down on the gravestone so that the church appears below his feet, and then puts him upright again, a graphic indication of the role this mysterious stranger will play in the young boy's life. Dickens called this relationship "the pivot on which the story will turn . . . the grotesque tragi-comic conception that first encouraged me" (*Letters* 9.325). The convict demands that Pip bring him some food and a file the next day and Pip complies, stealing from Joe and his sister to do so. The convict and another escapee are then arrested and returned to the ship. The plot of the novel depends upon Pip's attempts to repress this early association, but recurring symbols indicate to a careful reader that the "fearful man" is anything but removed from Pip's life.

Pip is invited to play at Satis House, where the eccentric and reclusive Miss Havisham lives with her ward, Estella. Satis House is exactly as it was years ago, when, on her wedding day, Miss Havisham was jilted by her fiancé. Pip falls for the beautiful Estella, who looks down on him as a lowly blacksmith's boy. When Miss Havisham's lawyer, Mr. Jaggers, tells Pip that a mysterious person is paying for him to go to London to become a gentleman, Pip presumes that the benefactor is his "fairy godmother," Miss Havisham, and that she is grooming him to be worthy of Estella.

Living the life of a London gentleman, Pip tries to distance himself from Joe and the other villagers, including Biddy, a companion from his young days. When his sister dies as a result of being hit over the head with a convict's leg iron, Pip returns to the forge for her funeral, but otherwise, he avoids Joe altogether. He and his good-natured roommate Herbert Pocket, a relative of Miss Havisham, get into difficulties with money and associate with a group of idle young men, including the brutal Bentley Drummle, who also admires Estella.

In the last chapter of "Stage Two," Magwitch reappears and once again turns Pip's life upside down when he reveals that he is Pip's benefactor; all those years he has been working hard in Australia to support the boy who fed him on the marshes. At first Pip is horrified, especially since Magwitch, if found, will be hanged for returning to England. But in caring for the old criminal and helping him escape, Pip forgets his own expectations. They discover that Compeyson, the other convict on the marshes, knows of Magwitch's return. Pip also learns that Compeyson was the man who jilted Miss Havisham and that Estella is the daughter of Molly, Mr. Jaggers's housekeeper, and Magwitch. The plan to smuggle Magwitch out of England is nearly foiled when Pip is nearly killed by Orlick, Joe's morose journeyman, but Pip is rescued by his friends. After sheltering Magwitch near the river, Pip and Herbert are rowing Magwitch out to a ship when Compeyson overtakes them in a police boat. The two convicts wrestle in the water and Compeyson drowns. Magwitch is tried and sentenced to death, but he dies of his injuries.

Before the attempted removal of Magwitch, Pip had been wounded, unsuccessfully attempting to rescue Miss Havisham from a fire at Satis House. Now he falls seriously ill, but Joe nurses him back to health. After some years abroad, Pip returns to find Joe and Biddy happily married with a son, a new little Pip.

After writing the beginning of "Stage Three," Dickens regretted that his readers could not read the whole of the last part at a sitting "because the general turn and tone of the working out and winding up, will be away from all such things as they conventionally go" (*Letters* 9.403). Dickens was referring here to the fact that he planned to end the novel with Estella happily married to a doctor (after a disastrous marriage to Drummle, who has died). However, when Dickens had finished the novel, he gave the last chapters of the manuscript to his friend and fellow novelist, Edward Bulwer-Lytton, to read. Bulwer-Lytton persuaded Dickens that he must have a happy ending for Pip if the book was to find favor with its readers. So Dickens rewrote the ending, expanding it and moving the chance meeting of Pip and Estella in a London street to the garden of Satis House, where recurring images of mists and shadows could be recalled for a final time. But does the revision end happily? For those who wish Pip to be married to Estella, such a reading is possible; but it is also likely that Dickens himself did not see such an outcome for his hero, and so the last line ambiguously suggests that they part now, never to meet again: "the evening mists were rising now, and in all the broad expanse of tranquil light they showed to me, I saw the shadow of no parting from her."[1] Dickens said of his revision, "I have put in as pretty a little piece of writing as I could, and I have no doubt the story will be more acceptable through the alteration" (*Letters* 9.433). Whatever Victorian readers may have thought, the two endings have certainly inspired much lively debate among later readers of the novel, many of whom agree with Forster (and Dickens?) that the original ending "seems to be more consistent with the drift, as well as natural working out, of the tale" (Forster 2.289).

CHARACTER DEVELOPMENT

Because Pip's great expectations involve becoming a "gentleman," many of the characters in the novel help Dickens define what he means by that term. According to British custom, the title of gentleman was an inherited one, based on family background and wealth acquired from property. It also implied the possession of good manners and morals, as typified by the knight, the gentle man of the Middle Ages. By the nineteenth century, though, the Industrial Revolution had made the title less easily defined because a new class of wealthy industrialists had risen from humble origins. Many of the new self-made men were disdainful of the class from which they had risen and were anxious to acquire respectability and gentility. And the old families continued to reject this new class on the grounds that they had no pedigree and they were engaged in "trade." Dickens satirizes the old family snobbery in Herbert's mother, Mrs. Pocket, who glories in her aristocratic background but is "perfectly helpless and useless" (187). To be "gentry" meant to be above earning a living, although the professions such as Law and the Church were acceptable occupations. But for Dickens, family and money did not confer gentlemanly status. The idle young "gentleman" who lives on family money is typified in Bentley Drummle, who has family and wealth but is no gentleman. Only when Herbert and Pip become employed do they achieve some measure of happiness.

If Victorian society wrongly identified family background with gentlemanly status, so did many mistake wealth and possessions with moral superiority. The villain Compeyson has managed to pass himself off as a gentleman because he has the right schooling, accent, and clothes. These externals bring him a lighter sentence than the uncouth Magwitch when they are tried together. It is understandable that Pip also mistakes possessions for character, because the village has taught him to do so. Magwitch is equally taken in by the trappings of the gentleman, having seen its power in the courtroom. In a fine touch of irony, Magwitch mistakes Herbert for a working man because of his humble dress, and he assures Pip that he will "make" a gentleman of him too. But Herbert's father, Matthew, never mistook Compeyson for a gentleman because "no man who was not a true gentleman at heart, ever was, since the world began, a true gentleman in manner" (179). Recalling the original meaning of "gentility," derived from the chivalric code of the knight, "heart" (compassion), and "manner" (breeding), are the key to Pip's search for his place in society.

The "true gentleman at heart" in the novel is Joe Gargery, but Dickens deliberately distinguishes Joe, a "gentle Christian man" (458), from the "true gentlemen in manner," Matthew and Herbert Pocket. Dickens told John Forster that the opening scene between Pip and Joe was "in its general effect exceedingly droll. I have put a child and a good-natured foolish man, in relations that seem to me very funny" (*Letters* 9.325). Like most wholly good people in literature and life, such as Dostoevsky's Prince Myshkin (the Idiot), Joe is foolish and unsophisticated in comparison with the more worldly characters. He has a childlike clearsightedness, like Hans Andersen's boy who sees that the emperor has no clothes: On seeing Pip's grand new London residence, Joe comments, "I wouldn't keep a pig in it myself—not in the case that I wished him to fatten wholesome and to eat with a meller flavour on him" (218). As a child, Pip sees Joe as his equal, and he soon surpasses Joe at reading and writing. But he acknowledges "a new sensation of feeling conscious that I was looking up to Joe in my heart" (49) when Joe explains that he cannot physically restrain his wife when she is pursuing them with a cane she calls "Tickler." He had seen his father beat his mother and he will not raise his hand to a woman. During the course of the novel, Pip loses his sense of "looking up to Joe"; only when he recovers it, does he become a "gentleman."

Combined with Joe's gentlemanly heart, Pip must also acquire the manners of the Pockets through education. Lacking money and caring little for clothes or possessions, the Pockets are clearly gentlemen because they combine Joe's compassionate heart with education, high principles, and social grace and ease. A true gentleman treats everyone with respect, regardless of class, and is comfortable in all social settings. Joe remains uneducated and unmannered, and desperately uncomfortable away from the forge; at Miss Havisham's, he is unable even to talk to her directly and his visit to Pip in London is one of the most comic but also painful scenes in the novel. Pip's embarrassment is contrasted with Herbert's ease and is partly responsible for Joe's clumsiness; but Dickens deliberately makes fun of Joe's limitations, and at the end of the novel, Joe still has difficulty writing. Dickens's point is not that Pip should have stayed at the forge; he had greater potential than Joe long before he learned of his Great Expectations. But he can fulfil that potential without rejecting and despising his roots.

Several characters in the novel are defined by their surroundings. Miss Havisham, in particular, exists in a richly symbolic landscape, Satis House. Estella explains to Pip that "satis," or "enough," suggests that whoever lives there could need nothing more. But the name "Have-is-sham" makes clear that the possession of wealth can provide only greater need. The decaying and moribund house and garden are the external expression of Miss Havisham's imprisoned mental state and the destructiveness of her failure to forgive and move on after being jilted on her wedding day, many years before. She is trapped in her own misery and desire for revenge, just as she is trapped in a decaying bride's dress and a house where the clocks have stopped and the light of day never penetrates. Miss Havisham's death-in-life existence represents the psychological neurosis of a mind arrested by events that cannot be accepted or forgiven. The destructive effect of such isolation from the real world of change and growth is vividly worked out in Estella's stunted emotional life, as is the effect of Miss Havisham's enjoyment of wielding power over Estella and Pip. A compound of several "white women"—some real and some fictional—Miss Havisham is connected to a story Dickens wrote for *Household Words* in 1857 entitled "The Bride's Chamber," in which a young man causes his rich young bride's death simply by telling her to die. For eleven years, she slowly pines away in a decaying mansion very similar to Satis House. Dickens recast Miss Havisham as both the bride and the groom, who, through a sheer act of will, gains control over other minds and hearts and destroys them.

John Wemmick's unusual house also defines his personality and comments on the novel's theme that we must not separate ourselves from our fellow men. Wemmick is essentially a kind man; his home is warm and loving, a haven of peace where he and his father, the Aged P., eat buttered toast in comfort and harmony. But Wemmick, Mr. Jaggers's clerk, can only sustain such a loving home by barricading it from the rest of London. In 1845 Friedrich Engels, a German philosopher who visited and wrote about England in the nineteenth century, noted that in the new urban society, "everyone turns his house into a fortress to defend himself—under the protection of the law—from the depredations of his neighbours."[2] Wemmick takes great pride in his "castle," which is comically defended by drawbridge and cannons so that it will be safe from the outside world, especially his criminal clients. Unfortunately, Wemmick barricades his kind heart also, reserving it for his home and hiding it away at the office. He refuses any kind of human contact with his clients, preferring to deal with them on a purely material level, as does his master Mr. Jaggers. His clients may be criminals, but Dickens reminds us that they deserve a little of the kindness that is found in Wemmick's castle.

THEMATIC ISSUES

The central theme of *Great Expectations* is that we are all connected in our humanity: Wealthy gentleman, humble blacksmith, hardened criminal, all share in the human potential for good and evil, and none can cast the first stone or assume they are free from the faults of others; we share a common guilt. *Great Expectations* reiterates this observation, and Dickens's warning to his society and the solution can be found in Pip's blessing on Magwitch at his death:

"Mindful, then, of what we had read together, I thought of the two men who went up into the Temple to pray, and I knew there were no better words that I could say beside his bed, than 'O Lord, be merciful to him, a sinner'" (455).

Pip's blessing comes from St. Luke's gospel, Chapter 18, the source of two other themes in the novel: the value of the child and the dangers of worshipping wealth or allowing money to take the place of human affection. The "two men" to whom Pip refers are the Pharisee and the publican in one of Christ's parables. The Pharisee, a rich man, self-righteously thanks God for making him better than other men because they are sinners and he is not. But the publican, or tax collector, is a humble man who meekly prays, "God, be merciful to me a sinner." Then Christ exhorts his listeners, "Suffer little children to come unto me, and forbid them not: for of such is the kingdom of God. . . . Whosoever shall not receive the kingdom of God as a little child shall in no wise enter therein." Dickens also reminds his readers of a third passage in St. Luke, Chapter 18, through a comic reference of Joe's in the chapter that follows Magwitch's death. Joe is trying to tell Pip about Miss Havisham's death and the "great expectations" of her greedy relatives who have been waiting impatiently for her death in order to inherit her fortune. Unable to remember the name of Matthew Pocket's sister Camilla, he refers to her as Mrs. Camels. Dickens's readers, as familiar with the Bible as he was, would certainly have recognized Dickens's reference to Christ's advice to the rich man in Luke 18: "It is easier for a camel to go through a needle's eye, than for a rich man to enter into the kingdom of God." Dickens had made a humorous reference to this passage earlier in the novel, when Pip has just received news of his new fortune but is still living in the village. He goes with Joe to church and thinks to himself that "the clergyman wouldn't have read that about the rich man and the kingdom of Heaven, if he had known all" (144). Newly discovering himself a rich man, the young Pip does not like to think that Christ really meant him; later, he learns that the possession of wealth is not the answer to all his hopes, as he had believed.

These three biblical passages provide us with the key to understanding the themes of human interconnectedness and shared guilt. Every aspect of the novel is integrated into the working out of Dickens's view of the proper relations between people, whether they are convicts, blacksmiths, or London "gentlemen." The publican's recognition that we are all guilty in some way provides one answer to Pip's question, "what is a gentleman?" Christ's love for children and recognition of their value is another answer; and his warning about the dangers of accumulating wealth and admiring those who have it is a third.

At the beginning of the novel, Dickens establishes the conflict between the self-righteous Pharisees, who set themselves apart from their fellow man, and the characters in the novel who, like the publican, recognize their human fellowship with all people regardless of class or circumstances. Typically in Dickens children and childlike adults are the least self-righteous, and the most victimized, so Pip and Joe are the innocent recipients of authoritarian blame. Christmas dinner at the forge typifies the conflict. It is anything but "Christ-massy" for the child, squeezed into a corner of the table, fed the most unappetizing parts of the pork and fowls, and further tortured by a barrage of criticism from the adults, who are all the time tucking into a large meal. Pip is accused of "crimes" of which he is quite innocent, especially the crime of ingratitude because he is an orphan and therefore a burden to his sister, Mrs. Joe. Pip is then told that he is "naterally wicious" (25), another tenet of the Victorian Calvinists who believed in the doctrine of original sin but who were inclined to absolve themselves from a share in it. To counteract the self-serving adults at the table, Joe, the good Christian, heaps Pip's plate with gravy to show his sympathy with the child.

Pip is innocent of the charges laid against him by the adults, and central to the novel is the distinction between real guilt and guilt that is determined by a hypocritical society that, like the Pharisee, is quick to find fault in others. Many scenes draw attention to this theme, such as an episode at the Three Jolly Bargemen, when Pip and the others are discussing the reporting of a murder trial in the newspaper and are unanimous is declaring that the accused is guilty of Wilful Murder. Mr. Jaggers, the criminal lawyer, overhears their verdict and reminds them that the essential tenet of English law is that we are innocent until we are proven guilty.

Pip knows that the adults are unjust to find him guilty of being an orphan and a glutton, but the confusion of innocence and guilt has become more complicated because he is eating his Christmas dinner while harboring the guilty secret that he has stolen from the forge to feed an escaped convict. Pip was terrified of him, and he stole the food as much out of fear as out of a child's sense of what is right. But when he feeds him out on the marshes, the rightness of this Christian meal is contrasted very forcibly with the un-Christian formal dinner at the forge. Pip tells the rough and dangerous outlaw that he is glad that he is enjoying the meal; the convict replies just as politely, "Thankee, my boy. I do" (19).

Pip identifies with the convict for two reasons: He is now a criminal himself, and he has formed a human bond with him because he has fed him. The bond is evident in his reference to the convict as "my fugitive friend." When they encounter the two runaways, Pip distinguishes Magwitch as "my convict." Pip's sympathy also helps him recognize the hypocrisy and lack of charity of the self-righteous dinner guests, who are excited at the prospect of a chase to catch the escaped convicts from the prison ship. Joe, however, reinforces Pip's innate sense that he was right to take the food when they track the convict down. Joe tells him he was "welcome to it . . . We don't know what you have done, but we wouldn't have you starved to death for it, poor miserable fellow-creatur" (39). So Pip is guilty but innocent: In the eyes of society and the law (represented very graphically by the hand-cuff-wielding soldiers who burst in on the Christmas dinner), he is certainly guilty of both theft and aiding an escaped convict; but according to Christian duty (represented by Joe's childlike moral sense), he did the right thing in recognizing his human bond to a starving man.

The barriers put up between the self-righteous and the outcast are physically present at Satis House, which is barricaded against robbers. But at Satis House, Pip also discovers that, to the upper classes of society, a blacksmith is as much an outcast as is a criminal. Miss Havisham and Estella represent a social class that Pip has never encountered before. The Hubbles, Mr. Wopsle, and Mr. Pumblechook are snobs and hypocrites, but they are village people. Miss Havisham represents the gentry, the landed families whose money is largely unearned. For the first time, Pip sees himself through the eyes of another class, and, unfortunately, those eyes belong to the beautiful but unattainable "star," Estella. When Pip falls under her spell, he understandably starts to judge himself against her view of him; he begins to share her contempt for his speech, dress, and hands, all visible manifestations of the difference between the working and leisured classes. And, naturally, Pip blames Joe for his contemptible state, so Pip's separation from Joe begins. At this point in the novel, Dickens now carefully links Pip's new sense of shame at his social class with his guilt at being a young criminal. Estella's contempt not only makes him feel ashamed of his coarse hands, thick boots, and ignorant language; it also makes him feel that he "was in a low-lived bad way" (64). His life at the forge thus becomes identified for him with his criminal connections, and both are totally unacceptable to Estella.

Pip's sense that it is a "crime" to be a blacksmith is evident when he is formally apprenticed to Joe by appearing before a magistrate. Mr. Pumblechook pushes him forward so much as though he were a criminal that the bystanders assume he is one. For Pip, becoming a blacksmith is the equivalent of a prison sentence because he feels trapped now in that life, just as the young Dickens saw no escape from the blacking factory. But Pip sees it as criminal as well; he is marked out for public notice and contempt as much as he would have been had he really committed a crime.

The connection between Pip's criminal past and his present life surfaces menacingly throughout the novel, most forcibly when Mrs. Joe is attacked and beaten with an iron filed from a convict's leg. Pip has just been associated with the famous murderer George Barnwell when Mr. Wopsle acts out his biography for Pip and Mr. Pumblechook. Again, Pip is found guilty of something of which he is entirely innocent when the two adults regard him as though he were the guilty Barnwell himself. Barnwell's crime was the murder of his uncle, so when Pip returns home after the play-reading to find his sister unconscious, hit by "his" convict's leg iron, he immediately feels responsible for the attack. He is innocent of committing the crime, but he is guilty of murderous feelings toward his sister that are acted out through Orlick, Joe's morose assistant at the forge. Once again he considers telling Joe the whole story, but does not, considering that "the secret was such an old one now, had so grown into me and become a part of myself, that I could not tear it away" (119).

When Pip's new fortunes take him to London, he expects to leave crime behind on the marshes; he expects the city to provide the genteel life that he thought he had found at Satis House. But just as Miss Havisham's decaying and barren surroundings are far removed from Pip's sense of them as having "something to do with everything that was picturesque" (107), so London is not at all the golden city of which he had dreamed. Once again, he is immediately surrounded by crime. He is taken to Mr. Jaggers's criminal law office, next door to Smithfield cattle market, a "shameful place, being all asmear with filth and fat and blood and foam" (163), which seems to stick to him. Beside the market and dominating the London landscape is Newgate Prison. Pip's attempts to separate himself from crime are futile; Wemmick even tells him, "You are one of us, as I may say" (197).

Estella considers convicts "wretches," and she tells Pip that his village friends are not suitable companions for him now. So he avoids visiting Joe, but avoiding crime is more difficult. When he meets her for tea, he bitterly regrets that he has been visiting Newgate while waiting for her. Just as the dirt of Smithfield seemed to stick to him, he now feels contaminated by his association with crime and desperately tries to rid himself of it before meeting Estella: "I beat the prison dust off my feet as I sauntered two and fro, and I shook it out of my dress, and I exhaled its air from my lungs. So contaminated did I feel, remembering who was coming, that the coach came quickly after all, and I was not yet free from the soiling consciousness of Mr. Wemmick's conservatory, when I saw her face at the coach window" (261). Once again, guilt and shame are intermingled through Pip's associations with the lower classes and with the criminal classes, and Estella encourages his desire to separate himself from both.

Pip finds it strange that he should be "encompassed by all this taint of prison and crime"; after his early encounter with the convict on the marshes, it is strange that the taint keeps reappearing, "starting out like a stain that was faded but not gone"; strange that "it should in this new way pervade my fortune and advancement" (260–61). Dickens demonstrates that it is a stain common to all and is often an innocent stain; one becomes a "gentleman" only by recognizing that all are tainted in some way. The ironies of the novel, far from being farfetched coincidences, are intended to show that we are all connected in our humanity to the causes of crime. One such irony is Estella's parentage. Brought up at Satis House, Estella considers herself apart from and superior to the village people and the criminal classes; but we learn that she is the daughter of a convict and a murderess. The one whom Pip is most anxious not to contaminate with the dust of Newgate could not be more a product of it.

The culmination of the themes occurs in the brilliant closing chapter of "Stage Two," when Magwitch returns, holding out his hands to his "son." Pip of course is horrified at this overturning of all his assumptions: His benefactor is *not* Miss Havisham, so Estella is *not* destined for him after all. Dickens prepares for the revelation very carefully, in a scene shot through with irony. Pip does not at first recognize his convict, but when he does he assumes that he can rid himself of this unkempt and unwelcome guest by paying him back the money that the other convict had returned to Joe:

He watched me as I laid my purse upon the table and opened it, and he watched me as I separated two one-pound notes from its contents. They were clean and new, and I spread them out and handed them over to him. Still watching me, he laid them one upon the other, folded them long-wise, gave them a twist, set fire to them at the lamp, and dropped the ashes into the tray. (313–14)

Great Expectations contains many telling exchanges between characters, but none is so startling as this one. Pip the gentleman hands over new notes to the man who earned those notes by very hard work in Australia, depriving himself of the comforts they could have supplied in order to keep Pip in new clothes and expensive watches and rings. When two pounds exchanged hands earlier, they were hard-earned notes also; Magwitch could ill afford to send two pounds back to the blacksmith who had fed him, and the convict who carried them down to the village could just as easily have kept them himself. But now they mean nothing. Pip has not earned them, and does not even know who has supplied them. Most importantly, Magwitch does not want them; hence, he burns them. Magwitch powerfully rejects the "cash nexus" in this scene, just as Joe rejected payment for Pip when he left the forge and Herbert and his father refuse to have any monetary dealings with each other. Since becoming a gentleman, Pip has often replaced human contact with money, sending Joe presents instead of visiting him, and admitting that if he could have kept Joe away from London by paying him, he would have paid him. Now he thinks that he can get rid of an embarrassing figure from his past by giving him money. But Magwitch wants something much more valuable from Pip. He wants love from the boy who was the first to offer him a kindness in a hostile world and whom he thinks of as his son.

Pip's abhorrence for Magwitch is understandable, and it is shared by the true gentleman, Herbert Pocket. Magwitch is a violent, uncouth man who sleeps with a pistol at his pillow. But Pip's abhorrence is also understandable because it stems primarily from Magwitch's sense that he "owns" Pip. He looks on Pip as a possession that he has made; he admires his clothes, his watch, his education, and "would stand before the fire surveying me with the air of an Exhibitor" (335). Magwitch has used Pip as an instrument of revenge on the wealthy Australians whom he felt had looked down on him as both a convict and a common man. When they passed him on their fine horses, he would think to himself, "If I ain't a gentleman, nor yet ain't got no learning, I'm the owner of such. All on you owns stock and land; which on you owns a brought-up London gentleman?" (317).

Dickens parallels Miss Havisham's ownership of Estella with Magwitch's ownership of Pip. Both regard themselves as surrogate parents, but both use the child for their own ends. The effects of such ownership are devastating for both Pip and Estella: Pip is deprived of the satisfaction and fulfilment of earning a living, which causes his "inability to settle to anything—which I hope arose out of the restless and incomplete tenure on which I held my means" (308); Estella grows up without a heart. But both Miss Havisham and Magwitch also had the best of intentions for their adopted children, wishing to protect them from the evils that had damaged their own lives.

Magwitch's love for Pip returns us to the opening of the novel, when the child fed the starving and hunted man. "Stage Three" of the novel details the gradual return of that sympathy, and it begins when Pip learns that Magwitch (appropriately called Abel), is not as guilty as society and the law have found him. An orphan like Pip, but with no family or friends, the young Magwitch was forced to steal food and quickly became known as a "hardened" criminal with little chance of changing his reputation.

Once again, Pip is made to feel guilty for something of which he is really innocent when he feels responsible for Magwitch's life; by returning to see Pip, Magwitch risks being hanged. As the narrative speeds up through the hiding of Magwitch, his attempted escape from England, his capture, trial, and death, Pip takes on this responsibility and, at the same time, confronts his real guilt and reconnects with the classes, which, as a "gentleman," he had rejected: the convict, Magwitch, and the common working man, Joe.

Pip's path to redemption is full of obstacles, and like the heroes of old, he has to journey to the underworld to distinguish innocence from guilt and acknowledge his responsibility as a free, not an "owned," man. First, he is burned in the fire that destroys Miss Havisham and the dangerous attitudes of vengeance and failure to forgive that have crippled her life and Estella's. Then, he is forced to face his guilt and repent of it in the old sluice house on the marshes, where he is confronted by Orlick and threatened with death. Full of regret for his treatment of Joe and Biddy, and praying for their forgiveness, he is spiritually redeemed and then rescued by friends who recognize that he has now earned the title of gentleman. Trabb's boy, who works for the village tailor and who had been such an astute critic of Pip when he was a gentleman externally only, comments, "ain't he just pale though!" (425). Pip has just fought off Orlick, and Dickens intends us to recall an earlier fight with a "pale young gentleman," Herbert Pocket. Pip is now, finally, a pale young gentleman, too.

Pip's redemption at the sluice house makes him fully human and able to feel compassion for Magwitch as he nears his death. Pip's silent recognition of his cruelty to Joe is made possible by his growing love for Magwitch, and he acknowledges his human bond with the old convict, a bond forged by the little boy on the marshes: "For now, my repugnance to him had all melted away, and in the hunted wounded shackled creature who held my hand in his, I only saw a man who had meant to be my benefactor, and who had felt affectionately, gratefully, and generously, towards me with great constancy through a series of years. I only saw in him a much better man than I had been to Joe" (441).

Through his unselfish love for Magwitch, Pip has become the gentleman he desired to be, but it is a very different gentleman from the one he originally sought. All the trappings of wealth, possessions, and status have to be stripped away from him; thus, after Magwitch's death, he is again taken into the valley of the shadow through illness, to return in a childlike state that allows him to make his peace with Joe. He fancies he is "little Pip again" (461), and he finds Joe "just as simply faithful, and as simply right" (462). The three passages from Luke are fulfilled when Pip regains the moral sense that prompted the child to feed a convict whom the adult world could only condemn.

STYLISTIC AND LITERARY DEVICES

Great Expectations is particularly rich in symbol and imagery. Much of the imagery is atmospheric: to create suspense and a sense of foreboding in a novel that abounds in mystery. Because the same images keep recurring, they also tie the events of the novel together but in a subtle and understated way that reflects Pip's gradual understanding of the web of connections in his life. Such a passage occurs at the *peripeteia*, or turning point, when Magwitch comes back into Pip's life at the end of "Stage Two." Pip is alone in his lodgings at the top of a house near the river. The weather has been stormy and wet for days, with a "vast heavy veil" of rain driving over London. The wind is howling ominously around his high windows, blowing directly from the marshes where he first encountered Magwitch. Looking out, he sees "that the coal fires in barges on the river were being carried away before the wind like red-hot splashes in the rain"

(309). The image recalls Pip's last glimpse of Magwitch, when he is taken away in the prison boat, back to the Hulks: "the ends of the torches were flung hissing into the water, and went out, as if it were all over with him" (40). Listening nervously to the wind and rain, Pip hears a footstep that he connects with the footstep of his dead sister. He does not yet know that it belongs to the convict whose leg iron was responsible for his sister's injury, but the connection is made subtly for the reader. As he goes out to see who is coming up the stairs, Pip leans over the rail with his reading lamp, and the apparently unknown visitor climbs up into the circle of light: "he was in it for a mere instant, and then out of it" (310). Then "as he ascended the last stair or two, and the lamp light included us both, I saw, with a stupid kind of amazement, that he was holding out both his hands to me." The light of the lamp graphically illustrates this stranger's place in Pip's life. At the beginning of the book he was there for "a mere instant"; when he disappeared into darkness for some years, he was still connected to Pip; now he has returned and the light "included" them both because, from now on, Pip will remain at Magwitch's side.

That Magwitch has been intimately connected with Pip all those years without Pip's knowledge is central to Dickens's point that we are all connected, whether we are gentleman or convict. These connections are highlighted throughout the novel by the use of light and darkness, as in the many occasions when the faces of Estella and her mother, Molly, are illuminated by flares of light. That we are connected when we least expect to be is graphically illustrated when Compeyson is sitting behind Pip at Mr. Wopsle's play. For the first time in days, Pip is not thinking about Magwitch's enemy, but Mr. Wopsle sees Compeyson in the audience. Dickens's imagery again ties together the marsh scenes with the present danger when Mr. Wopsle reminds Pip of their last meeting with the convicts, at their capture: "I am particular about that; with the torchlight shining on their faces, when there was an outer ring of dark night all about us" (381).

Chains, links, and other bonds are the chief motifs in the novel, both highlighting the criminal element and emphasizing the theme of human interconnectedness. Early in the novel, Pip asks the reader to "think for a moment of the long chain of iron or gold, of thorns or flowers, that would never have bound you, but for the formation of the first link on one memorable day" (71). The notion of being "bound" is double-edged for Pip. He feels bound to the convict because he fed him, and he is "bound apprentice to Joe" (102) when the indentures are signed, making him a blacksmith. Pip resents both connections and denies them throughout "Stage Two," when he is in pursuit of gentlemanly status. But to be "bound" or "attached" to someone has moral implications as well: the implications of affection and moral responsibility. Pip feels connected to the convict when he stuffs bread and butter down his own trouser leg and the weight of it reminds him of the iron on the convict's leg. The leg iron continues to haunt him throughout the novel, and when Magwitch returns, their close connection is abhorrent to Pip. But now the connection is ironically a monetary one because the chain connecting them is Pip's expensive watch chain: "Nothing was needed but this; the wretched man, after loading wretched me with his gold and silver chains for years, had risked his life to come to me, and I held it there in my keeping!" (318). When Herbert returns, Pip tells him that Magwitch is "attached to me, strongly attached to me. Was there ever such a fate!" (338). Magwitch is "attached" because his life is in Pip's hands; but he is also "attached" because he loves Pip like a son. Dickens emphasizes this double "attachment" through the word "bound," when Pip tells Herbert that Magwitch is "so bound up with [Pip's] fortunes and misfortunes" (340). Herbert replies that Pip is "bound to have, that tenderness for the life he has risked on your account, that you must save him." (340). Pip does indeed learn to accept that he is "bound" to the convict and to Joe in the best possible way: through human sympathy and compassion.

Dickens emphasizes the human condition also through continual references to hands. Handshaking is the universal sign of fellowship, a recognition of fellow feeling and sympathy, and Dickens uses hands to differentiate between the characters who recognize their common bond and those who put up barriers of class or prestige or moral superiority. When Pip returns to the village for his sister's funeral, the ceremony is stripped of all meaning because of Mr. Trabb's concern with appearances: More important than the emotion behind the funeral are the clothes and trappings that surround it. So when Mr. Trabb holds out his hand to Pip, wanting Pip's hat so that he can decorate it with black ribbon, Pip, "misled by the action, and confused by the occasion, shook hands with him with every testimony of warm affection" (275). Mr. Trabb's obsession with display rather than fellow feeling contrasts strongly with Joe's warmth, when he "clasped [Pip's] hand and said no more" (276). Mr. Wemmick, too, in his position as Jaggers's clerk, does not shake hands with his criminal clients except once, when they are destined for hanging the next day. Mr. Jaggers washes his hands with scented soap after meeting with clients to rid himself of their contamination and separate himself from them. But perhaps the action also signifies his recognition that he is guilty of not taking more interest in them. Like Lady Macbeth after the murder of Banquo, and Pontius Pilate, who washed his hands of the responsibility of Christ's death, Jaggers is unconsciously acknowledging that he does have a responsibility to his clients that goes beyond paying Wemmick. Just as Wemmick has an affectionate side, Jaggers, too, has had "poor dreams," and while his hold over Molly is uneasily sadistic, he did act in her case out of a sense of responsibility for the child, Estella.

Mrs. Joe's hardness and lack of affection is represented by the hardness of her hands, which hurt Pip more than they comfort. Pip is brought up "by hand," or by bottle rather than breast, and is expected to be grateful to her for it, but it is a "hard and heavy hand" (8) to the small boy. The apron that covers Mrs. Joe's chest is stuck full of pins and needles that get into the bread that she holds against her chest when she is buttering it; the pins are then transferred to the mouths of Pip and Joe as they eat their suppers. Far from wanting to feed and nurture her child, Mrs. Joe actually arms herself against him and damages him dangerously in the feeding. In contrast to Mrs. Joe is Biddy, the good mother of a new young Pip at the end of the novel. While Mrs. Joe's wedding ring hurts Pip's head when she roughly washes his head, at the end of the novel, Biddy, the nurturing mother, shakes Pip's hand and the "light pressure" of her ring "had a very pretty eloquence in it" (476).

A PSYCHOANALYTICAL READING OF *GREAT EXPECTATIONS*

Like *David Copperfield* (and in the chapter on that novel, readers will find a description of psychoanalytical criticism), *Great Expectations* lends itself to Freudian analysis because it is a first-person narration in which aspects of the speaker's psyche are projected onto other figures in the novel. Dolge Orlick operates as Pip's *id*, the dark side of Pip that he does not want to face. Orlick is the embodiment of evil, slouching out of the primeval mud of the marshes where he lives like Cain, the murderer of his brother, Abel (110); he tells Pip that he knows the Devil well. Orlick acts out Pip's repressed desires, the first being the attack on Mrs. Joe, for which Pip feels very guilty, as though he had done the deed himself. Orlick physically fights with Joe when Pip is desperately resentful of being Joe's apprentice; he is attracted to Biddy and later works at Satis House. Orlick lurks around the village spying on Pip like a "shadow," as the *id* is sometimes described. Bentley Drummle is Orlick's counterpart in London; like Orlick, he is Pip's double, often lurking in the background, a dangerous and brutish force.

Pip comes face to face with his repressed dark side in the sluice house scene near the end of the novel, when Orlick acts as his accuser. This encounter closely follows redemption scenes in symbolic literature such as *Sir Gawain and the Green Knight*. In this journey into the valley of the shadow of death, or the dark night of the soul, the hero encounters a mysterious figure, who, in religious works such as *Pilgrim's Progress*, is the devil, but who, in psychological terms, represents the dark side of the hero. Thus, Pip comes face to face with Orlick, the devil's friend and Pip's evil *id*. The approach to the house is desolate and fearful, surrounded by a "choking vapour" that warns of death (417). The encounter with one's evil side is essentially a recognition of guilt, which then leads the hero through five stages: admission of guilt, repentance, suffering, humiliation, and a final fight for life. Pip feels that he has "come to the brink of [his] grave" (420) when Orlick catalogues his grievances with him, telling him that the attack on Mrs. Joe that led to her death was done through Pip. At the same time, Pip silently admits to his real crime: his neglect of Joe and Biddy. In his repentance, he defeats his evil side and becomes active for good.

The journey through the nightmarish valley of the shadow of death always results in a spiritual rebirth into daylight and calm. Pip wakes after a long sleep to find the world renewed: "As I looked along the clustered roofs, with Church towers and spires shooting into the unusually clear air, the sun rose up, and a veil seemed to be drawn from the river, and millions of sparkles burst out upon its waters. From me too, a veil seemed to be drawn, and I felt strong and well" (428). While Pip is freed from his evil side, Orlick remains in the novel as a threatening presence, suffering a minor setback when he is sent to jail for breaking into Mr. Pumblechook's house. This mild retribution (similar to the imprisonment of Uriah Heep, David Copperfield's *id*) suggests that the darker impulses of mankind can never be fully dealt with; so no one can cast the first stone.

NOTES

1. Dickens rewrote the new last line several times. In manuscript, he wrote, "I saw the shadow of no parting from her but one." He removed the last two words before publication, and the line that appeared in *All the Year Round* and in the 1861 edition read: "I saw the shadow of no parting from her." In 1862, the line was changed again to, "I saw no shadow of another parting from her." The World's Classics edition is based on the 1861 edition.

2. From Friedrich Engels's *The Condition of the Working Class in England*, trans. by W. O. Henderson and W. H. Chaloner (Oxford: Basil Blackwell, 1958), 31.

10

The Other Novels from
Dombey and Son (1848) to
The Mystery of Edwin Drood
(1870)

DOMBEY AND SON (1848)

The last installment of *Martin Chuzzlewit* appeared in June 1844; Dickens began writing the first installment of *Dombey and Son* in June 1846. In between the two novels he wrote three Christmas books, *A Christmas Carol*, *The Chimes*, and *The Cricket on the Hearth*, short novellas that, unlike the novels written in weekly or monthly parts, were planned as a whole and written with the end in mind. The Christmas books also gave him an increased realization of time and change and the effect of the passing of time on character development. Although he used the supernatural to allow for a character's movement into the past of his memory or into an imagined future, the books still show him thinking more profoundly about how the past impinges on the present and is ever-present to the character as he develops. For this reason, the years between these two novels are usually seen as a turning point in Dickens's career between the early, more picaresque and loosely structured novels and the carefully planned and intricately structured later works, starting with *Dombey and Son*. For the first time, Dickens started using "number plans" or notes that he made while writing the novel, to help him keep the threads of the plot and character development firmly in mind.

Dickens's intention in *Dombey and Son* was to examine pride just as he had examined selfishness in *Martin Chuzzlewit*. But while the major transformation in that novel (Young Martin's recognition of his own better nature) occurs suddenly, at the sick bed of his friend Mark Tapley, Mr. Dombey's transformation is carefully prepared for and embedded in the novel. As Dickens explains in his preface, "Mr. Dombey undergoes no violent internal change, either in this book, or in life. A sense of his injustice is within him all along. The more he represses it, the more unjust he necessarily is. Internal shame and external circumstances may bring the contest to the surface in a week, or a day; but it has been a contest for years, and is only fought out after a long balance of victory."

Mr. Dombey is a Victorian businessman, the head of a family firm (the novel's title refers to the firm rather than to father and son, as his little son recognizes) and a pompous, cold, and proud man, instantly recognizable as a type by Dickens's readers. The book opens with the birth of his son and the death of his wife, the latter unimportant to Dombey except as the source of his son's nourishment; couldn't something temporary be done with a teapot, Mr. Chick helpfully suggests. Dickens explained to Forster how Mr. Dombey's intense pride in his son would be thwarted by the boy's early death, and how his resentment at his daughter Florence's continuing presence and affection would fester into positive hatred. He continued:

So I mean to carry the story on, through all the branches and off-shoots and meanderings that come up; and through the decay and downfall of the house, and the bankruptcy of Dombey, and all the rest of it; when his only staff and treasure, and his unknown Good Genius always, will be this rejected daughter, who will come out better than any son at last, and whose love for him, when discovered and understood, will be his bitterest reproach. For the struggle with himself, which goes on in all such obstinate natures, will have ended then; and the sense of his injustice, which you may be sure has never quitted him, will have at last a gentler office than that of only making him more harshly unjust. (Forster 2.20–21)

Pride is the controlling passion of Dombey's second wife, Edith, who humbles Dombey by eloping with his business manager, James Carker, whose deviousness is embodied in his very white and symmetrical teeth and his smile that resembles the snarl of a cat. Carker's intention is to destroy Dombey's financial and personal lives; he succeeds in the former, but Edith humbles him in turn by revealing that she had no intention of becoming his mistress. With Dombey in hot pursuit, Carker flees back to England but dies violently, mowed down by a train.

Florence, the embodiment of love and self-sacrifice, always recognizes that her father cannot accept his own emotional core, and her understanding of him makes his fear of her all the greater. But she is supported by a variety of loving and exuberantly comic characters including Walter Gay, Dombey's office boy, who was originally to be blighted by Dombey's influence (as Tom Gradgrind is by his father in *Hard Times*) but who, instead, is shipped overseas, presumed drowned, but returns to marry Florence. His uncle, Solomon Gills, and Sol's friend Captain Cuttle provide an alternative to Dombey's method of business in their nautical instrument shop, The Wooden Midshipman, where eccentricity, love, and human emotion flourish. Kindness flourishes also in Mr. Toots, school friend of Paul and devoted follower of Florence.

Paul Dombey is one of Dickens's most successful child characters whose death greatly affected Dickens's readers and whose precocious wisdom and understanding (combined with childish egotism) is carefully drawn. Dickens's memories of his own childhood are evident in the characterization of Paul, and he based the formidable but essentially understanding Mrs. Pipchin, with whom Paul stays at the seaside, on Mrs. Roylance, with whom Dickens boarded when his father was in the Marshalsea Prison. The memory of those days and Dickens's powerful sense of abandonment enter the novel in Florence's desperate attempts to soften her father's heart.

Dickens's concern for "fallen women" and his genuine desire to help them to a better life (rather than condemn them, as Victorian society in general did) is evident in the novel also in the characters of Alice Marwood, who is seduced and abandoned by James Carker, and her mother, "Good Mrs. Brown," a frightening figure who appears from time to time and is a threat to Florence, capturing her in the streets and stealing her clothes. She, too, had been seduced and abandoned as a young woman.

Dombey and Son was the first of Dickens's novels to use the railway, and it was as symbolic of the ambiguities and tensions of the Victorian Age as the stagecoach had been symbolic of an earlier, rural and more settled age in *The Pickwick Papers*. The railway was both progressive and exciting and dangerously tied to a new age of industrial smoke and destruction. It kills Carker (and nearly kills Dickens nineteen years later), but it is also the way of the future. No one had a more intense dislike for people who glorified "the good old days" than Dickens.

Dombey and Son was also the first of Dickens's novels to employ a coherent and carefully planned plot, with consistent and powerful imagery through which the theme of pride evolves. Dickens had dealt with the closed and emotionally repressed man of business before, in Scrooge and several of the other Christmas-book protagonists. But while these characters were released from their prisons by means of the supernatural (recalling the past to them and even foretelling bleak futures), Dombey's internal struggle and deliberate self-deception is powerfully evoked and developed, until his financial and personal defeat forces him out of his isolation. It was a character that Dickens considered so quintessentially English that, in his 1862 Christmas story, "His Boots," he calls such a repressed man Mr. L'Anglais (Mr. the Englishman) as the French villagers' pronunciation of Mr. Langley. The isolation of the emotionally repressed character (not always, but usually masculine—a little girl in the Christmas story *Tom Tiddler's Ground* similarly turns in on herself), was to become central to his novels from then on.

Dombey and Son restored Dickens's faith in his powers as a novelist, which had been shaken by the comparatively lukewarm reception to *Martin Chuzzlewit* (which he had considered at the time "immeasurably the best" of his books thus far). *Dombey and Son*'s first installment sold out its entire 25,000 copies within hours; in no time, the numbers were selling well over 30,000 copies each month.

BLEAK HOUSE (1853)

David Copperfield followed *Dombey and Son* in monthly installments in 1849 and 1850. A year later, in the autumn of 1851, feeling "intolerably restless" and "wild to begin a new book," Dickens began *Bleak House*, its first installment appearing in March 1852. Many consider this sweeping panorama of the "condition of England" in the 1850s Dickens's finest work. Its memorable second paragraph, which begins "Fog everywhere. Fog up the river, where it flows among green aits and meadows; fog down the river, where it rolls defiled among the tiers of shipping, and the waterside pollutions of a great (and dirty) city," strikes the keynote metaphor for the whole novel. Fog is the Court of Chancery, where the delay and obfuscation of the legal system stunt lives and destroy hopes. Everyone in the novel is connected in some way to the case of Jarndyce and Jarndyce, which has been mouldering in the court for many years before the novel opens. *Bleak House* achieves its remarkable coherence through an extraordinarily complicated plot, threads of related imagery, and a dual narrative that was innovative in the novel form.

Esther Summerson, the first-person narrator who alternates irregularly with a third-person omniscient narrator, is an illegitimate child raised by a woman (later revealed to be her aunt) who takes the view that Esther's parents' sins are visited upon her. Esther does not know what her parentage is, but deprived of love she takes comfort from her doll (as the orphan Jane Eyre also did, a few years earlier). Esther never fully recovers from this early deprivation; she remains self-doubting and at times pathetically grateful when people are kind to her. She is adopted by her kind guardian, John Jarndyce, for whom she becomes the housekeeper of his home, Bleak House. He is also the guardian of two wards of court in the Jarndyce case, Ada Clare and Richard Carstone. Ada and Richard fall in love, but Richard, after trying and failing at various callings, becomes caught up in trying to settle the lawsuit (despite Mr. Jarndyce's warnings), thinking that it will make him rich; instead, it gradually undermines his mental and physical health.

The secret of Esther's parentage is gradually revealed as the story proceeds through the chance recognition of handwriting and the similarity between her and her mother, Lady Dedlock. Many hints arise along the way as various characters glimpse a mystery and try to solve it. There is a mysterious man, known only as Nemo (no man), who dies of an overdose of opium in his forlorn rented room in the house of Mr. Krook, an eccentric keeper of a rag and bottle shop. Another tenant is Miss Flite, a brilliant study of a hanger-on in the courts of justice. Her family have all been ruined by the Court of Chancery, but she attends every day, expecting a judgment; her companions are caged birds who will be released when that judgment occurs.

Behind the search for the secret surrounding Esther's birth is Tulkinghorn the lawyer, who notices that Lady Dedlock recognizes the handwriting on some documents. He discovers that the writer is Nemo, now dead, and that Jo, the young crossing sweeper despised by everyone except Nemo ("he wos wery good to me, he wos!"), has been asked by a veiled lady to show her Nemo's grave. When Tulkinghorn discovers that Nemo was Captain Hawdon, Lady Dedlock's lover and Esther's father, he threatens to tell Sir Leicester Dedlock, but he is murdered in his rooms that evening. Inspector Bucket (the first police detective in English literature) arrests the kindly George Rouncewell by mistake; the murderer is actually Hortense, Lady Dedlock's estranged maid who has been in the employ of Tulkinghorn. When Sir Leicester is told about his wife's affair, he has a stroke, and Lady Dedlock is found dead at the gates of her lover's burial place.

There are many related sub-plots surrounding the main mystery. Esther contracts a disfiguring illness from Jo, who dies of it. She has been pursued unsuccessfully by Guppy, a law clerk, but he changes his mind when he sees that she has lost her looks. In another January/May marriage (a favorite theme in Dickens's work), John Jarndyce proposes to Esther and she accepts out of gratitude to him, although it is evident that she is in love with Alan Woodcourt, a noble young doctor who attended Nemo and then went abroad. The reader is clearer about Esther and Alan Woodcourt's mutual attachment than she is, and it is no surprise that when he returns, they marry with Mr. Jarndyce's blessing. Ada and Richard also marry, but he dies as a result of pursuing the Jarndyce and Jarndyce case, which is finally settled, with any remaining money having been eaten up in costs.

As usual, there are a large number of minor characters who weave in and out of the main narrative. Mrs. Jellyby is Dickens's most memorable portrait of the misguided philanthropist who is so busy with "projects" for the natives of Borrioboola-Gha that she fails to look after her own chaotic house and her neglected children. Dickens based her—rather unfairly—on Caroline Chisholm, a philanthropist whose mission was to help families emigrate to Australia. The plight of Mrs. Jellyby's own children and Jo, the crossing sweeper and lost child of London, who is constantly forced to "move on" and eventually dies of disease, is Dickens's warning to a complacent and smug England, glorying in its position as the center of the new industrial world. Jo was probably based on a real boy, George Ruby, who testified in a well-publicized legal case in 1850. His "home," the sickening slum known as Tom-All-Alone's, has become the symbol for the corruption at the heart of Victorian London. Endless government reports catalogued the horrific living conditions of the urban poor, where the drinking water was contaminated and the ditches overflowed with filth and sewage. That Captain Hawdon is buried there, that Lady Dedlock dies there too, and that Esther contracts a nearly-deadly fever from it demonstrate Dickens's point that all humanity is interrelated and interdependent, however much Chesney Wold, the ancient seat of the Dedlocks, may deny the existence of Tom-All-Alone's. Dickens was to use mysterious parentage to make the same point again in *Great Expectations*.

LITTLE DORRIT (1857)

Originally to be entitled *Nobody's Fault*, *Little Dorrit* followed *Hard Times*, but it returned to the twenty-issue format of the earlier novels rather than being published weekly in *Household Words*. It appeared in installments from December 1855 to June 1857. Although it was set earlier in time, like *Bleak House* (the Marshalsea Prison, which is the setting for much of the novel, had closed down in 1842), it was also like *Bleak House* in being inspired by the worst aspects of English life in the 1850s. But like the novel that followed it, *A Tale of Two Cities*, it blended a personal love story with a powerful evocation of public events, a love story deeply influenced by Dickens's own emotional turmoil in the 1850s.

The inspiration for both *Hard Times* and *Little Dorrit* can be found in Dickens's 1853 Christmas story, "Nobody's Story," in which "nobody" is ordinary hard-working English people who are beset with burdens and obstacles imposed by the Bigwig family, or the ruling aristocratic class, who, despite the Reform Act of 1832, still held the reins of power in the country. The Christmas story finds the Bigwigs guilty of depriving the poorer classes of education, literature, Sunday recreations, and wholesome life while patronizing them with the attitude that the Bigwigs know what is good for the working classes. Even when cholera swept through the slums (as it did in 1831 and again in 1848–1849 and 1853–1854, killing thousands of people), "not a man among [the Bigwigs] ever admitted, if in the least degree he ever perceived, that he had anything to do with it." It was "Nobody's Fault," as *Little Dorrit* was to reiterate.

Since the evils decried in the 1853 Christmas story, England had been engaged in the Crimean War, a "nobody's fault" of disastrous proportions. Sheer incompetence and adherence to pointless rules and regulations had resulted in the deaths of hundreds of British soldiers from cold and hunger in the winter of 1854–1855. Six hundred soldiers were killed unnecessarily by a Russian ambush, a "blunder" that Tennyson dramatized in his "Charge of the Light Brigade." In Dickens's view, the Bigwigs, or aristocratic Tories, were responsible for most of the ills of the country, and the ordinary working people, soldiers and countrymen alike, were the victims of aristocratic conceit and neglect. The Bigwigs are the Barnacle family in *Little Dorrit*: Barnacles because they cling tenaciously to the ship of state but are totally useless and deliberately prevent its progress; Barnacles because they are everywhere, clinging with their large families (with all the privilege of inherited position) to every surface of government and especially the Circumlocution Office, which specializes in "how not to do it." Lord Decimus Tite Barnacle was based on Lord Palmerston, the elderly prime minister whose bungling ineptitude in the Crimea was the cause of a public outcry.

The Circumlocution Office is one of the many prisons that form the dominant setting and metaphor of *Little Dorrit*: Prisons of body, mind, and spirit cramp and distort the characters, from Miss Wade, a self-pitying orphan who distrusts all offers of kindness, to Mrs. Clennam, self-imprisoned in her room as a religious penance. The Circumlocution Office is as prisonlike as the Marshalsea itself, as Arthur Clennam and Daniel Doyce, partners in an engineering firm, discover when they try to patent Doyce's invention and encounter the endless red tape that strangled the inventiveness and ingenuity of the English working man.

There are real prisons, too, from the one in Marseilles, where the novel graphically opens, to the Marshalsea Prison in London, the setting of the first half of the novel and familiar to Dickens because his father had been imprisoned there for debt in 1824. Little Dorrit is the child of the Marshalsea because she was born there, daughter of the Father of the prison, William Dorrit, who is imprisoned for debt for over twenty years. He is released halfway through the novel when it is discovered that he is the heir to an unclaimed estate. Dickens's exploration of Mr. Dorrit's complex psychological state is profound and compelling. A gentleman reduced to the circumstances of the common thief, Mr. Dorrit clings to a perverted gentility and dominance in the prison by becoming its "Father." He accepts money from the other inmates under the pretense that it is "tributes, from admirers, to a public character" (55). His children work outside the prison to support him but he pretends not to know of it so it will not disturb his status as a "gentleman."

In the second half of the novel, released from the Marshalsea, Mr. Dorrit takes his pride and position into the world, as far from the London prison as he is able; he and his family tour Europe in a sojourn that incorporates Dickens's extensive knowledge of the Continent. At his side always is Little Dorrit, who recognizes her father's intense snobbery and pathetic concern with gentility but who protects and shelters him out of pity for his long imprisonment. But the stranglehold of the prison follows him around Europe (and is graphically represented by the frozen bodies stored in eternal snows at the Great Saint Bernard pass); to Little Dorrit, the genteel travellers they encounter on their grand tour behave exactly like the Marshalsea prisoners and are captive to their couriers, poor accommodations, and aimless lives. Mr. Dorrit ensures his daughters' imprisonment by hiring Mrs. General to teach them gentility; her method is to "varnish" life, avoid discussion of anything important, and cultivate a surface by repeated practice of the words "prunes and prism." Mr. Dorrit's daughters survive Mrs. General, but their father is held captive by his desperate desire to appear genteel and keep secret his shameful past. The conflict reaches its inevitable climax in a brilliant scene (which foreshadows the portrait of Doctor Manette in *A Tale of Two Cities*) just before his death, when he thinks he is back in the old prison and addresses the dinner guests as though he were still the Father of the Marshalsea.

Keeping up appearances is a mental and even a physical prison that enslaves those who aspire to gentility, including Little Dorrit's sister Fanny, who inherits her father's snobbery and marries a rich fool. Mr. Merdle, the wealthy banker, appears to be in control not just of his own life, but of everyone else's in the moneyed world; but even his chief butler intimidates him, and his secret "complaint" turns out to be a systematic fraud that eventually leads to his suicide and the financial collapse of everyone associated with him. Dickens based Merdle on George Hudson, whose railway-based financial empire crashed in 1849, and John Sadleir, who poisoned himself in 1856 when his fraudulent practices became known through the collapse of his Irish bank.

At the heart of the novel and the plot is Arthur Clennam, in a powerful study of middle age that derived from Dickens's own restless sense of loss and regret that he first described in *David Copperfield* but that had continued to haunt him. Like *Bleak House*, *Little Dorrit* contains many secrets bound up in Arthur's mother's house, which creaks and whispers and finally collapses under the weight of its burden of guilt. It is revealed at the end of the novel that Mrs. Clennam is not Arthur's mother; before their marriage, her husband had had an affair with a young singer whom he was forbidden to marry. When the girl died, Mrs. Clennam took on their child, Arthur, and raised him, as Esther Summerson was raised, in a grimly Calvinistic and self-righteous way to expiate the sins of his parents. Mrs. Clennam has voluntarily imprisoned herself in her room for many years, but the mental prison of narrow Calvinistic doctrine is, in many ways, worse. The damage such restrictive upbringings did to children in the name of Christianity was a favorite theme with Dickens, and it was central also to Pip's development in *Great Expectations*.

Dickens's identification with Arthur Clennam enters the novel comically in the affectionate portrait of Flora Finching, Arthur's delightful childhood girlfriend who is then (on his return from twenty years in China) a large and silly matron, just as Maria Beadnell mysteriously turned into Mrs. Winter in Dickens's own life. More pervasive, though, is Dickens's sense of growing old, captured especially in Clennam's unrequited love for the young and pretty Pet Meagles (which he tries to deny to himself by calling himself "nobody") and in his failure to recognize Little Dorrit's love for him—and his for her—because she seems like a child to him. He is imprisoned by his own view of himself as old and weary and by his sense that his mother is hiding a guilty secret that casts a shadow on him as well. The secret turns out to be Mrs. Clennam's hiding of the codicil to a will that leaves money to Little Dorrit, a favorite Victorian plot device that is here very powerfully tied to Clennam's restless and troubled state of mind.

Like David Copperfield, Arthur Clennam awakens to the realization that he loves the woman who has loved him for years, and the novel ends with a poignant blending of the lovers with the hustle and bustle of Victorian life, with its Barnacles and bustle and dirt and disease. Despite the problems of the city and the new Industrial Age, human life and activity are to be found here and cherished in open and loving hearts: "They went quietly down into the roaring streets, inseparable and blessed; and as they passed along in sunshine and in shade, the noisy and the eager, and the arrogant and the froward and the vain, fretted, and chafed, and made their usual uproar."

OUR MUTUAL FRIEND (1865)

Between writing *Little Dorrit* and his last complete novel, *Our Mutual Friend*, Dickens wrote *A Tale of Two Cities* and *Great Expectations*, both shorter novels for weekly publication in *All the Year Round*. Readers who dislike the dark intensity of *Our Mutual Friend* often contend that it reflects Dickens's failing health and exhaustion. But his conception for the novel, which he described in January 1864 as "a combination of drollery with romance," indicates that he was still full of humorous and imaginative ideas for this expansive and dense work, which appeared in monthly parts from May 1864 to November 1865. His condemnation of a foolish aristocracy, central to all his work, is as biting as ever, but at the heart of *Our Mutual Friend* is also a fascinating study of identity and double lives, no doubt influenced by his own double life in hiding his mistress Ellen Ternan (and at times adopting a pseudonym himself). Ellen can also be seen as an influence on the physically powerful and assertive Lizzie Hexam, the waterman's daughter whose skill with boats and water allows her to save the effete young gentleman, Eugene Wrayburn.

The plot of *Our Mutual Friend* is complicated, and like all the novels of Dickens's maturity (beginning with *Bleak House*), revolves around a mystery. The main character is John Harmon, who has been left a fortune by his father (a dust, or refuse, dealer) on condition that he marry Bella Wilfer, a clerk's daughter whom he has never met because he has been in South Africa for some years following an argument with his father. When John is drugged, beaten, and robbed on his return to England by a double-crossing shipmate (who drowns), he takes advantage of the situation by identifying the dead shipmate's body as his own and taking on a new identity. Under the name John Rokesmith, he takes lodgings with the Wilfers in order to decide if he wants to marry Bella. At first, he finds her mercenary and spoiled, characteristics that old Harmon had noted in her as a child, leading him to consider her a suitable match for his wilful son.

The central themes of *Our Mutual Friend* are established in this plot and are worked out through the interrelated characters who enter John Harmon's disguised life. Greed for money—especially money derived from unsavory sources, such as old Harmon's garbage heaps—motivates much of the action, beginning with the opening scene, in which Gaffer Hexam drags the river for drowned bodies to plunder. The Harmon fortune has passed to old Harmon's kindly foreman, Noddy Boffin, who becomes known as "the Golden Dustman" and who is preyed upon by Silas Wegg and his accomplice Mr. Venus, a dealer in bones and skeletons as a taxidermist. Mr. Boffin employs John Rokesmith as a secretary, but he and Mrs. Boffin soon recognize him as the boy they once knew. They also take in Bella Wilfer and carry out an elaborate plan to make her less mercenary by having Mr. Boffin pretend to be corrupted by his newfound wealth (another case of double identity). The plan works, Bella's better nature triumphs, and she marries John Rokesmith without knowing of his true identity as the heir to a fortune. When Silas Wegg discovers an old will in the dust heaps, leaving old Harmon's property to the Crown, he plans to blackmail Mr. Boffin but is thwarted by Mr. Venus, who tells Mr. Boffin of the plot. The will turns out to be useless anyway, having been superseded by the one that leaves the property to John or Mr. Boffin.

Two other groups of characters are woven into Harmon's story. The satire on aristocratic families in *Little Dorrit*, graphically represented by Mrs. General's varnish, centers on a varnished couple suitably named the Veneerings, whose "surface smelt a little too much of the workshop and was a trifle sticky" (6). Their "bran-new" house and money attracts a following of society toadies, including the Lammles, who marry on the mistaken assumption that the other is wealthy. The Veneerings's circle includes both the titled families and the nouveau-riche like themselves and Mr. Podsnap, an insurance broker whose name has become synonymous with the worst kind of smugly patriotic pig-headedness and pride. He patronizes everyone, especially anyone who is not English. Dickens also satirizes Victorian prudishness in Mr. Podsnap, who judges everything by whether it will raise a blush to the cheek of a young person.

Eugene Wrayburn and Mortimer Lightwood, two young lawyers, are members of the Veneerings's set also, and at first, they are in the long line of idle young gentlemen satirized by Dickens in Jack Maldon (*David Copperfield*), James Harthouse (*Hard Times*), Henry Gowan (*Little Dorrit*), and many others. But like Sydney Carton, who drags himself out of dissipation into heroism, Eugene and Mortimer are restless and dissatisfied with their indolent lives. When Eugene falls in love with Lizzie Hexam, the beautiful but illiterate daughter of Gaffer, he at first resists it, and their friends fear that he is another Steerforth, a gentleman preying upon a girl from a lower class. Lizzie is also pursued by Bradley Headstone, a once-poor boy who has risen to the status of schoolmaster and who teaches Lizzie's self-serving brother Charley. (Charley's disgraceful treatment of Lizzie recalls Tom's similar treatment of his sister Louisa in *Hard Times*.) Headstone's name suggests his character: a pent-up, furiously repressed, and jealous man whose passion bursts out when he finds that Eugene is a rival for Lizzie's affections. Eugene deliberately torments Headstone, using his position as a "gentleman" to demean the headmaster, who finally attacks Eugene and casts him into the river to drown. Lizzie, using her strong skill at the oars, saves Eugene; his journey through the valley of the shadow of death is in every way a baptism, and he returns to life and strength a humbled and loving husband to Lizzie. Mortimer learns from it, too, and both men turn their backs on the "Society" that disapproves of a gentleman's marriage to a river girl.

Like many of Dickens's novels, *Our Mutual Friend* is about being restored to life as were John Harmon and Eugene Wrayburn; like *A Tale of Two Cities*, it offers redemption and renewal with the river and drowning as the source of baptism and rebirth. The river is a powerful antithesis to the surface triviality of high society, represented by the "veneer," or false sheen, of the Veneerings and their friends. Many of Dickens's motifs and concerns reappear, even the Poor Law of *Oliver Twist*, and as usual, the novel teems with characters and incidents who support the themes of the corruption of money and the evils of social snobbery. "Fancy," so important to Dickens, is found in many places, including the dolls' dressmaker Jenny Wren, a crippled girl whose vivid imagination allows her to transcend her miserable existence looking after her foolish drunk of a father. Parents and children have a central position, too; many of the problems in the novel arise once again from inadequate or misguided fathers.

THE MYSTERY OF EDWIN DROOD (1870)

It is one of literature's great ironies that Dickens's only true "whodunit" was interrupted by his untimely death. The mystery of who did what to whom has puzzled readers ever since, because Dickens left no clear indication of his plot, and like all good mystery writers, he provides all sorts of clues and red herrings. According to John Forster, Dickens told him that the story "was to be that of the murder of a nephew by his uncle; the originality of which was to consist in the review of the murderer's career by himself at the close, when its temptations were to be dwelt upon as if, not he the culprit, but some other man, were the tempted. The last chapters were to be written in the condemned cell, to which his wickedness, all elaborately elicited from him as if told of another, had brought him" (Forster 2.366). Not until the end would the identity of the victim, Edwin Drood, and his killer, John Jasper, be revealed, through the discovery of a ring that survived the corrosive effects of the lime into which the body had been thrown.

Like all of Dickens's later novels, the story opens dramatically, in an opium den in the East End of London where John Jasper, the young choirmaster of Cloisterham Cathedral, is indulging his addiction. Jasper is secretly in love with Rosa Bud, but he knows that she is engaged to Edwin Drood according to the wishes of their fathers (just as old Harmon's estate was bound to John's marrying Bella in *Our Mutual Friend*). What Jasper does not know is that Rosa and Edwin have agreed to be just friends, so if he does murder Edwin out of jealousy, it is unnecessary, as Dickens told Forster the murderer would quickly realize. After Edwin's disappearance, Jasper declares his love for Rosa, who takes fright and runs away to her guardian's house in London, suspicious that Jasper may have something to do with Edwin's disappearance.

Other people are implicated in the disappearance, including Neville Landless, a handsome young man who quarrels with Edwin over Edwin's apparent disregard for Rosa. Neville and his twin sister, Helena, are newcomers to Cloisterham, orphans from Ceylon who are dark-skinned and athletic. That Helena is unusually brave and once disguised herself as a boy was probably going to have some bearing on the plot. When Jasper throws suspicion on Neville because Edwin disappeared after their violent quarrel, the twins leave for London. Thickening the plot is a mysterious stranger, Dick Datchery, who then arrives in Cloisterham. From his description, he is clearly someone in disguise, but who? Readers have found hints that suggest any number of identities. Datchery's detective work in the town is halted before he can discover the secret of Drood's disappearance; in the last line Dickens wrote, Datchery notes down his most recent discovery and then sits down to dinner.

Forster's version of the plot—that Drood is murdered by Jasper—would certainly lead to a prison-cell scene that Dickens would have enjoyed writing. He was always fascinated by the psychology of the murderer and the effects of a guilty conscience after the crime. Dickensian also is the idea of a double identity, the murderer hiding his evil nature from the world and then in his cell developing into a split personality to divorce himself from his crime. The "originality" of this idea, as Dickens described it, would be a natural progression from the exploration of double identities in *Our Mutual Friend*. John Jasper appears to be another Bradley Headstone, quietly pursuing a respectable calling while harboring passionate love for a woman and murderous designs against a rival.

New to Dickens's work but central to his friend Wilkie Collins's mystery novel *The Moonstone* (published in 1868) is opium addiction. The theft of the moonstone is committed by someone under the influence of opium, who then has no recollection of stealing it. The stone is found when he is drugged again. Princess Puffer, the haggard old woman who runs the opium den in *Edwin Drood*, mysteriously visits Cloisterham and appears to have some secret knowledge about her client Jasper.

Many people have taken up the challenge to finish the novel, and the range of interpretation attests to the success of Dickens's "mystery." Some believe that Dickens deliberately gave Forster a red herring to keep the story a secret; Drood may not have been murdered at all, but just disappeared, to reappear at the end of the novel. Throughout his fiction, Dickens had been intrigued by the idea of returning to life, symbolically or in reality. It was not uncommon in Victorian times for people to disappear and be assumed dead, especially if they went overseas, as did Walter Gay in *Dombey and Son*. According to the illustrator of *Edwin Drood*, Dickens told him that John Jasper, Edwin Drood's uncle, must have a double necktie because he uses it to strangle his nephew. But this too is inconclusive, as Drood could survive strangling just as other characters in Dickens's novels survive attempted murder, including Eugene Wrayburn in *Our Mutual Friend*. Dickens's suggested titles for the novel certainly suggest more strongly than "mystery" that Edwin Drood does indeed survive: He considered titles such as "the disappearance," "the loss," and even "the flight" of Edwin Drood. Another clue is the title page, which includes a vignette of Jasper holding up a lantern and discovering a very live Drood.

Dickens returned to his favorite childhood place, the cathedral town of Rochester, for the setting of his novel. He also infused a surprising energy into it, despite his own failing health. Many of the characters are athletic and active, especially the Reverend Septimus Crisparkle, one of Dickens's good clergymen, who rises early and loves nothing more than a brisk swim in the river. His friend Lieutenant Tartar, retired from the navy, with sunburnt face and twinkling eyes, tends to his windowboxes by climbing up rigging as though he were still on board a ship. Miss Twinkleton, the schoolmistress, becomes "sprightlier" at night, away from her duties. There is darkness and foreboding in the smoke of the opium den and in the crypts of the old cathedral, where Durdles the stonemason takes Jasper on a moonlight expedition. But there is light and movement also, as the cathedral spires rise into the clear air in the passage that Dickens wrote just before he died:

A brilliant morning shines on the old city. Its antiquities and ruins are surpassingly beautiful, with a lusty ivy gleaming in the sun, and the rich trees waving in the balmy air. Changes of glorious light from moving boughs, songs of birds, scents from gardens, woods, and fields—or rather, from the one great garden of the whole cultivated island in its yielding time—penetrate into the cathedral, subdue its earthy odour, and preach the Resurrection and the Life. The cold stone tombs of centuries ago grow warm; and flecks of brightness dart into the sternest marble corners of the building, fluttering there like wings.

With its emphasis on strong, athletic people (the triumph of Lizzie Hexam over Eugene Wrayburn's apathy in the previous novel), *Edwin Drood* demonstrates its author's unflagging energy, interest, and vitality right to the end.

Bibliography

ABBREVIATIONS

Forster: Forster, John. *The Life of Charles Dickens*. (1872–1874). Ed. A. J. Hoppé. 2 vols. London: Dent, 1966.

Letters: The Letters of Charles Dickens. Pilgrim Edition. Ed. Madeline House, Graham Storey, and Kathleen Tillotson. 10 vols. to date. Oxford: Clarendon Press, 1965– .

Memoranda: Charles Dickens' Book of Memoranda. A Photographic and Typographic Facsimile of the Notebook Begun in January 1855. Ed. Fred Kaplan. From the Original Manuscript in the Berg Collection, New York Public Library, 1981.

Nonesuch: The Letters of Charles Dickens. Nonesuch Edition. Ed. Walter Dexter. 3 vols. Bloomsbury, London: The Nonesuch Press, 1938.

The Oxford University Press World's Classics Series is the source for quotations from the following:

Bleak House, ed. Stephen Gill (rpt. 1998).

Christmas Books, ed. Ruth Glancy (rpt. 1998).

David Copperfield, ed. Nina Burgis; introduction by Andrew Sanders (rpt. 1997).

Great Expectations, ed. Margaret Flint; introduction by Kate Flint (rpt. 1994).

Hard Times, ed. Paul Schlicke (rpt. 1989).

Little Dorrit, ed. Harvey Peter Sucksmith (rpt. 1982).

Oliver Twist, ed. Kathleen Tillotson (rpt. 1998).

The Pickwick Papers, ed. James Kinsley (rpt. 1988).

A Tale of Two Cities, ed. Andrew Sanders (rpt. 1998).

The Penguin English Library (Harmondsworth, England) is the source for quotations from *Barnaby Rudge*, ed. Gordon Spence (rpt. 1997).

The Everyman Library (J. M. Dent) is the source for quotations from the following:

American Notes and Pictures from Italy, ed. F. S. Schwarzbach and Leonee Ormond (1997).

Christmas Stories, ed. Ruth Glancy (1997).

Dombey and Son, ed. Valerie Purton (1997).

Martin Chuzzlewit, ed. Michael Slater (1994).

The Old Curiosity Shop, ed. Paul Schlicke (1997).

Important recent editions of the novels are the Norton Critical Editions Series (New York: W. W. Norton).

MAJOR WORKS BY CHARLES DICKENS

American Notes for General Circulation. London: Chapman and Hall, 1842.

Barnaby Rudge: A Tale of the Riots of 'Eighty. London: Chapman and Hall, 1841.

The Battle of Life: A Love Story. London: Bradbury and Evans, 1846.

Bleak House. London: Bradbury and Evans, 1852–1853.

A Child's History of England. London: Bradbury and Evans, 1852–1854.

The Chimes: A Goblin Story of Some Bells That Rang an Old Year Out and a New Year In. London: Chapman and Hall, 1844.

A Christmas Carol, in Prose: Being a Ghost Story of Christmas. London: Chapman and Hall, 1843.

The Cricket on the Hearth: A Fairy Tale of Home. London: Bradbury and Evans, 1845.

David Copperfield. London: Bradbury and Evans, 1849–1850.

Dombey and Son. London: Bradbury and Evans, 1846–1848.

Great Expectations. London: Chapman and Hall, 1861.

Hard Times: For These Times. London: Bradbury and Evans, 1854.

The Haunted Man and the Ghost's Bargain: A Fancy for Christmas Time. London: Bradbury and Evans, 1848.

The Life and Adventures of Martin Chuzzlewit. London: Chapman and Hall, 1842–1844.

The Life and Adventures of Nicholas Nickleby. London: Chapman and Hall, 1837–1839.

The Life of Our Lord. 1849. London: Associated Newspapers, 1934.

Little Dorrit. London: Bradbury and Evans, 1855–1857.

The Mystery of Edwin Drood. London: Chapman and Hall, 1870.

The Old Curiosity Shop. London: Chapman and Hall, 1841.

Oliver Twist; or, The Parish Boy's Progress. London: Bentley, 1838.

Our Mutual Friend. London: Chapman and Hall, 1864–1865.

Pictures from Italy. London: Bradbury and Evans, 1846.

The Posthumous Papers of the Pickwick Club. London: Chapman and Hall, 1836–1837.
Sketches by Boz, Illustrative of Every-Day Life and Every-Day People. London: Macrone, 1836; second series, 1837
A Tale of Two Cities. London: Chapman and Hall, 1859.
The Uncommercial Traveller. London: Chapman and Hall, 1861.

BIOGRAPHIES

Ackroyd, Peter. *Dickens*. London: Sinclair-Stevenson, 1990.
Allen, Michael. *Charles Dickens' Childhood*. Basingstoke, England: Macmillan, 1988.
Forster, John. *The Life of Charles Dickens*. 3 vols. London: Chapman and Hall, 1872–1874. Ed. A. J. Hoppé, 2 vols. London: Dent, 1966.
Johnson, Edgar. *Charles Dickens: His Tragedy and Triumph*. 2 vols. Boston: Little, Brown; London: Hamish Hamilton, 1952. 1 vol. revised and abridged. New York: Viking, 1977; London: Lane, 1977.
Kaplan, Fred. *Dickens: A Biography*. London: Hodder and Stoughton; New York: William Morrow, 1988.

PERIODICALS

The Dickensian. London, 1905– .
Dickens Studies. Boston, MA: Emerson College, 1965–1969. Continued as *Dickens Studies Annual*. Carbondale, IL: Southern Illinois University Press, 1970– .
Dickens Studies Newsletter. Louisville, KY, 1970–1983. Continued as *Dickens Quarterly*. Louisville, KY, 1984– .

GENERAL STUDIES

Andrews, Malcolm. *Dickens and the Grown-up Child*. Basingstoke and London: Macmillan; Iowa City: University of Iowa Press, 1994.
———. *Dickens on England and the English*. Hassocks, England: Harvester Press, 1979.
Butt, John, and Kathleen Tillotson. *Dickens at Work*. 1957. London: Methuen, 1968.
Charles Dickens: A Critical Anthology. Ed. Stephen Wall. Harmondsworth, England: Penguin, 1970.
Charles Dickens: Modern Critical Views. Ed. Harold Bloom. New York: Chelsea House, 1987.
Chittick, Kathryn. *Dickens and the 1830s*. Cambridge, England: Cambridge University Press, 1990.
Collins, Philip. *Dickens and Crime*. 1962. New York: St. Martin's Press, 1994.
———. *Dickens and Education*. London: Macmillan, 1963.

The Dickens Critics. Ed. George H. Ford and Lauriat Lane, Jr. Ithaca, N.Y.: Cornell University Press, 1961.

Fielding, K. J. *Charles Dickens: A Critical Introduction.* 1958. Boston: Houghton Mifflin, 1965.

Ford, George H. *Dickens and his Readers.* 1955. New York: Gordian Press, 1974.

Garis, Robert. *The Dickens Theatre.* Oxford: Clarendon, 1965.

Gold, Joseph. *Charles Dickens: Radical Moralist.* Minneapolis: University of Minnesota Press, 1972.

House, Humphry. *The Dickens World.* 1941. London: Oxford University Press, 1965.

Leavis, F. R., and Q. D. Leavis. *Dickens the Novelist.* London: Chatto and Windus, 1970.

Miller, J. Hillis. *Charles Dickens: The World of His Novels.* Cambridge, MA: Harvard University Press, 1958.

Page, Norman. *A Dickens Chronology.* London: Macmillan, 1988.

———. *A Dickens Companion.* London: Macmillan, 1984.

Patten, Robert L. *Dickens and His Publishers.* Oxford: Clarendon, 1978.

Schlicke, Paul. *Dickens and Popular Entertainment.* London: Allen and Unwin, 1985.

Slater, Michael. *Dickens and Women.* London: J. M. Dent, 1983.

———. *Dickens on America and the Americans.* Sussex, England: Harvester Press, 1979.

Smith, Grahame. *Charles Dickens: A Literary Life.* New York: St. Martin's Press, 1996.

Stone, Harry. *Dickens and the Invisible World: Fairy Tales, Fantasy, and Novel-Making.* London: Macmillan, 1978; Bloomington: Indiana University Press, 1979.

———, ed. *Dickens's Working Notes for His Novels.* Chicago: University of Chicago Press, 1987.

Wilson, Angus. *The World of Charles Dickens.* London: Secker and Warburg, 1970.

OLIVER TWIST

Dickens, Charles. *Oliver Twist.* Ed. Fred Kaplan. Norton Critical Edition. New York: Norton, 1993.

Dunn, Richard J. Oliver Twist: *Whole Heart and Soul.* Twayne Masterwork Studies No. 118. New York: Twayne, 1993.

Paroissien, David. *The Companion to Oliver Twist.* New York: Columbia University Press, 1992.

———. Oliver Twist: *An Annotated Bibliography.* New York: Garland, 1986.

CHRISTMAS BOOKS AND CHRISTMAS STORIES

Butt, John. "Dickens's Christmas Books." *Pope, Dickens, and Others.* Edinburgh: Edinburgh University Press, 1969, 127–48.

Glancy, Ruth. *Dickens's Christmas Books, Christmas Stories, and Other Short Fiction: An Annotated Bibliography.* New York: Garland, 1985.

Slater, Michael. Introduction to *Christmas Books.* 2 vols. Harmondsworth, England: Penguin, 1971.

Thomas, Deborah A. *Dickens and the Short Story.* Philadelphia: University of Pennsylvania Press; London: Batsford Academic and Educational, 1982.

DAVID COPPERFIELD

Collins, Philip. *Charles Dickens*, David Copperfield. Studies in English Literature No. 67. London: Edward Arnold, 1977.

David Copperfield and Hard Times. Ed. John Peck. London: St. Martin's Press, 1995.

Dickens, Charles. *David Copperfield.* Ed. Jerome H. Buckley. Norton Critical Edition. New York: Norton, 1990.

Dunn, Richard J. David Copperfield: *An Annotated Bibliography.* New York: Garland, 1981.

Storey, Graham. David Copperfield: *Interweaving Truth and Fiction.* Twayne's Masterwork Studies No. 68. Boston: Twayne, 1991.

HARD TIMES

David Copperfield and Hard Times. Ed. John Peck. London: St. Martin's Press, 1995.

Dickens, Charles. *Hard Times.* Ed. George Ford and Sylvère Monod. Norton Critical Edition. 2d ed. New York: W. W. Norton, 1990.

———. *Hard Times.* Broadview Literary Texts. Ed. Graham Law. Peterborough, Canada: Broadview Press, 1996.

Easson, Angus. Hard Times: *A Critical Commentary and Notes.* London: University of London Press, 1973.

Manning, Sylvia. Hard Times: *An Annotated Bibliography.* New York: Garland, 1984.

Simpson, Margaret. *The Companion to* Hard Times. Westport, CT: Greenwood Press, 1997.

Thomas, Deborah A. Hard Times: *A Fable of Fragmentation and Wholeness.* Twayne Masterwork Series No. 166. New York: Twayne, 1997.

A TALE OF TWO CITIES

Charles Dickens's A Tale of Two Cities: *Comprehensive Research and Study Guides.* Broomall, PA: Chelsea House, 1997.

Glancy, Ruth. A Tale of Two Cities: *Dickens's Revolutionary Novel.* Twayne Masterwork Studies No. 78. Boston: Twayne, 1991.

Newlin, George. *Understanding* A Tale of Two Cities: *A Student Casebook to Issues, Sources and Historical Documents.* Westport, CT: Greenwood, 1998.

GREAT EXPECTATIONS

Critical Essays on Charles Dickens' Great Expectations. Ed. Michael Cotsell. Boston: G. K. Hall, 1990.

Dickens, Charles. *Great Expectations*. Ed. Roger D. Sell. New Casebooks. New York: St. Martin's Press, 1994.

———. *Great Expectations*. Ed. Janice Carlisle. Case Studies in Contemporary Criticism. Boston: Bedford Books of St. Martin's Press, 1996.

———. *Great Expectations*. Ed. Edgar Rosenberg. Norton Critical Edition. New York: W. W. Norton, 1999.

Great Expectations. Ed. Nicholas Tredell. Icon Critical Guides. Cambridge, England: Icon Books, 1998.

Hornback, Bert G. Great Expectations: *A Novel of Friendship*. Masterwork Studies No. 6. New York: Macmillan, 1987.

Sadrin, Anny. *Great Expectations*. London: Unwin Hyman, 1988.

Worth, George J. Great Expectations: *An Annotated Bibliography*. New York: Garland, 1986.

Index

About the Author

RUTH GLANCY is Assistant Professor of English at Concordia University College of Alberta. She is author of several books and articles on Dickens including a companion to *A Tale of Two Cities* and two bibliographies. Best known for her work on Dickens and Christmas, she has edited his Christmas books and Christmas stories, and is regularly interviewed on the subject at Christmas time.